SUGAR DADDY DIARIES

Helen Croydon is a freelance print and broadcast journalist who specialises in investigative reports and features on sex, the sex industry, dating and relationships. She has written for various publications, including *The Times*, the *Sunday Times*, *The Guardian*, *The Independent*, the *Daily Mail*, *Company* magazine and *The Erotic Review*. She has produced and presented programmes for various broadcasters, including ITN, Channel 4 and Current TV.

SUGAR DADDY
DADDY
Diaries

When a Fantasy
Became an Obsession

HELEN CROYDON

MAINSTREAM
PUBLISHING

EDINBURGH AND LONDON

First published in Great Britain in 2011 by
MAINSTREAM PUBLISHING COMPANY
(EDINBURGH) LTD
7 Albany Street
Edinburgh EH1 3UG

ISBN 9781845967666

This book is a work of non-fiction based on the life, experiences and
recollections of the author. In some cases, names of people, profile names,
places, dates, sequences or the detail of events have been changed to
protect the privacy of others and for artistic reasons. The author has
stated to the publishers that, except in such respects, the contents of this
book are true.

A catalogue record for this book is available
from the British Library

Printed in Great Britain by
CPI Cox & Wyman, Reading RG1 8EX

1 3 5 7 9 10 8 6 4 2

Acknowledgements

Thanks to everyone at Mainstream Publishing for their hard work and enthusiasm. Special thanks to Bill for the gin and tonics and to my editor, Claire, for her impressive focus and for keeping up with the changes.

Thanks to my wonderful lodger – sorry, friend – Suki, for reading bits of this in its early stages and for feeding my enthusiasm as I launched my writing career. Thanks for your wit and for laughing at my jokes! Thank you to my happily married friends for their insights and, OK, their lectures – I did listen. Thanks to my dying breed of single friends for their entertainment and their interest in my stories, which led me to write this. Thanks to the men who feature in this book for their lessons in life. Warmest of those thanks to 'Malaysian Sugar Daddy'. Thanks to my mum for – gulp – taking news of this book so well. And thanks to my sister and her family for advice on breaking that news.

Contents

Prologue

One Saturday evening in the spring of 2007, home alone with a glass of Sainsbury's finest Chardonnay, I guiltily googled 'younger women, older men, dating'. I felt embarrassed even though there was no one there to see what I was doing. I think I shiftily glanced up and around my empty open-plan living room to check no one was there – the reflex reaction of shame.

You see, I'd always had a thing for older guys. When I say 'thing', I mean a preference. But I say 'thing' because back then I didn't really understand it. The word 'preference' seems too bold – as if I openly admitted I wanted to pursue older guys. But I wasn't brave enough to say that. No one else seemed to have a preference for older men. Most girls my age gravitated to the boy-band types; you know, the guy with the toned body, trendy, gel-spiked haircut and an obsession with mixing decks. Harbouring non-conventional sexual preferences isn't something we like to advertise, is it? Sex is a mysterious and uncomfortable enough topic as it is, so most of us like to think that we're doing it pretty much the way everyone else does (only slightly better).

So, I kept my lustful thoughts about older men to myself, boxing them off as just a harmless 'thing'. That made my tastes seem less absolute – like I could be persuaded to swing both ways. That way, I felt I still belonged safely in the realm of normality.

Before I go any further, actually, I'd just like to stop any Freudian analysis right here, in case you're doing any armchair theorising. I lost my father in my mid-20s and I was devastated – obviously. It had a big impact on my world on many different levels. We were – and are – a close, secure, loving, supportive family. But that had no bearing on my thing for older men. I liked them way before that happened. My first crush was on a teacher. My first boyfriend, when I was 18, was 33. I met him in Japan during my gap year. Amid the alcohol-fuelled expat lifestyle, the 15-year age gap was hardly noticed. Ever since, nearly all my eye-wanderings have tended towards the older, self-assured model, usually in a suit, looking important. You know the type – a Richard Gere, a Pierce Brosnan.

So why did it take me until I was 29 years old to google 'dating older men'? It was embarrassment, primarily. I was alone with my computer, but it seemed such a definitive step to acknowledge my semi-conscious sexual preference and type it into a search engine. Talking of which, yes, dating sites. That was the other part of it. I hadn't done – what do you call it? – 'online dating' before. While the likes of Match. com were becoming almost a must-have tool for any noughties singleton looking for romance, I felt there was still a residual stigma of desperation attached to anyone who resorted to cyberspace to find a partner. I was looking for excitement, not true love, and that had kept me well away from the conventional matchmaking sites.

But this one Saturday evening, I seized the reins to my tame little fantasy and decided to embrace my hidden dating desires. Finally getting round to clicking the 'Google Search' button after all those years of repressing what I really wanted in a man – maturity, finesse, assuredness, wisdom – was fuelled by three things.

First, the Chardonnay. I never drink that cheap supermarket stuff any more, by the way; that's one of the side effects of spending all your time with rich people (keep reading, you'll understand).

Second, I was fresh out of a stifling three-year relationship – with someone my own age, actually. Three years was by far the longest I had ever been with someone. One and a half years of it was lovely. The other one and a half years felt like one big living compromise. We worked different hours and had different priorities. I didn't want to start watching a film with him at eleven at night, skip the gym to eat bagels with him on a Saturday morning or hang out with his friends and their games consoles. I didn't want to justify every pair of shoes I bought or feel I should dress down because he preferred me like that. I didn't want to run every diary entry past someone else.

Like most halves of an unhappy couple, it took me a while to break away – the poignant moments of honeymoon-period romance obviously have deep enough claws to pin us to the person we shared them with long after love dissipates. I dreamed about being single again. I craved the freedom and my old identity. I remembered myself being much sparkier than I had become. But I wasn't bold enough to get out for ages. When I did, finally, I decided I was absolutely never going to be tied down to someone else's routine again.

I was approaching 30 and had suddenly been awakened to my sex drive – quite startlingly so. I had never been the promiscuous type; in fact, I was quite the prude at university. But now I could think of nothing else. *Sex*. It was like my unused teenage hormones whirled themselves up and exploded in the emotions of the break-up. Put simply, I was a horny, newly single female, thirsty to try out my new-found freedoms.

I was working as a middle-level broadcast journalist at

ITN, producing and presenting video reports and bulletins for multimedia outlets such as Internet TV channels, vodcasts and mobile phones. It sounded good at a dinner party, but really I felt frustrated with the pace of my career development and wanted to get into real TV. I could do my job drunk and standing on my head (except for the on-camera stuff – that would have caused problems). I did have plans to work on getting my career moving, of course, but first, while my sex drive was soaring and I had a very exciting new single status, my wardrobe space all to myself and a cool new lodger in my spare room, I wanted to make the most of my gloriously commitment-free lifestyle.

So I bounded onto the dating scene with bags of enthusiasm for the exciting encounters that lay ahead. But I found the typical bar hook-ups uninspiring: guys in their late 20s with big dreams and unrealistic ideas of romance. Most seemed keener to get settled down than my girlfriends of the same age. And the last thing I wanted was a man I had to phone every day, some guy who'd want me to learn all his friends' names! I wanted to be wined, dined and seduced in a hotel suite – or in the lift on the way there. And then I wanted to repeat it a couple of weeks later, without the obligatory texts and exchanging of life stories in between. I wanted to meet someone who knew how to flirt and where to go for dinner, someone who had achieved something in life and could impress me with his wisdom. I didn't want a boyfriend, I wanted a lover.

Friends tried to fix me up with 'nice guys'. Family tried to steer me towards the idea of a long-term relationship. How could they not see I didn't want that? I wanted adventure. I fantasised about someone older, sophisticated, distinguished. I wanted a man in an Armani suit, oozing confidence and sexual assertiveness. I wanted to be given a glimpse into his intriguing executive world and then to go back into my own safe little shell until we met again. Given that my social life revolved around after-work drinks with disgruntled broadcast journalists going nowhere, engagement parties, weddings, hen dos and baby showers, what I wanted wasn't coming to me.

And third – you thought I'd forgotten the third reason, didn't you? – third, I had developed a crush on a very senior boss at work. He was more than 20 years older than me, and to me he represented all the great things about a mature man I described earlier. I was in awe of him at first. He was this unattainable figure, safe to fancy. He had an air of authority and a devilishly handsome yet comforting, friendly, almost familiar face. The few times I had talked to him, he had made me laugh. His aura of power was mixed with a quirky humour and a boyish playfulness. My crush grew. It wasn't until much later that I found out he had a long-term partner. My feelings turned to frustration. I had all these keen younger single guys on the periphery of my social world, but I didn't want them. And then there was this older guy in my everyday working environment whom I desperately wanted but couldn't have.

And it was due to those three reasons – two-thirds of a bottle of Chardonnay, a determination to be single and *freeeee*, and a crush on an older man I couldn't have – that I found myself hitting the 'Google Search' button.

When I'd taken the leap, I discovered that there were quite a few websites specifically based on the model of successful older men looking for younger women. I joined what looked like the largest. It was called Sugardaddie.com and I adopted the profile name 'Perrier Jouet'.

I didn't know it then, but that capricious moment of googling would change my life for ever. And my wardrobe, actually, but we'll come to that later. I never intended it to be anything more than a few fun dates, but I soon discovered that my relaxed ideal of an emotionally low-maintenance open relationship was regarded as quite a treasure by the time-poor, cash-rich gentlemen on the site, so much so that they were willing to pay, in many different ways, to preserve that dynamic.

Over a three-year period, I met scores of extremely wealthy, colourful and often influential characters. At first it was for kicks, then out of journalistic curiosity about moral and social boundaries. And then, inevitably, I became driven by the material gains that were thrown my way, though it was the realisation that this latter incentive had taken over, with poisonous side effects, that eventually made me stop. This book, based on my diary, charts my journey of personal, moral and sexual discovery as I question modern ideals about relationships, examine the role of power in relationships between men and women, confront my commitment-phobia and try to work out if we really do need love at all.

Chapter 1

My Nervous Start

♥ **Early May 2007**

My phone vibrated in my clenched hand. There was a text:
'Get the lift straight to the 42nd floor. Booked under Garrison.
In blue suit.'

I have to give his name? I thought. Is that the protocol in
these posh places? I was walking – or hurrying, more likely,
knowing me – along Old Broad Street from Liverpool Street
Tube station, heading towards Vertigo 42, a decadent
champagne bar on the 42nd floor of a tower building in
London's financial district. I was on my way to meet Date
One. I could feel my heart beating fast. This was my first-ever
Internet date – my first blind date, actually – and the first
time I had ever taken an active step towards living out a
fantasy. My fantasy. Of dating an older man – an experienced,
seasoned real man, someone of a higher calibre than the men
I came across in normal life.

I had texted my lodger – or friend, as she understandably
preferred to be called – before I left. I told her I had written
down my date's website profile name, his real name (or at
least the one he'd given me), his phone number and the name

of the bar where we were meeting in a notebook on the coffee table. That book became a fixture in which I wrote all my dates' details. My lodger said that some nights she would come home and flick it open to see if I was going to be in or out that night.

I forced myself to walk on, conscious of the click-clacking of my tall, slender heels on the tarmac – such a salacious sound! How have I ended up on this expedition? I thought. A well-brought-up girl from a happy family with a good job – what was I doing, going to meet a man who had put himself on a website with such an unsavoury name as Sugardaddie.com? I suddenly wished I was on my way to meet a girlfriend for a bottle of wine. I could sit down, relax, put the world to rights over too much Chardonnay and giggle about boys. That was the form my nights out usually took, and right then I wanted very much to be in that comfort zone.

I had to pass through what looked like an office reception to get up to Vertigo 42. A glamorous female receptionist who looked more like an air stewardess checked the booking for Garrison before she let me through the barriers and directed me to the lift. I hit the only button, marked 42, and my ears popped as the lift blasted upwards. The doors opened and I was greeted by a backdrop of sound that would become familiar to me: the soft murmur of low voices mixed with piano music and distant clinking of cutlery and glasses.

'Can I take your coat, madam?' asked an unnaturally upright waiter in black tie.

'Thank you.' I took off my cream Topshop mac. I was dressed in a brown and cream dress – nice but definitely not expensive – with a chunky belt. The dress showed the perfect peep of cleavage. And I was wearing heels, of course, though they were a bit worn and shabby if you got up close.

'What is the name of your party, madam?'

The waiter led me to my first date – a 45-year-old property lawyer – saving me the task of having to recognise a stranger from the one picture he had sent. As with all the men I went on to meet, he didn't look at all how I'd expected him to in the flesh. Several times during the evening, he tilted his head in a certain way that recaptured the angle of the pose in his photo, so I knew the picture had been real. But the general, overall look of a person, I found, can never be captured in one snapshot.

Not exactly Richard Gere or Pierce Brosnan, I thought, but definitely not unattractive.

We greeted each other with a polite peck on both cheeks.

'Sorry, have I kept you waiting long?'

That day I had been off the newsroom rota, which meant the only things I had to do were go to the gym and get ready for my date. But I was still late. No matter how hard I train it, my brain refuses to accept that time is inflexible. I always try to squeeze 30 minutes into 25. (If I could change one thing about myself, it would be not to be always in a mad rush wondering why on earth I didn't get time to do all the things I planned to do.)

'Not at all,' Date One replied. 'What do you do?'

'I'm a journalist,' I answered innocently.

'You're not doing an undercover sting on the site, are you?'

I was surprised at his joke because back then I didn't do that type of exposé at all. There was little scope for exclusives in the area of broadcast journalism I worked in, and, unlike in print journalism, you needed a camera and a crew to get a story. I had told him my true profession because I was eager to give a respectable impression of who I was. I wanted to allay any fears that I was some drifting wannabe bimbo looking for a rich man. But, of course, my level of intellect was of no interest to him. He was far more concerned about protecting himself. We were both so paranoid about our little Internet secret that we were paying more attention to ourselves than each other.

We were sitting side by side on comfortable swivel chairs aligned in front of full-length windows, which lined the entire perimeter of the circular bar, looking out onto the most spectacular dusky view of central London.

He told me he was married. I didn't judge him. Maybe his wife was adulterous, maybe she was ill or possibly she accepted an open marriage. But I thought he should have divulged the fact before we set the date. It might have changed my expectations slightly. Actually, given all the high-pressure conventional dates I had had recently with over-eager guys my own age who wanted to camp out at my flat for two days at a time, it made me feel more comfortable.

This seemed a good time for the question I had been dying to ask: 'Why did you join the site?'

'Well . . . younger girls. I find them beautiful.'

I looked at him suspiciously. I admired his open admission, but if he was looking for nothing more than a pretty face, I wasn't sure I wanted to be pigeonholed in that role.

'And have you had much luck?' I enquired, fishing for an idea of how often he did this and what exactly he considered to be a successful date.

'Well, yes,' he shrugged. 'I've met lots of beautiful women. The site's known for the calibre of women who use it.' He paused and sipped his Veuve Delaroy, wondering if he could get away with stopping there. I looked at him expectantly, forcing him to go on, and he added, 'But no one I have wanted to see more than once.'

I was warming to the conversation now. I wondered if

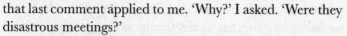

that last comment applied to me. 'Why?' I asked. 'Were they disastrous meetings?'

'Not at all. It's just that . . . the moment's easily lost.' He looked at me as if he didn't want to have to explain. But I didn't know what he meant. 'A young girl is the ultimate trophy for a man,' he continued, reading my expectant face. 'She's a beautiful, pure creature. Plump skin, innocent eyes, firm body.' He looked around the room and his gaze rested on a young strawberry-blonde girl in a long backless dress. 'But she isn't a real woman yet. She's just beautiful to look at. As a woman gets older, she gains wisdom and intuition and a strength of character that men don't develop. It's very powerful. But then she loses her looks. She substitutes one attribute for another. I find a mature woman captivating but in a very different way from a young, beautiful, innocent girl.'

Those words have always stayed with me. Every time I find myself fearing growing old and wrinkly and untoned and varicose-veined and ridiculous in leather trousers, I think of Date One's consolation. My strength of character, my *savoir faire*, will replace all that in one fell swoop. It will say, 'Take that, lost youth. I'm much more powerful than you!'

But it also struck me that what Date One was seeking was the fulfilment of a chunk of his sexual and romantic desires. The vacancy for a strong, supportive female role was already filled by his wife; it was the young, blue-eyed picture of innocence that he was wanting. But whenever he came near to getting it, the reality that his sexual ideals were just girls – vulnerable prey – prevented him taking things any further. I wondered how many other men faced this conflict: driven and teased by beauty and fantasy but too riddled with guilt to go in full force.

After our third Veuve Delaroy, we parted company. He

asked if he could see me again. I remembered that he'd said he had never wanted to see anyone else more than once. I said yes, but I was thinking no. He had been pleasant enough company, but I didn't feel quite ready to be anyone's 'ultimate trophy' just yet.

♥ ♥ ♥

I made a point of checking that my next date was single.

He was a 47-year-old sports events organiser and keen poker player. I laughed when I read that in his message and replied asking him if he'd be taking me to a football match or a casino on our first date. He replied: 'LOL. Not a football match organiser as such. I deal with corporate hospitality at high-profile sports events. F1, international golf tournaments and the like. I travel to all the major world competitions and negotiate the best deals for clients looking to send whole teams of staff over. Got one in Brazil next week.'

Sports Man picked me up outside Hampstead Tube station in an open-top vintage Chevy. It was a bright, white, cute little thing and made a huge *brummm* noise as he pulled out. I had come straight from work, in a long-sleeved, button-up, leopard-print dress and was again wearing my cream mac. I climbed in, swinging my legs around ostentatiously. 'Great outfit,' he remarked, without a moment's hesitation. Thankfully, my office was staffed predominantly with under-30 TV-presenter wannabes and so resembled a catwalk most days. My turning up in a leopard-print mini-dress didn't raise any eyebrows. It was only when I came in the following day in the same outfit that it became a talking-point.

Sports Man had apparently 'forgotten his wallet', so we had to pop to his flat before going to the restaurant. I trusted him, but it did dawn on me just how much of a risk I was taking by going into his flat before we had so much as clinked

20

glasses. He opened a bottle of rosé Louis Roederer. I was glad of the alcoholic fix to relax me. I was nowhere near as nervous as when I had gone to meet Date One, but, oh yes, I was still anxious. I wasn't so much worried about him not being attracted to me, because this wasn't about me looking for love, but I still wanted to impress. I didn't want him to think I was a little girl looking for a father figure to make her life complete. And I had the same uneasy feeling in my gut as last time, like I was setting out to do something ignoble.

I think Sports Man invited me upstairs because he wanted me to see his bachelor pad to ensure that I was suitably impressed by his financial status before going to dinner; it might also have been a ploy to make me feel comfortable enough to come back later. It was a four-bedroom, spacious modern build with a roof terrace the size of a whole garden. The doors onto the terrace were open, letting in fresh air and orange rays of evening sun.

Sports Man sat a respectable distance from me on his mauve suede couch, but still I felt angry with myself for getting into this potentially dangerous position. The golden rule of Internet dating, which I'd read in every magazine known to woman, is not to go to the home of a man you meet online until you've built up trust. Not only was I drinking champagne in this stranger's flat, I was also a good way out of central London on a quiet street. It wasn't as if I could easily flag down a cab if things got uncomfortable.

The Louis Roederer all but finished, we went for a cocktail in a stately country clubhouse on the edge of the Heath. He paid. It seemed that this was implicit with dates arranged through the website. Until now, I had always offered to pay half of any bill when on a date, but with Date One and Sports Man, I didn't even consider making the gesture. It felt hugely inappropriate. In the messages that preceded any meeting, the men would always suggest the location to meet.

It was assumed that the man booked and the man paid. In the whole three years of my sugar daddy dating craze, there was never any question of me having to pick up half the tab. I loved that, not because it saved me money or anything as calculating as that but because it gave me a sense of being looked after, of being provided for and wanted. It seemed to accentuate our gender roles and I found that massively sexy.

Sports Man did everything to lead me to believe he was a gentleman, opening doors and taking my coat. As the mojitos slowly started to ease our inhibitions, talk inevitably turned to the site. Who had we met and why were we on there? My answer was an honest one, and the same as what I had said to Date One: 'I'm bored of meeting the same types of people my age. I don't want a relationship, but I do want someone to share a few adventures with and to be taken out and shown a good time every now and again.'

'That's refreshing,' said Sports Man. 'There are a lot of girls on that site who just want money. Some are pros.'

I was stunned, naively. 'You mean they ask for cash? Upfront? How? What do they say?' I spluttered.

'Oh, all sorts of ways. One girl – she was Eastern European – asked me on the phone before I met her if I'd "sponsor" her. I know what that means. I've wised up now. That means they want me to pay them.'

I was fascinated. I wanted to know who these girls were, what they looked like, what they did for day jobs. Were they professional escorts or just regular girls sick of student debts? I've always been curious about the secret world of call girls and escorting, and I found myself feeling strangely turned on.

'One girl I met twice and we just had dinner, that's all,' Sports Man continued. 'The third time, she came back to my flat. I kissed her and she told me that if we were going to have "that sort of a relationship" she wanted £1,500 a month.'

Good God, I thought. But Sports Man didn't think that was unreasonable. 'She suggested getting together once a week, so that works out at something like three to four hundred pounds per meeting. It's actually not a huge amount, considering it would obviously be much more than just a dinner date.' Sports Man told me he hadn't taken her up on the offer. 'I'm not into that side of things. I think a lot of people on the site are, but I can have fun without writing a cheque. That's why it's such a relief to meet you.'

Chapter 2
A Word with Myself

♥ Mid-May '07

I told the story of Sports Man and his previous encounters to my only remaining single friend a few days later.

'He was probably trying to open a negotiation,' she said calmly.

'Oh, don't be ridiculous. I hadn't so much as hinted that was what I was looking for,' I replied.

'But if everyone on that website does it, he probably presumes you do too. You should have said, "Fifteen hundred? Well, I'll do it for a thousand!" Did you fancy him?'

I laughed, not knowing if Only Remaining Single Friend was being serious or not. I don't think she was, but it made me realise how easy it could be to trade sex for money – and how surprisingly understanding other single females might be. I'd never mention the temptation to my happily married friends, of course. Women, in my experience, go through a startling tightening of morals once they consider themselves one half of a couple.

'Course I fancied him,' I told her. 'I wouldn't have stayed the night if I didn't.'

'What's it like, sleeping with someone that much older? Could he still, you know . . . perform?'

I couldn't understand why Only Remaining Single Friend didn't see the attractive qualities – physical as well as mental – of an older man over a younger one. I remembered getting back to Sports Man's apartment. He slipped his hands around my waist and delicately but assertively pulled me towards him. My leg sent the empty champagne bottle flying across his glass coffee table. We laughed as he wrestled me down to the thick soft cream carpet. It was deliciously decadent. I felt reassured by his boldness as he unbuttoned the leopard-print dress.

He wasn't embarrassed about being hungry for me – not like inexperienced men who would so often ruin an erotic moment by pausing for verbal confirmation, putting the human back where I wanted the animal to be. He smelled different from the young men I was used to – less sweet and more manly. Those delicate fine lines around his eyes and the feel of his slightly toughened skin as my fingers pressed on his back, pulling him towards me – they all added to what seemed like his elevated status in the world, and I wanted him to want me.

'Yes, he could perform,' I replied.

Whether or not Sports Man had been trying to open a negotiation, I was glad I hadn't bitten. That would have ruined the whole point of what I was doing. It would have removed the element of choice. And I didn't want to be tied to an arrangement that would oblige me to see him regularly. After all, I'd gone on that site to seek a low-maintenance relationship in the first place. I didn't want to belong to anyone. Ugh, no, no. The ultimate liberation for me was to feel I could date high-profile, influential men with no incentive other than pure, hedonistic pleasure.

Actually, let me embellish on that. In fact, let me embellish quite a lot because well . . . it's complicated. I had actually done committed before, remember, with The Ex. But I hadn't liked my first taste of it. I wilted under the constraints of a long-term relationship. It felt like he lurked in every corner of my life, from breakfast to the next day's breakfast, needing attention, love, reassurance, time, commitment, physical contact and sex. I didn't want to take days out and 'do things' together when we had other things we had to do.

My most vivid argument with him – and this is reflective of how we were – was two years into our relationship on a day he returned from a two-week work-related trip. A group of my university friends had arranged a reunion – a proper one with people I hadn't seen since graduation. That was seven whole years! But when I told him I would be in a pub with them for the afternoon, he was incredulous that I would not be at the train station to greet him. That's what I would do if I had really missed him. So I left the pub – the pub where my long-lost friends were – and went to Victoria train station to meet the Gatwick Express. Yes, I really did.

But I resented it, and he resented me for having hesitated. We argued right up until we went to bed. I didn't sleep that night while my poor distressed mind tried to comfort itself that no, honestly, you really haven't done anything wrong. You just wanted to see old, loyal friends. But my trust in myself was shaken. I must be . . . surely I can't be . . . maybe I'm . . . selfish!

And, you see, that's the scariest, most petrifying thing about being in love. You believe in that person so much that sometimes you stop believing yourself. By default, you become undermined. You are imprisoned by your attachment to him.

Well, that's what my subconscious concluded anyway. The rows increased and I felt my freedom edge further out of reach every day, and eventually we broke up. And my subconscious sent a write-up of the whole awful, tearful, furniture-dividing, ugly, angry, confusing process to my consciousness.

It said: 'Miss Helen, whatever you do, don't ever put me through that again! Don't ever, ever, ever get deeply involved with another person again, because in the deep end you are at the mercy of someone else. Stay in the shallow end where you can swim unaided and where you can get out quick if someone tries to pull you in. If you really must exercise your lust, just focus on the sex. Go and live out a few fantasies, you know, a hotel liaison with some older, dashing, sophisticated, seductive gentleman on business. Yes, that one, I think I've mentioned it before. And if you feel yourself getting sentimental and you really must direct your romantic feelings somewhere, then for goodness' sake find a man who is unavailable. All best, your subconscious.'

And my conscious mind said: 'Gosh, since this break-up, all I seem to want to do is have fun. Now, I'm not sure where it's coming from, but suddenly I've got this burning desire to experiment with my sex life – I've never really done much of that. I don't think I want to be in a relationship again for a long time. In fact, I don't think I want to be in one ever. This thing I have for older men keeps getting stronger, so I think I'm going to do something about it. In fact, I even fancy my boss, who's more than 20 years older than me! Hmm, yes I really do like him – far more than just sexually, actually – but he's totally out of reach, so that's that. I'll just keep him as my private, pleasant fantasy and flirt occasionally to brighten up my working day. In the meantime, I have a plethora of men to date from that sugar daddy website. And, in fact, these sugar daddy dates are perfect for me. I can't believe how lucky I am to discover a new breed of man who doesn't suffocate me. All best, your consciousness.'

Chapter 3

Totally Addicted to Dating

♥ Late May to June '07

So now you know the kind of zeal with which I took to Internet dating. And I kept up this kid-in-a-sweetshop wonder for months. I used to associate online dating with all sorts of negative labels – desperate, lonely, no friends. But now that I had found a niche site that perfectly matched my tastes and my agenda, I became an addict. I had a database of men at my fingertips; I could search by their age, the colour of their eyes, where they lived and even their salary. It was like entering a virtual room with a limitless supply of attractive men and an open licence to flirt with as many as I liked, all from the safety of my laptop. Finally, I was in touch with guys I was actually interested in! For years, I had dated my contemporaries, listened to their boorish tales of beer and football and tried in vain to find something sexually attractive about their fresh young faces. But thanks to this age of technology, I was now meeting men in a different league, with confidence, experience and interesting backgrounds. Nearly all were responsive, too, and that made me feel sexy, naughty and alive.

Every day when I logged on I would have at least eight new messages. I had never before experienced so much attention from so many different people. I had to log on every day – *had to*. I took a sneaky look as I left for work or after I got home from those Chardonnay evenings with girlfriends.

These men were the antidote to the trapped feeling I had when I was in a relationship. At last, I felt I was at liberty to do the simple things I wanted with my day – the gym, reading a chapter of a novel before bed, Sunday lunch with a girlfriend – without having to convince a man that I wasn't prioritising other things over him. These men allowed me to run free. I saw Sports Man two more times after our first date, but he didn't seem to mind that I didn't phone between meetings. He didn't try to map out my Saturdays or get me to meet his friends, as I feared a conventional date might do.

Being new to Internet dating, however, meant I had to pick up the etiquette. At first, I treated all messages like work emails. I thoughtfully and promptly responded to each one. I gave a polite one-sentence summary of why their application hadn't been successful, without actually outright telling them that, although their profile picture was taken in front of a Lamborghini, I just don't do fat and bald.

Then I realised that I couldn't keep up with all the messages, such is the desire of older men to meet a younger woman. One day, I had three offers to be whisked away – to Florida, the Côte d'Azur and someone's boat in Marbella. I didn't feel quite brave enough to venture on an international blind date just yet, but it was good to know that I could fuck on a yacht if I wanted to.

I got people mixed up, too. They all had such similar profile names, things like 'wealthyman100', 'Cityboy44' and 'Legaleagle89'. Most men didn't upload photos to their profiles. 'I'm very well known in my industry and don't want to risk being seen on here,' was the typical excuse. The protocol seemed to be that women unfailingly posted a photo on their profile but men emailed one on request once a correspondence had been established. Since their email addresses never tallied with their profile names, I couldn't keep track of whose photo I had seen, what conversations we had had and whether we had arranged to meet or not. It was simply impossible, unless I logged progress on a spreadsheet, and that seemed obsessive.

Then there was the new phenomenon of cyber-rejection. Many times I messaged a member and got no reply. I wanted to know why! What was wrong with my photo and what was I saying in my profile that they didn't like? Knowing that everyone on the site was open to attention from the opposite sex made being rebuffed online feel more personal than being ignored in a bar, where we can all reassuringly blame rejection on the possibility that our object of desire is taken.

My profile was to the point. There was a sexy photo, taken when I'd dabbled in modelling as a teenager (really, I didn't look *that* different 12 years on!). It said: 'Attractive, slim, bubbly blonde: I love life, laughter, decent wine and even more decent conversation. Oh, and gin and tonics! I'm simply bored of younger guys and want to meet someone older, wiser, more interesting and more confident. I'm a journalist with my own flat, based in north London, so I'm quite self-sufficient. I enjoy the freedom of single life, so am just looking for something fun and casual but with some genuine chemistry – a new adventure!'

The huge number of responses made me feel like a sex goddess. Of course, I knew it was a virtual world and that an inbox full of lustful messages from men who had never met me was by no means a reflection of real life, but still, it was pretty addictive to an Internet-dating newcomer.

I checked out some of the other girls, or 'Sugar Babes', as they are known on the website, and was pleased to find they sounded unattractively high-maintenance. They wrote things like, 'I want to be treated like a princess. I don't like anything cheap – I am a designer girl.' One bolshie 24-year-old wrote, 'If you are a man that thinks doors are for walking through first, then don't get in touch.' Another listed her favourite perfumes and preferred restaurants. Others had written their life stories – and not interesting ones at that. It made me realise that I am pretty simple in my requirements of a man: wit, charm, a suit and some sophisticated seduction.

However, many of the men who fuelled my online high never had any intention of meeting. I had yet to learn that in the Internet dating world there are many fantasists who thrive on the thought that they can attract the opposite sex, but when it comes down to arranging a meeting they shy away in fear of shattering their illusion, a phenomenon not dissimilar to Date One's recurring failure to take his young beauties beyond a first date.

Cybersex Writer was one of these. He contacted me because he had picked up on the reference in my profile to being a journalist. He was excited, he said, because he was a keen writer in his spare time and we clearly had something in common.

I was impressed and curious, so I asked for links to his stories. As I read the first few paragraphs of the first one he sent, my stomach tightened with arousal. I replied asking him whether his stories stemmed from imagination or experience. He said it was a combination and that the one he chose to send me had been sparked by a crush on a friend's 16-year-old daughter. My first reaction was shock – that's only just not criminal, isn't it?! – until I reflected that it was only the action, not the thought, that was unacceptable. Like Date One, Cybersex Writer was brave enough to confront sexual feelings that most men panic themselves into repressing.

I playfully suggested he centre his next story on meeting a girl from London on an Internet site; he sends erotic stories to her and then he comes to visit her. The rest was up to him to invent. Oh, the expectation of hearing someone's personal fantasy about me! Days later, I emailed him to ask him to hurry up. He said that maybe he could get inspiration for a storyline if we both logged on to Messenger and 'chatted to set the scene'.

Messenger. I hate instant messengers of any sort – MSN, iChat, all of them! It's a fruitless activity that takes up as much time as a face-to-face chat but reaps less than a tenth of the rewards. The majority of the website's members used to suggest we 'move to Messenger to chat'. I would always avoid it if I could. I feel the same way about phone calls. I can't stand the thought of being tied to a computer or handset for 20 minutes making small talk when you can say what you need to say in one email or text. I'd rather save the frivolities for in person, with a bottle of wine.

'I don't have Messenger,' I typed.

He sent me a link to download the software. This is what I don't understand: presumably one uses Messenger because it's quicker than email (which is instantaneous anyway), but in order to save just fractions of seconds, you have to wait while a huge file downloads and then set up a username and password and start adding contacts.

But Cybersex Writer insisted that if we were going to write something together he needed to see where our conversation went. I agreed to grant an exception and downloaded Yahoo! Messenger. After which everyone who had ever saved my Hotmail address got a message saying, 'Perrier Jouet just joined Messenger!' I was instantly flooded with pop-ups of 'hey wanna chat?' They appeared every time I logged on to my computer, even when I hadn't specifically opened the software. 'No, I don't want to chat! I have a life – an increasingly hectic one!' I would scream at my machine until I figured out how to uninstall the stupid software for good.

Cybersex Writer even suggested we switch to video chat,

which nearly gave me a small hernia. Telephones and Internet messengers are intrusive enough, shrieking for your attention at unexpected moments, but if people start demanding to see each other as well as hearing their voices, then, gosh, when will we ever be free from others' grasp? My home is where I put face masks on and pad around in fluffy slippers. I do not, under any circumstances, welcome unplanned video guests.

I pretended to be technologically hopeless, so we stuck to the basic messenger software and began to construct our erotic fiction via the keyboard.

'I need to set the scene first,' he wrote. 'What are you wearing?'

'A silk nightie. Salmon pink. Shiny, tight, short. It gapes at the back where it isn't quite tied tightly enough.'

'How does it fall over your bust?'

'Loosely. Sometimes when I move around, one breast pops out and I don't even realise.'

'Where are your hands?'

'Resting gently in my lap, but the nightie is riding up so my hands are resting half on silk and half on the flesh at the top of my thighs.'

'I'm fast-forwarding,' he tapped. 'I've arrived in London, you are coming to meet me on a date. What are you wearing now?'

We continued like this until he said he had enough erotic material to produce a story based on a fictional meeting between us – a cyber-relationship turned real. Then he suddenly announced he had to leave – to go and see his children who were performing in a piano concert.

I was bemused more than annoyed. To me, all these experiences were fascinating insights into the mature man's world, and I was hungry for endless variety. 'Until next time,' I wrote, and settled down to watch the news, smug in the knowledge that I had lost my cybersex virginity.

Chapter 4

My First Non-Committal Relationships

♥ *July '07*

The first man who I felt really fitted with my desired model of a low-maintenance, high-fun relationship came to me via a morning date. Yes, morning. I found the idea simply exhilarating.

> Nothingbutthebest: 'You are quite beautiful. I enjoyed reading your profile – it sounds direct and genuine. I too enjoy being single but would love to share some fun, casual moments with a kindred spirit. What would your ideal date be?'
>
> Perrier Jouet: 'Hmmm . . . what a question. Sushi, cocktails and a non-set agenda for the evening. Does that come close to your ideal?'
>
> Nothingbutthebest: 'I'd do cocktails first and move on to champagne with the sushi. Followed by a dimly lit bar for more cocktails and then . . .'

Using 'dot dot dot' was obviously the 'in' euphemism to refer to sex. I was picking up all this cyber-dating code. We couldn't seem to set a date for the sushi, champagne and 'dot dot dot', though. My shift patterns and his travel itinerary made it seemingly impossible. Either he was in the south of France, Sicily or St Lucia or I was working the dreaded night shifts. Every ten weeks, my work roster gave me a three-week run of nights. I can't think of anything more hellish about the broadcast-news industry than the unavoidable roster patterns. I didn't see friends, didn't drink, didn't see daylight and didn't wax for the entire three weeks. They never tell you about that at journalism school.

I jokingly suggested we would have to meet for a champagne breakfast after a night shift if we couldn't fix a day, but he took the suggestion seriously. So, one Tuesday morning at 8 a.m., after I'd finished a producer shift in the newsroom, working on the early-morning bulletins and reports, I told the ITN-paid taxi that I wasn't going to my home address, as booked, but to the Langham Hotel behind Regent Street. Champagne Breakfast Guy was waiting in the doorway. I was wowed by his looks. He had short, dark hair and strong, chiselled features. He was head and shoulders above any of my other dates so far. In fact, at 6 ft 6 in., he was head and shoulders above most things. I felt tiny as he walked ahead of me, leading me to the morning room, checking politely that I wasn't too tired after my night shift.

'I'm absolutely fine,' I assured him. The excitement had kept me alert all night. In fact, I had even bypassed the usual 3 a.m. lull. The dining area was bright, airy, pristine and noticeably quiet. He ordered scrambled eggs and smoked salmon for us both and two glasses of Bollinger. I wished he had ordered a bottle. I'd have been less conscious of my drinking speed then.

He told me he was taking a 'career break' and using his free time to travel and to visit his villa in Sicily. Actually, it transpired that he had been suspended from his role as chairman of an insurance company while it was investigated over premium-fixing allegations. He told me how the Serious Fraud Office had searched his home. The press had doorstepped him several times and he was constantly being pursued for comment by journalists from financial titles.

'Was it a big case? Would I have heard of you?'

'Being a journalist, you probably would, so I'm not telling you my surname.'

He should have known that was a fatal thing to say to anyone, regardless of whether they are a journalist or not. Naturally, I became convinced there was an exciting story to be discovered and already I was scheming how I could find out his last name. He told me he had to wait two months for the result of the SFO inquiry. In a worst-case scenario, he could end up spending two years in jail.

'Another glass?' My body's reaction to the bubbles was sped up by the effects of the long night shift, and once we were off the subject of the investigation we started talking and giggling louder and louder.

'I think we should go somewhere less quiet,' I whispered, suddenly aware of the guests glancing up questioningly from their cappuccinos and copies of the *Financial Times*. We must have made an odd sight at 8.30 a.m. in a hotel, drinking six glasses of Bollinger and asking obvious first-date questions.

It was clear we needed to get out of the breakfast room, but which one of us was going to be daring enough to suggest we go to his room? 'Do you fancy a morning-cap?' doesn't really have the same ring. We walked awkwardly through the lobby, both thinking it, not saying it. I felt drunk on tiredness. My mind felt pleasantly out of focus. I seemed to have been stripped of any decision-making abilities, but I was enjoying the sensation. I opened my mouth to say, 'Shall we get a coffee?' but before I could speak, he grabbed my arm and without saying a word guided me assertively to the lift and then his room.

It smelled of fresh linen. The neutral decor and gold satin bedding made it feel like walking into a sanctuary, a sensation my addled brain welcomed. The only evidence that Champagne Breakfast Guy had checked in was his silver laptop sitting on a polished oak desk beside a bulging fruit hamper.

Still without saying a word, we turned to each other and kissed, making our way to what looked like a quadruple king-size bed, and I gently undid his buttons. It felt so natural. I could feel his warm breath against my lips as he reached behind me and undid the zip on my dress. It fell to the floor just as I undid his bottom button and his shirt glided off. I embraced my sleepiness and sank into the bed, pulling him down near to me. He was gentler, quieter and more passionate than Sports Man. He kissed more but had that same air of self-assurance. I lay on the bed, trusting him to know what to do. He made love like he was in love. He was rhythmic, gentle and he felt warm and comforting – but maybe that was my own sleep-deprived body drawing itself into relaxation.

I didn't leave the hotel until 2 p.m. I stopped off at reception to 'confirm the spelling of the surname of the gentleman in Room 301'. Bingo! I went home, googled his name and read the coverage on the inquiry into his company. From what he had told me over the Bollinger and what I was sleepily scanning over now, he seemed pretty innocent to me. I woke up at 9 p.m. and went straight to the office for another night shift.

♥ ♥ ♥

Usually on night shifts I would hibernate from life for three weeks. This time, though, spurred on by my new Internet dating high, I was determined not to let my unwelcome shift patterns prevent me from going on all the dates I had put so much effort into setting up. Yes, more dates with more fascinating people with fascinating, glamorous lives.

And so I arranged to meet Munich Man one evening before work. I called him Munich Man because he had business there and was only in the UK for around ten days a month, which, to me – still fiercely embracing my freedom – was a great big plus. He suggested meeting on a Monday evening for a drink and dinner. I warned him from the start that I had a curfew, that a night shift loomed at the end of our date and so I would not be able to indulge in more than one glass of wine. If I'm upfront, I thought, there won't be any false expectations.

We met on the fifth floor of Harvey Nichols, the second most upmarket department store in Knightsbridge after Harrods. I was excited as I walked in heading for the lift. Harvey Nicks was the sort of place I went to only to browse, knowing I could never afford anything. I had always thought of those little champagne bars dotted around upmarket department stores as places where other people went – people in higher-earning industries than journalism. I felt the same in airports; I would always be on the metal chairs with the masses, eating a packet of sushi from Boots, never at the oyster bars where the less financially challenged people sat.

The fifth floor of Harvey Nicks was laid out around a white-leather-lined circular bar. An expensive delicatessen occupied half the floor and various restaurants, including a sushi conveyor belt, took up the rest. I saw a man sitting directly in front of me. He was wearing a dark-grey suit that stood out against the white bar. He looked slick, with a briefcase tucked neatly by his feet, sipping from a champagne flute, reading the *Evening Standard*. His silver-grey hair was standing on end, which he seemed oblivious to. I hope that's

him, I thought, and it was.

'Ah, Helen?' He looked right at me, warmly, and I remember thinking that he had kind eyes. I joined him for a glass of champagne and then we crossed to the other side of the department-store floor for sushi, which we washed down with another glass. He was full of chatterbox energy, jumping from subject to subject, and had an air of amicable chaos about him.

He was a walking anthology of funny stories from the website. One girl he'd met, apparently, wasn't used to drinking and virtually collapsed on him after two glasses of champagne. 'She was slurring and spluttering and losing control of all her limbs,' Munich Man giggled. 'She was a total nightmare. One minute she'd have a fit of hysterics and the next minute she'd collapse on my shoulder. I had to get the concierge to call a cab before they accused me of drugging her or something!'

I loved the fact that he made light of using the site rather than guiltily referring to it as if it were some sort of sinister secret, as so many of my other dates had done. Munich Man's only drawback as far as I could tell was that his voice was so posh and he talked so fast that I couldn't always understand what he said.

'How did you discover the website?' I asked. I meant, 'Why did you join?'

'Well, I tried to meet people through normal channels,' Munich Man continued in the same unashamed tone, 'but that's awfully difficult because I'm in Munich one week, London the next and then San Francisco after that. As soon as we get to the second or third date, they start asking where it's going and they want promises that I can't make.' He spoke rapidly, his voice high-pitched and his eyes wide, and he used words like 'frightfully' and 'awfully' all the time.

'Same with men,' I replied, remembering my first date after my break-up, before joining Sugardaddie.com. Straight away, it had been clear that the guy expected at least three meetings a week. I'd felt cornered, fearful that I'd end up back in a lifestyle where I struggled to find the time to see my friends or spend time on my own, so I hadn't contacted him again. 'If someone isn't in a position to commit, it's much more honest to advertise for short-term fun on a website set up for that than to prey on a poor real romance-seeker in a bar under the false pretence that you're open to falling in love.'

We went for another cocktail at nearby Zuma, a trendy, expensive Asian fusion restaurant. Munich Man was a 42-year-old fund manager. He was going through the end stages of a divorce and had no permanent home. He lived between a hotel in Munich and the Jumeirah Carlton in Knightsbridge. Every second weekend he would go back to his estranged family's home in Cambridgeshire to take over childcare duties from his wife. He was matter of fact about the logistics – as were all divorcees whom I had encountered from the website – but reading between his high-speed lines, there was a tone of bitterness.

'What happened between you?' I asked, judging him to be man enough for such a personal question.

'I tried awfully hard to make the marriage work,' he began, more slowly now, looking down, not at me. And he told me about the long and painful process of falling out of love. I felt an urge to put my hand on his shoulder but I was scared that he would find it intrusive.

He raised his arm to attract the attention of the barman for a refill and then I remembered, with horror, that I had to go *to work*! I had my car with me. We were usually provided with taxis for night shifts but that was only useful if I was going to the office straight from home. And I'd thought that if I drove to my date it would stop me getting tipsy. So much for that optimistic theory.

Two glasses of champagne and a dirty Martini was really pushing the limit as to what I could safely consume and still manage a news desk, but driving was definitely out of the question. I abandoned my little old banger in Knightsbridge, got a cab and made a mental note to collect the car in the morning before the parking meters kicked in.

As I raised my arm to flag a cab, Munich Man grabbed me, pulled me in and kissed me passionately. I was left in a dizzy whirlwind. I liked this man more than any of the others to date. He seemed more fun than Champagne Breakfast Guy, who, although daring, had, I thought, a tendency to be over-serious. In the taxi, his kiss whirred around in my head. There was a stubborn smile on my face that I couldn't suppress. I hadn't felt this kind of giddy, elated lust for a long time. Already, I was thinking of meeting him again, kissing him again. I just had to get off those goddamned night shifts. Talking of which, I hoped there was somewhere open that sold awfully strong black coffee.

Chapter 5

A Cash Offer

♥ **July '07**

The recompense for having to work night shifts was that once the hideous three-week run of them was over we were awarded five days off – five glorious days to recover from disturbed sleeping patterns, SAD, sub-zero office temperatures and, worst of all, twenty-one days of sobriety. I always used those five days to get some dignity back after spending weeks in a fleece, glasses and flat shoes. I'd get a haircut, have my highlights touched up, book a month's worth of waxing and get my toes painted.

So I was feeling thoroughly rested and glowing when I turned up to meet Munich Man again, a week after our first date, on the fifth floor of Harvey Nicks. We had two cocktails and moved on to a seafood restaurant in a fashionable area of the Fulham Road in Chelsea. It was quiet and brightly lit. That didn't bother Munich Man; he was still talking loudly and, I noted, at an alarming pace. Our seafood platter arrived, but he hardly touched it. I tucked in to lashings of crabmeat, prawns bigger than the palm of my hand, bright amber mussels and juicy chunks of crayfish.

'I'm eating all this. Do help me,' I said, interrupting his 70-mph account of a recent visit to his brother's villa in Provence.

'Well, the truth is,' he replied, making no effort to lower his voice, 'I had a little line earlier. I think I did it too close to dinner. Gosh, awfully silly, really. I've ruined my appetite.' He paused, beginning to look worried by his awkward predicament. 'Do you want one? Here you go.' He tried to force a small pink square of folded paper into my hand under the table.

'Erm, maybe later,' I said. I by no means frowned on cocaine. I had dabbled in it, like most people my age, but that was on special occasions – a party, a birthday, a club night – when there were a few of us doing it together and we knew we had a weekend to recover. I didn't think that a Michelin-starred restaurant was the time or the place for a relative Class A novice like me to be experimenting. It seemed a waste. And he hadn't even tested how liberal my views were on it. It is, after all, illegal.

'Well, if you want it, just say.' He nibbled on a prawn, but other than that the entire platter was consumed by me. Not the oysters, though – hideous, foul-smelling things.

Despite his startled-rabbit expression throughout dinner, I found Munich Man endearing company. I was becoming smitten by his eccentric, bumbling manner and I was still thinking about the kiss before I had got into the cab. Mmmm, The Kiss. He got the bill and I rested my hand on his leg. 'Shall we go for a drink somewhere?' I asked.

'My hotel's awfully close. I have some nice wine. We could go back there,' he suggested, acting innocent.

The Jumeirah Carlton Tower is on a quiet corner of Cadogan Place, right by the designer shops that line Sloane Street and near to Munich Man's favourite meeting place, Harvey Nicks. Two doormen in beige tails, cravats and comically tall hats opened the cab door and a third held open the hotel door. We walked through a glitzy reception to the lift. Munich Man's room was on the fifth floor, right at the end of a corridor. He nearly always had the same room. I clocked a bottle of wine in a bucket of now-melted ice and two fresh glasses already laid out. That was presumptuous preparation, I thought, but I was secretly flattered by his optimism.

Munich Man chopped up two huge, heavy-duty lines of cocaine and, away from the formality of the restaurant and surrounded by the decadence of his five-star hotel room, I took up his offer this time. It hit me instantly, filling me with a happy energy and a fervent urge for him. We couldn't get our clothes off quickly enough. He kissed me and ran his hands up the sides of my whole body, over my bra, stopping at my neck, where he pressed hard on the pressure points at the back of my head. It sent a secondary cocaine rush through me. Cocaine makes your body feel slightly numb but at the same time it makes you crave extreme sensations. So it makes you kiss, fondle and fuck furiously. He was extremely well endowed and stayed in the same rock hard state for hours. I couldn't understand how that had outlasted the cocaine.

I stayed the night, too exhausted to go anywhere when we eventually collapsed at around 4 a.m. I awoke to the sound of singing in the shower. When I felt I could face opening my eyes, before me was a sweet-smelling figure in a neatly pressed suit, bursting with energy, furiously tapping away on a BlackBerry. He hoovered up a leftover line of cocaine from the bedside table, pausing with a twenty-pound note poised by his left nostril to ask if I wanted any. I told him I would rather manually dislocate my nose than put anything else up it. And, with that, he trotted off to an 8 a.m. meeting, reminding me to take down the 'do not disturb' sign when I left.

I was just dosing off again when I was rudely awakened by my phone. It was Champagne Breakfast Guy texting to confirm our meeting in three days' time. Really? Had I arranged that? I would answer him later. I switched my phone to silent, put my head back on the pillow and went back to sleep. After the night before, I felt sexually satisfied enough for the next month.

♥ ♥ ♥

I still had three days of my post-night-shift break left and I chose to spend them drinking wine with Only Remaining Single Friend, to whom I divulged all the intimate details of the night with Munich Man.

'He must take Viagra,' she concluded.

'I asked him. He said not. He said he was just turned on by a beautiful girl,' I insisted proudly.

'No way. No man can do cocaine all night and, you know . . . last!'

By the Sunday evening, I was exhausted. The following morning was my first day back to working daytime office hours. I would see The Boss tomorrow. After not being in for so long, I'd have an excuse to go in and talk to him – to ask him about his holiday, to ask him about business, to flirt. I wanted to feel and look good, so I started preparing for an early night. As I did, I sneaked a look at my messages on Sugardaddie.com. When members log on, a little banner pops up on their profile to tell other members that they are online. One guy evidently saw my flashing online marker and fired off a message in stilted English.

'I had a booking tonight at Mandarin Oriental restaurant. It is a Sasha Gausselmann restaurant, I assure you the best of quality. My date for the evening has said she has cancelled at last minute. I have a booking for 9pm. If you would like to join me, I assure you I am genuine SD and to prove it I will give you £500 for evening. I promise I am true gent and I will not expect any more than dinner this first time.'

I reread it. Gosh. 'A genuine SD,' he said. That was the abbreviation for 'sugar daddy'. Is that what they were expected to do? Pay women to have dinner with them? This was what Sports Man had been referring to, and this guy, by the name of Andre, thought I was one of those girls. I had never had an overt cash offer like that. I had had members who had emailed things like, 'Can I interest you in Paris mid-June?' or 'Can I take you for dinner? What perfume do you wear?' but never anything like this.

Could I accept money from a stranger for dinner? He'd clearly stated in black and white that there would be no expectation of anything more. He obviously wasn't a native English speaker. His language reminded me of one of those scam emails that open with 'warm greetings from Africa' and offer to deposit half a million US dollars in your bank account. What if he was running some scam like that, scheming something dreadful? Or what if he was a crazed Russian who would get obsessed, try to control my life and send mafiosi to follow me whenever I left my flat?! But then, if I was in a public place and I didn't agree to go anywhere with him in private and I filled out the coffee table book with his details for my flatmate to see, what could go wrong? On the other hand, I have greasy hair, chipped toenail polish and a four-day hangover, shouted my voice of reason. But £500! And dinner in a celebrity chef's restaurant with an interesting man. I wonder what he does and where he's from, said my voice of opportunity. Besides, I recognised his profile. I had seen it before and noted that he looked attractive and that I must message him some time. Well, fate had done it for me.

I tied my unwashed hair back, topped up my toenails with a near-match colour and jumped on the Tube. The Mandarin Oriental is a grand hotel in Knightsbridge directly opposite

Harvey Nichols. The bar was buzzing, but the restaurant was serene. Other than two Indian businessmen who looked like they were engaged in a very important and heated discussion, there was no one there but him. I easily recognised him from his profile picture, but it was clearly at least ten years out of date.

'Thank you so much for coming at short notice.' He was French. He stood up to kiss me. It was an air kiss. He was tall with long limbs and a long neck. I could see that he had once been a handsome man – as his out-of-date photo had suggested – but he now looked like he had aged beyond his years. He was probably only in his mid-50s, at a guess, but there was a frailty about him and at times his gestures reminded me of an old man's. His movements came with an effort and as he ate he would suddenly pause, holding his fork upright on the table, and stare into space with lifeless, sunken eyes, like a man who's given up on the present and lives by reflecting on what was.

He ordered the tasting menu – seven small courses. I had actually already eaten when I'd received his message, but I imagined I would easily manage to politely tuck away a few delicate foie gras wafers and prosciutto-wrapped scallops.

Before the first course arrived, he handed me a brown envelope, saying, 'This is for you.' I didn't know what to do. What was the etiquette? Should I gush with delight as though he'd just given me a divine Gucci watch? Or should I put it in my bag with nothing more than a nod and give the impression that I did this sort of thing all the time? Or, worse still, I suddenly thought in horror, was this intended as some sort of deposit and was he expecting me to allude to continuing the evening's services after dinner?

Ignoring that screaming thought, I chirped away with banal chatter. He was quiet and didn't talk back much. He gave an occasional uninterested nod and would look around the room. His English was poor, but his French accent somehow made the conversation seem less strained. I could be sent to sleep by the voice of a Frenchman; their speech is like a lullaby. I don't care what they say, I just like to listen to it.

After the fourth course – herb-rolled Suffolk sheep's cheese with land-cress salad – I excused myself to go to the Ladies. Locked safely inside a cubicle, I counted the cash. There were ten new and fresh-smelling fifty-pound notes. I held them between my thumb and fingers for a few seconds, rubbing the layers together gently, liking the way the rough texture felt as the notes glided against each other. I felt as if I was in possession of a precious stone that I shouldn't really have. Why had Andre given me this? He wasn't acting in the least bit suggestive. In fact, he could hardly even hold eye contact.

When the tasting came to an end, I was still wary of him springing a surprise second phase of the evening on me. We got up from the table and walked to the reception area. I was still half expecting him to say, 'Shall we go upstairs?' or something equally terrifying. What would I say then? But he simply held up my coat and said, 'Well, er, I 'ad better be calling you zee taxee.' I thanked him for the evening and disappeared, my brown envelope tucked away safely in my oversized handbag. I never heard from him again.

♥ ♥ ♥

'So there really is a God,' I concluded, telling a happily married girlfriend the story a few days later.

'He obviously thought you were an escort when he first contacted you, then, as the evening went on and you chatted away obliviously, he realised you weren't. He was probably too much of a gentleman to ask for his money back, but I bet he's really pissed off he's wasted 500 quid.'

'Oh, you think so?' I love Happily Married Girlfriend.

Sometimes she says the most sensible things that just never occur to me. In the happy bubble of my new and exciting dating life, I presumed everyone on the site was like me – looking for fun, adventure and new ways to satiate their curiosity about the world. Surely all the girls had the same thirst for life and new experiences as I did, and the same attraction to older men. There couldn't have been a blatant culture of money for dinner with a 'happy ending', could there? Surely men would go to a very different sort of website for that. Or maybe Andre, having quite clearly passed his peak, felt like he needed to make a down payment to secure a second date.

'You really shouldn't have accepted the money, though,' continued Happily Married Girlfriend.

'Why?!'

'It lowers you. You don't need that. You're better than that.'

Oh, here we go – moral pep talk and we're still on bottle number one. I often got those from Happily Married Girlfriend. Usually they were on the subject of casual sex, which she considered to be an unladylike pursuit; she thought my time would be better invested in looking for potential future husband material.

She believed anyone happily single to be in denial. I, however, was beginning to believe that anyone who was contented and *not* single must be in denial. My new-found freedom had given me a radiance that many people had commented on. I saw more of my neglected friends; I'd even made new friends; I could wear a dress and heels every day without having to explain myself; I chose when I ate and what time to set the alarm for. I was finding more and more evidence to back up my theory that independence was the elixir of life and relationships were a poisoned chalice.

'It's not like I slept with him!' I argued. 'I didn't even touch the guy's hand. He wanted a dinner companion; I had dinner. I was very polite. It's not like I ran off with his money. He could phone me if he wants something else. He hasn't.'

'He won't respect you for taking the money.'

Oh, I see, I thought. That's what all this is about: respect. Happily married friends always have this thing about needing respect from the opposite sex. That's why they advise things like withholding sex on the first date. And that's why they always ask excited questions like, 'Are you seeing him again?' They are convinced that every romantic encounter must in some way aspire to the continuity of marriage. They seem to have forgotten that there are perfectly acceptable models for forming short-term relationships.

'But it doesn't matter whether he respects me or not,' I insisted. 'I'm not looking for a relationship with this guy. I went on a whim. I went with an open mind to see what he was like, not to try and formulate a deep, everlasting relationship with him.'

'Would you tell the guy you do marry that you'd taken money from someone in the past?'

'Oh, for fuck's sake. I should stop doing things because of what an imaginary person who doesn't even exist yet may think?'

She was basing her argument on moral standards that society inflicts on us, not on her own independent, intelligent judgement. Over the next bottle of wine, we continued to disagree. The whole evening was horrid. When we eventually agreed to stop talking about it and move on to another topic, we couldn't get back to our earlier jovial tone. The conversation was strained as we tiptoed around sensitive subjects. I was conscious of everything I said for fear of being judged again, and she was conscious of everything she said for fear of offending me again. We parted with wooden hugs. There was a clear dent in our friendship, and I was upset.

Chapter 6
My Inbox

♥ August '07

As time went on, I realised that offers like Andre's weren't that uncommon. While it was a given that the man would always pay the way on dates from Sugardaddie.com, some wanted to get the competitive edge by offering gifts or promising shopping trips. Around 20 per cent of messages alluded to direct financial assistance. Take this one, from CharmingMystery, which was waiting in my inbox when I logged on one rainy afternoon: 'Hi, nice photo. What are you looking for? Do you like to travel? Am open to exploring new forms of relationship. Happy to help with finances/education fees etc. Get in touch if you want to discuss.'

Most didn't actually allude to financial help in the first email. Often they'd say in the third or fourth message that they were happy to 'help with rent/bills/luxuries'. Usually the ones who made offers like that were married or they were much older – 60-plus. When I say I preferred older men, I liked sophistication and the look of a mature face, but I struggled to find anyone above mid-50s attractive. I always deleted those types of offers, anyway. It wasn't that I agonised over the morals of it. It just never occurred to me that I – a professional from a respectable family with my own income – was in a position to entertain them. That sort of behaviour was for other girls, girls who didn't have careers or ambitions or their own busy schedules, perfectly manicured girls happy to become kept women and spend their afternoons lunching in Chelsea. For the rest of us, the only valid basis for romantic relations was mutual affection, surely?

Some men would just go silent for no apparent reason. Twice I'd got as far as organising a date right down to the time and the place and then found that there was no reply to my confirmation email sent on the morning ahead of our planned meeting. I wasn't sure whether to turn up or not. Thankfully, I didn't. I later learned that no confirmation definitely means no date, because everyone in Internet dating is terrified of being stood up, so everyone always makes an effort to double-confirm.

Above CharmingMystery's email was one from Krug. We had exchanged messages since the week I'd joined, but we hadn't met. He sent long, rambling emails describing his activities in detail. His photo was eye-catching, though. He looked like he was in his late 40s. I always paused to look at it whenever I read or sent an email. It had an extraordinary effect on me. It seemed to be erotically charged and I couldn't help imagining him in bed every time I looked at it.

In my last message to him, I had asked how his weekend was. He replied: 'I took part in a charity tennis tournament. It comprised six ladies' matches and six men's matches over the two days. The ladies played two matches before lunch and four after and the men played four before lunch and two after. The teams taking part were made up of local residents and business owners who get together every month to help a local charity . . .' It went on like that for another six paragraphs, all equally monotonous.

Whenever I suggested meeting, he would either give me a rundown of his schedule to explain why he couldn't meet or he would fail to acknowledge my suggestion at all. Krug was one of the many men whom I was to come across who seemed to be interested only in the thrill of online flirting, never actually intending to meet anyone.

'It's because they can pretend to be a different person online,' Happily Married Girlfriend had suggested once. 'They can pretend to be a millionaire, attracting the beautiful young women they fantasise about. When they get round to planning to meet for real, they panic because they can't live up to the image that they've portrayed.' Like I said before, Happily Married Girlfriend always says sensible things that I haven't even considered.

Next came an email from a girl, or Sugar Babe, called 'MissPenelope': 'Hi babe, how's this site for you? It isn't really going for me. Full of jokers. Awful!'

I had never had an email from a girl on the site before and I was naturally curious. What experiences had she had? Was she one of those girls that Sports Man had told me about? Gosh, I hoped so. It seemed somehow splendid that I could be talking to one. I replied: 'A little mixed, really. Lots of time wasters! Lots of cancellations! Why is it awful for you? x'

She came back to me within two minutes: 'I know another site where you can get 10,000 a month, this is SHITTTT!!! I'm off. XX'

There were no messages after that, so I didn't find out who she was or any more about the website she claimed to be joining, but I remembered her profile name.

Then there was the message I had been looking out for, from Greg:

Hey Helen,
I have emailed you yet another option. I was thinking

53

that if you leave UK on the night flight on Thursday, it makes for a full functional day on Friday instead of a recovery day. I think it is a better schedule for you . . . but not sure? Maybe sleeping a full night in your own bed on Thursday is better tho? Too much thinking! Anyway, it is an option. I need to confirm tomorrow. Let me know.

PS Just FYI, I leave for US tomorrow afternoon. I will be in Seattle on a different time zone.

That was a message finalising our plans for *New York next week*! We'd started arranging it three weeks ago. When Greg had contacted me initially, I'd ignored him. He said he was a Canadian living in Toronto and travelled regularly to New York for meetings, and he'd asked if I wanted to join him on one of his trips.

Anyone who opens dialogue with an invitation to join him on a business trip to a mutually foreign city must be either desperate, dangerous or another fantasist with no intention of following through on the offer, I concluded. Why not select a girl who already lived in NYC? He didn't have a photo on his profile, either. But he was persistent and his messages articulate and pleasant to read. He was one of the only people who bothered to punctuate his messages and spell words correctly.

After his third message, I responded, asking for a photo. He was in sportswear with a baseball cap. He was stocky and broad-shouldered in a toned, muscular way. I could see an attractive face beneath the cap, but in his pose, in those clothes, he looked a little like he could be guarding the door of a nightclub. I can't go to New York to meet this guy, I thought. This was ridiculous.

But still he persisted, and, after allowing myself again to be persuaded to chat on that wretched messenger thing, I was charmed by him. He was more emotionally astute than anyone from the site I had dated so far. I was drawn in by his eloquence and what seemed like a genuine interest in and an ability to listen to me. I'm still not sure when the exact 'fuck it' moment came, but suddenly I found myself checking the work roster for a weekend off and we were discussing e-tickets.

Chapter 7

Two Nights in New York

♥ August '07

Flying first class is amazing. I used to think that paying up to eight times more than the price of an economy ticket was something I would never do, on principle, even if I could afford it. The disproportionate ratio of cost to increased comfort could never justify it, I said.

I have since changed my mind.

In first class, you get your own personalised service. You get to choose five courses, you get to dictate when you want to eat and whether you want to be woken up. You get to choose your wine. You get extra films. And you get space – absolutely loads of space. Those moments in economy class when you need to rummage through your bag for lip balm, tissues, book, pen for the landing card and end up elbowing the person next to you or when you have to hold on for as long as possible for the toilet because you really can't climb over that person *again* – those moments just don't happen, because you can neatly lay out everything you need for the entire flight on not one but several side shelves and tables. And you don't have to fold them away when you get up to go to the toilet. And you get a duvet and proper toothpaste. And you get off the plane first so you reach the customs line first. I felt like I *belonged*.

I'm certainly glad I didn't drop out of this trip, I thought, as I sipped Pommery champagne from an American Airlines branded champagne glass, moving the chair back into the reclining position and then up again for the 15th time before take-off. I had had a mini-panic the night before leaving. I had texted Only Remaining Single Friend: 'What am I thinking flying across Atlantic to meet stranger?! Should I call off? He could be nutter. If not, should I take black pencil skirt and lace top or purple dress? Require diff shoes so can only take one.'

She had replied: 'Don't cancel. If he's awful go shopping. Dollar v good against pound now. Take the lace top.'

Greg had booked a junior suite at a hotel in Nolita, a fashionable, arty part of New York, the streets lined with boutiques, next door to SoHo. He told me to get a cab from the airport and text when I was five minutes away. He rushed out, paid the driver, despite my feeble attempts to tell him not to, and took my bags.

Service in America never fails to impress me. Staff are friendly and helpful and nothing is ever too much trouble. Within minutes, the team at the front desk knew my name, where I was from, how my flight was, when I was going back and whether this was my first time in New York. You'd never get this in a London hotel, I thought.

Greg was like his photos. He was dark, stocky and muscular and average height. Without his sportswear uniform, he was, as I had hoped, much more attractive. He beamed when he saw me; I noticed he smiled a lot. 'Oh, you look even better in the flesh than in your photo!'

'And so do you!' I laughed in reply.

A moment is all you need to establish if you are likely to be 57 attracted to someone. In the first ten seconds, you probably make more judgements than you do during the next ten hours. In those initial seconds, what ran through my conscious mind was: 'I don't think I've done at all badly for a random shot at an international blind date.'

It was strange meeting someone for the first time knowing we would be sharing a hotel bed for the next two days. It didn't make me feel nervous, though. I suppose I must have done some semi-conscious risk assessment of the weekend and concluded that the possibility of not finding him attractive was balanced by the chance that I would have a fantastic all-expenses-paid trip to New York with a charming, interesting and interested new date.

One of the overwhelmingly friendly front-desk staff showed me to the room. Greg said he'd finish off what he was doing in the lobby on his laptop and be up in ten minutes. Very considerate, I thought. He obviously wanted to give me some privacy while I settled in.

I looked around the suite. It was decorated in a mixture of English Georgian and modern styles. There was a glass dining table at one end of the room and two sofas facing each other with a glass coffee table in the middle on the other side. Through a double door at the end was the bedroom and his 'n' hers en suite bathrooms. The late-afternoon sun was pouring in through three large windows. I felt a surge of elation. I was in New York! No one knew I was here other than Only Remaining Single Friend and my lodger. How *brave* I had become with my dating!

I splashed water on my face and, typically, my mascara ran down my cheeks. Shit. I hadn't planned on a full face wash and reapplication of make-up. Where was my toiletry bag? In my case. Which hadn't been brought to the room yet. Shit. Greg knocked on the door. I wiped the mascara away with some wet toilet tissue and went to open the door.

Greg was smiling. 'How do you like it?' He was relaxed, non-intrusive, uncomplicated. He poured two gin and tonics from the minibar and we sat down on the two sofas opposite each other. Greg managed the world network of suppliers for a huge chain of fashion houses, a role that took him all around North America, Asia and recently into South America. Although he had claimed to be 39 in his profile, he was actually 46. 'I find that once you go over 40 you get eliminated from lots of searches,' he said. 'You've got something white on your cheek. Right there.' He leaned forward to wipe it off. It was half-dissolved toilet tissue.

He listened well, I noticed, and asked lots of questions. He seemed to have an analytical mind, like me. As our conversation developed, I felt we were fully on the same wavelength.

An hour later, we went for a walk around SoHo, Greenwich and the Meatpacking District. I was getting distracted by the impressive array of shops and their awe-inspiring window displays. 'I take it you like shopping?' said Greg, as I lagged behind yet again, gawping up at a leggy mannequin in possibly the sexiest knee-high white boots I'd ever seen.

'I've wanted to come shopping to New York for *ages*,' I replied, unable to take my eyes off the boots. They were made of the softest, most luscious-looking leather, with a gold buckle at the top and a mouth-wateringly sexy gold heel.

'We'll have plenty of time for that tomorrow. Believe it or not, with my job, I happen to be a man who knows a lot about brands, labels and the best places to shop. So you, lady, are in luck.'

Greg suggested we 'drop in to Nobu' for sushi. Not having been to either of the London branches, I didn't realise what an understated way of putting it that was until I saw the prices on the menu and the number of waiting staff hovering over every table.

As soon as I started to eat – a platter of fresh sushi, Nobu's   59 signature dish of black cod with miso, sesame aubergine and delicately wrapped parcels of prawns – my jet lag hit me. I could feel myself phasing out of the conversation; Greg's sentences were starting to wash over me and my body was beginning to feel that long-haul ache. Darn jet lag. I didn't want to be tired.

Back at the hotel, I lay like a dead weight on the bed. He lay next to me, stroking me affectionately but not sexually over my nightdress. What was my family like, he wanted to know, my relationships with my siblings, where did I grow up, why did I choose to study Japanese at university. He asked simple but meaningful things, and each time I answered I felt he really listened and registered. I was amazed by how at ease and connected to him I felt. As I lay there on the cusp of sleep, I even forgot how much of a commitment-phobe I was.

Then I was wide-awake at 5 a.m., Greg breathing heavily behind me. I listened to the clock ticking slowly, waiting for it to become a decent enough hour for me to wake him. By 6 a.m., my stomach was rumbling too much to bear. I am always ravenous in the mornings and am used to eating breakfast immediately. I stepped out of the bed quietly, wondering if there would be a café or shop where I could get some fruit to tide me over until he woke and we got to go for a proper breakfast. But before I'd even got to my case to take out a top to throw on, he was awake, smiling sleepily, unperturbed by being woken so early.

'Are you ready for a day of shopping?'

Of course I was ready for a day of shopping, but I wasn't certain if he meant a day of shopping paid for by him or a day of shopping funded in the conventional manner – by my well-used credit card. Deep down, I knew that it was most likely the former, given that no date I'd ever met through the website had ever let me pay for anything in his presence. But

I didn't dare to be too presumptuous and, besides, it kept it more magical if I tried to keep that expectation to the very back of my mind. I think I wanted to feel surprised.

'Is there anything you really need?' Greg kept asking as we walked through the streets of SoHo. 'What do you like looking at? Do you need a dress for tonight? Or new jeans? I know a great jeans store; they have every make imaginable.' I didn't know what to say. I wanted to find a couple of smart work outfits – things that I could wear on camera now that I was doing more on-screen stuff. But I didn't want to give the impression that I had a checklist in my head.

'Do you like Louis Vuitton?' he continued, when I didn't specify anything or anywhere I wanted to go. 'What about Alexander McQueen? Or Chloé?' I think he was waiting for me to jump and say, 'Oh, yes, that one's my favourite!' But not only was I trying to avoid being opportunistic, I actually didn't know anything about designers. I had never dreamed of going into a clothes shop where the price tags went into three figures, let alone four. Like most people of my age and income, I was much more comfortable rummaging through the rails of Zara and Oasis.

I also didn't know what his expectations were for our shopping trip. Did he just want to get in and out of a shop after treating me to a gift, or did he have the patience for hours and hours of browsing, the way women usually shop? I suspect he noticed my awkward politeness; thankfully, he took things into his own hands. 'The Prada store,' he said, stopping suddenly and pointing at a large building across the road. 'We have to go in there, if only to see the architecture.'

New York's SoHo Prada store opens into a huge space that stretches over an entire block. In the centre, the wooden floor dips down in a bowl-like shape and there are steep steps down the side of the slope leading into the basement.

And that's where all the clothes are. A rail of red dresses 61 invited me to go leafing through them. Wow, I kept saying. Every dress, shirt and pair of trousers hanging delicately on its hanger was unique, thoughtfully and lovingly designed. Every stitch, every hem sang of quality. All the shades of colour seemed so new and beautiful I wondered if Prada had them patented. Prada outfits, it is safe to say, rarely find their way onto the shoulders of lowly paid multimedia journalists.

'Try it on,' said Greg, as I refused to let go of a thick, tailored red dress with which I appeared to have fallen head over heels in love. 'And grab some other things, too. What about this? And this?'

Suddenly, I was in the changing-room, with staff thronging around me, bringing the red dress, then a similar navy dress and a black leather dress, presenting glasses of champagne on a silver tray, offering their personal recommendations.

A camp male sales assistant was leading the pack. 'Oh, I have something that would suit your shape just perfectly, ma'am.' 'Oh, did you see our new collection of leather pencil skirts? Ma'am, you have to try them.' 'Oh my gosh, Prada fits you like a glove.' 'This belt, it just completes the outfit. You have to get this belt, ma'am.' 'Oh, ma'am, I've seen those pants on a lot of customers and, believe me, it doesn't fit anyone's butt like it fits yours.'

Soon, the changing-room was full. Greg stood calmly by, beaming as usual and telling me how wonderful I looked. It was all too much. I didn't feel comfortable saying, 'Yes, I'll take that and that and that.' It felt greedy. But I couldn't get out of it now. I'd drunk two glasses of their best Bollinger already. A dressmaker was involved, too, pinning up the length of some trousers that would apparently go with 'everything'. The staff, who had run out of recommendations for outfits, were now concentrating their charms on asking my life story. I felt obligated to take at least a few things to the checkout, but nothing I'd tried on had a price tag.

'Red is so your colour,' continued the camp sales assistant. 'Do you remember last year's Prada collection? We had a lot of reds.'

Do I remember last year's Prada collection? That's hilarious, I thought. Of course I don't remember last year's Prada collection. I could have told him all about Primark's, though. 'Oh, yes, you did,' I lied. 'Really nice shades, too.'

'Oh, ma'am, they would go with your colouring perfectly.'

Phew, I pulled that one off.

'Oh, what are those pants you're wearing, ma'am?' he continued, as I emerged from the changing-room wearing the outfit I'd entered the shop in. 'They look like they could be Marni. Or maybe Balenciaga?'

'Oh, these?' I said. 'They're from . . . they're from this cute little boutique shop in London.'

'They're gorgeous. They could definitely be Balenciaga.'

'Thanks,' I said. My 'pants' were actually £12 from New Look. I didn't even know what Balenci-whatever was!

We had been in the shop – sorry, 'store' – for nearly two hours. It was time to stop procrastinating and decide which outfits I wanted. Too much and I could come across as greedy and unappreciative; too little and I would cheat him of the pleasure of feeling that he had made me the happiest woman in New York, or it could lead him to believe I didn't like any of the things he'd been enthusiastically throwing at me.

'So, I suppose you'll be taking this, and this, and this?' asked the shop assistant.

'Er, yes, well . . . is that OK?' I said, turning to Greg.

'Of course. Take whichever ones you like.'

I took a deep breath. I had picked seven favourite items. The red dress was made from thick, heavy, expensive material; it was sleeveless, high at the nape of the neck and cut into a V-neck to my cleavage. It was modest, above the knee, with two subtle slits that came right to the very top of my thighs but were cut in such a way that they would only ever reveal a flash of flesh if I were to allow it. There was a black leather dress, slightly shorter but classically cut. It had a high neck and delicate short sleeves, with a panel of velvet running down the front and back. There was a pair of woollen high-waisted trousers and a cream shirt made of pure silk, which slipped through my fingers like liquid. It buttoned to the bust and had a built-in scarf that ran into silk tassels at the end, cut so finely they shimmered. There were two plain cotton shirts, one white and one black. And, most extravagant of all, there was a dark-red leather three-quarter-length coat, which I treasure deeply to this day. 'Well, I guess it's all this, then,' I said.

The shop assistant carried the items one by one to the counter and took our hotel details so that they could be hand-delivered to the hotel later that afternoon once the alterations had been made.

As Greg settled 'the check', I hung back awkwardly. I was near the perfume display. 'Oh, what do you wear?' asked the camp shop assistant cheerfully. Now, that I did know. The original Prada scent has always been my favourite. 'Carla,' he said, 'will you pop one of those in with the goods? Complimentary, of course. Oh, and put the men's one in too for this kind gentleman since he's been so patient.' He turned to me and asked, 'Have you tried the new one? It's got hints of orange.'

'I didn't know you had a new one.'

'Oh, Carla, put one of those in, too, will you, darling? With our compliments, of course.'

Gulp. You don't give away three bottles of Prada perfume unless the customer's spent a *huge* amount. Greg appeared from around the corner, beaming again. 'We're all set. Let's go.'

'Thank you so much,' I said, aware of how pathetic that sounded out loud.

'Oh, don't forget this,' said the shop assistant, handing me a small plastic card. 'You are now a Prada VIP customer. Every time you go into a Prada store in the future, show this and the staff will make sure you get the best service.' A fast-track ascent to VIP status within one transaction did not sound good – not for Greg's bank balance, at least.

As we walked back up the stairs and through the shop to the exit, the staff were all wishing us a good afternoon. In that moment, walking tall next to Greg, I felt so important, like I had become someone who had to be listened to, like I held a new power to get things I wanted. I don't remember ever having felt that kind of buzz before.

From there, we walked, we window-shopped and we talked. I had never talked so much to anyone. Greg tried to persuade me to buy more things, but I felt like I'd exhausted my share of his generosity and at first I declined. To take more would feel like having two desserts – I was sure I would love it at the time but then regret it and feel ugly about myself. But, by the end of the day, he had paid for a pair of Louboutin shoes (the ones with red soles so everyone knows what they are; I'd never owned a pair of shoes that came with their own individual cloth pouch before), a matching bag, a pair of Seven jeans, a swimsuit, a summer dress and . . . the white boots!

The Prada purchases had arrived at the hotel by the time we got back. Each item was wrapped in alternate layers of white and pale-blue tissue paper with the Prada logo on the front. When I packed the following day, I took the paper with me. I was thinking ahead to Christmas wrapping.

We poured gin and tonics and I declared excitedly that I would put on a fashion show. The plan was to choose the best outfit to go to dinner in. But we never got to dinner; instead, we got into a conversation.

'Tell me about your last relationship,' he said. I was buttoning up one of the new shirts and doing a half-turn in the mirror, inspecting myself from the side. I didn't have any trousers on. I sat down for a moment to give him my full attention.

'I look back and see myself living life in a straitjacket,' I said.

'What do you mean?'

'I didn't realise just how unhappy I was until I got out. I'm back to the old person who I was before. I have my spirit back. I've always felt more energised and more of a complete person when I've been single. It wasn't him. It was me. I find that being with one person sucks everything out of me.'

I was still there two hours later, my shirt half-buttoned, with the label sticking out, and nothing else on. That was the way it was with Greg and me. We'd get into a conversation and it would just run and run. Neither of us jumped on the sexual potential of the situation, although I was half-dressed. We were missing that current in our connection. We had sex, but only because we were sharing a bed and the script for how we met dictated that it should take place. I don't think either of us really felt like sex had a role in our bond, though. That had developed because we had a strange ability to connect our trains of thought. Everything he said made sense and I felt everything I said was understood.

Part of me probably felt like sex was some sort of unofficial payment for the airfare and the hotel and the meals and the breathtaking Prada till receipt. Making that a conscious thought would have been unbearable, however. I enjoy sex, I liked Greg, I felt connected to Greg, so I couldn't see a reason not to have sex with him. But what if he had been just some guy I'd bumped into in a bar and he hadn't flown me over here and hadn't taken me shopping? Would I have slept with him? I doubt I would have been bothered. If I had stopped to analyse that then, I would have noticed that I was, for the first time in my life, involved in some sort of sexual trade-off.

Greg moved the conversation on from exes to our views on relationships, to why he'd spent so much on me, to what that meant for his self-esteem, what that did for my feelings of self-worth, to the roles of men and women in general and then to the website. Why didn't we want conventional relationships like everyone else? What did my attraction to power mean? What about his attraction to younger girls with sweet-smelling hair and polished nails? His view was similar to that of Date One – that the physical beauty of youth signifies the ultimate prize but can be offset by an innocent, even gullible, outlook on the world.

Then we talked about the other types of people on the website: the demanding, crazy women he had met and the deluded fantasist men I had come across, the ones who never went through with meetings. We also discussed the few who, like us, seemed to be genuine people with an extreme curiosity about the world, using the site to explore a new type of relationship.

He had a lovely succinct way of phrasing things. At one point we were talking about whether relationships are the result of chemistry or timing. I said I thought it was timing, because if you're not ready for commitment, it doesn't matter who you meet. He replied, 'Well, I think chemistry forms the basis for whether you go on to decide if the timing is right.' I thought that was a perfectly articulated answer to an age-old relationship debate.

I remember thinking that if I could find someone with whom I had that level of intellectual connection as well as a sexual attraction, then even I would consider a relationship again. I was far too high on freedom to alter my views and go out and start looking for one, but Greg had made me pause. He had made me consider the notion that maybe I was skipping over something quite wonderful in all my shallow connections with sugar daddy dates. It had been ages since

I'd felt that hugely satisfying feeling of fully tuning in to someone's wavelength. I had that with Greg. He had reminded me of a different level of romance and for a moment tempted me to step back up to it. But, *stupid*, he lives in *Canada*. I couldn't possibly get any more involved than this whim of a weekend allowed.

On my final day, as I showered before leaving for the airport, Greg came into the bathroom and sat on the edge of the bath. 'I want to thank you for being such great company. I feel like I've grown,' he said. And I did too.

Chapter 8

Rumbled

♥ *October '07*

It seemed a lifetime since Champagne Breakfast Guy and I were disturbing guests in the breakfast room at the Langham Hotel, speeding through glasses of Bollinger. He had been busy travelling and I had been busy dating and being flown to New York.

Champagne Breakfast Guy and Munich Man were the only two people I formed a regular meeting pattern with. Sports Man had long slipped off my radar by now. In terms of the continuous but casual type of relationship I was looking for, Champagne Breakfast Guy and Munich Man were perfect. They were both incredibly good-looking – Champagne Breakfast Guy slightly more so, but Munich Man was always better turned out, making him look just ravageable. They were both intelligent and interesting conversationalists, though Munich Man talked so fast I could only understand about 60 per cent of what he said. They both provided that edge of glamour that I found so novel, by choosing exquisite restaurants and staying in top hotels – though Champagne Breakfast Guy always stayed at a different hotel, which added to the excitement, while Munich Man was always at the Jumeirah. They were both excitingly naughty – Munich Man in a cocaine-and-sex-binge way and Champagne Breakfast Guy in a may-go-to-prison-for-fraud way.

This seems a much healthier attitude to dating than getting all het up about one bloke, I mused. I was extremely fond of both men, but I didn't have a burning desire to embed them into every aspect of my life, from holidays to supermarket trips. Wouldn't the world be in a much healthier state if we stopped trying to shackle even the remotest trace of a romantic connection to an unrealistic ideal of exclusivity? Yes, I thought, people should be more practical about these things – like me!

For our next date, I met Champagne Breakfast Guy in the bar of the May Fair Hotel, behind Green Park station. I felt a million dollars in my new red Prada dress. There was a distinct autumnal feel to the evening, so I christened my red leather coat, too, and a pair of red leather gloves to which I had treated myself since my return.

Champagne Breakfast Guy had a flute of rosé Laurent Perrier waiting for me. I love it when guys dare to be decisive like that. We were about to set off for our booking at a nearby Italian when he told me he had left his wallet upstairs. It was, of course, a playful, euphemistic gesture to say 'I want you now'. Just for fun, I pretended not to get it and said innocently, 'Oh, OK. I'll wait here for you.'

'Come with me. I'll show you the room.' I had been curious to know what pretext he would use. He looked slightly awkward having to spell it out. I smiled to myself. I was loving being on this learning curve about men.

We got to his room and kissed, just like we had after our champagne breakfast, but I was more alert and more aware of him now. He was excited and that made me feel excited.

He took off my coat and I hung it up. I looked after that red leather coat. It was the probably the only garment I had ever owned that had never ended up strewn on the floor. I didn't take the dress off. He ran his hand right up the side-slit, over my hold-ups and we made love with our clothes on.

We were late for dinner and when we arrived my cheeks were still flushed and rosy – embarrassingly so. Champagne Breakfast Guy chuckled as I sifted through the menu, glowing like a Belisha beacon but pretending everything was normal. I blamed his stubble. That wouldn't have happened with Munich Man, who was always flawlessly clean-shaven.

With the sexual tension cleared at the beginning of the evening, our attention shifted to serious conversation. It's amazing how when two people are sexually satisfied the superficial flirting subsides and conversation becomes less frivolous. Champagne Breakfast Guy talked more about the investigation surrounding his insurance company and how he felt about the possibility of a custodial sentence if he was found guilty. 'It would be an open prison, which isn't too bad,' he said. 'You are actually free to leave in the day. But you have to stay there every night and there are strict curfews. I've resigned myself to that possibility. I'd have to treat it as two years' meditation, or a two-year break to read books, learn a language or something.'

He admitted that the chance that he might be confined to an institution for two years was holding him back from starting a relationship. He was unemotional about it, but it was clear that it preyed on his mind. I confessed that I knew his full name and had googled details of the investigation, so he started to explain how the whole thing had unfolded. As I listened to him in my post-coital haze, sipping Gavi di Gavi and feeling roasted artichokes melt in my mouth, he couldn't have seemed less like a criminal.

After dinner, it was clear we were both reluctant to go back 71 to the hotel room. We had already got our lust out of our system, and our conversation, although it had been stimulating, was exhausted. There was nothing more we wanted from each other, no other level to ascend to. I awkwardly said I should go home ready for an early start, and he, visibly relieved, said that he too had to get up early.

I was home by ten and, with the exciting details of the investigation fresh in my mind, I googled it again. Everything he had told me was true – the press camped on his doorstep, the court appearances, his suspension from the company. I genuinely believed in his innocence, but I felt excited by being close to it all.

♥ ♥ ♥

A few days later, I realised I was not the only one doing some investigative googling.

I was at work, hurriedly putting together a VT on the results of the Pakistani presidential elections, editing dramatic footage of protests in Lahore following President Pervez Musharraf's victory at the polls. I was alerted to my phone beeping by the buzzing noise of electrical interference in my headphones. I ignored it and carried on editing. I had a deadline to meet. It went off again and then again. The third time, I took a look. There were three messages from Champagne Breakfast Guy.

The first said: 'I just read your blog. Hilarious! I'm quite disappointed I'm not the main feature.' My heart skipped a beat and I urgently opened the other messages. 'I had actually shaved right before you arrived! And we drank a very nice Delamotte not Bollinger.' The third one read: 'How many have you clocked up now then? LOL.'

The last message was like a slap in the face. All of them were, actually, but the last one in particular because it was so judgemental.

Since joining Sugardaddie.com, I had started an online diary about my colourful dates. Being a journalist and having a love of writing, I felt compelled to record what I considered to be genuinely interesting stories and observations. Writing for pleasure was something I had let slip when I was in a relationship, and I wanted to revive it. Back then, blogs were the new big thing. So I started one, anonymously. It was more of an online diary, really, because I never tried to push for a readership. I didn't want recognition for it. I just wanted my story out there. It was therapeutic to preserve my experiences in words.

In fact, I never expected my blog to turn into risqué tales of my sexual exploits. When I started it, I imagined it would be filled with observations about the dynamics of age in a relationship. I don't think I envisioned that my antics would turn out to be so sexually charged.

I had adopted this new footloose approach to dating because I wanted to assert my independence as a contentedly single woman, explore my new-found sexuality and snatch glimpses into an elite world that mesmerised me. But Champagne Breakfast Guy's choice of the phrase 'clocked up' signalled that he had missed that reasoning altogether and took my adventures in multiple dating to be driven by nothing more than gratuitous promiscuity. It made me feel quite tawdry. I couldn't focus on anything. I took my headphones off and sat staring at my phone.

'How's that Musharraf package coming along?' prompted my editor.

'Nearly there.' My chest felt tight. I wanted to go outside and breathe fresh air, but I didn't think my editor would find the fact that someone had just discovered my erotic blog worthy of putting on hold the news that Pakistan had re-elected its president amid violent and deadly uprisings by the main opposition.

My mind was racing. How had Champagne Breakfast Guy found it? He wasn't working, so he must have had time on his hands. How did he know it was me who wrote it? What else had he read? How much had I written on there? I couldn't remember. Had I compared him with Munich Man? Said that he was better-looking but had not-very-sexy dress sense?

As well as feeling distressed at being rumbled, I also felt aggrieved. His reaction was a sad reminder of the double standard whereby women are always judged to have compromised a part of themselves if they are sexually liberal, while men who behave in the same way are thought to have achieved a goal.

For me, remaining free of emotional attachment to any one man was liberating. Feeling I could enjoy sex without being a prisoner to my own emotions was empowering. It was proof that sexual connections don't necessarily have to entail coupledom, DIY days and washing-up rotas. But, unfortunately, Champagne Breakfast Guy's derisive texts were a reminder that women can't enjoy hedonistic sexual pleasure without being judged, regardless of whether they actually hurt anyone. It seems to be assumed that if a woman agrees to let her body be used, she needs to receive some kind of emotional payment in return to be respected. Fun doesn't seem to be an acceptable currency.

When I got home I took my blog down. I saved the text safely into Word. I'm still going to write a diary of my dates, I thought, but it definitely won't be going online any more.

Chapter 9

Shopping Blunder

♥ **October '07**

Email from Happily Married Girlfriend:

> Hi babe
> Just wanted to say thanks for dinner last night, I didn't
> even know you had paid. My treat next time!
>
> My God. How much did we drinkkkkkkkkkkk?
>
> Am in trouble. [Husband's name] said I was singing
> to my iPod when I walked through the door and the
> room smelled so strongly of alcohol in the middle of the
> night he had to open the window!!

Reply from me:

> I didn't even know I'd paid!
>
> I look like death and just saw my sexy boss – typical.
> Have to present on camera today, too.
>
> Singing to iPod is nothing. Here is my scene this morn
> . . . wake up, sore head . . . see bucket by side of my bed.
> No memory of putting it there. Suspect it's because I

had room spins. Get up, Prada coat is on the living-room floor (yes, the Prada!), bra is on bathroom floor, two shoes are at the furthest possible points of my flat away from each other and my hat is in the fridge (!).

AND, biggest mystery of all, there is a screwdriver and a pair of scissors out on my sideboard! I seriously have no idea.

A funny email, you may think. Clothes strewn all over the flat is not that unusual for me after a few tipples, and even the hat in the fridge can be explained, probably, by drunken haste to get a bottle of water when I got home. But when I saw the screwdriver, I was worried! I had woken up at 6 a.m. that morning with a splitting headache. I discovered my hat in the fridge when I went looking for a carton of fruit smoothie. I gulped down the entire litre, direct from the carton, while staring in fuzzy disbelief at my hat balanced on a half-dozen box of eggs. Then I went back to bed to try to piece the night together. I was still trying when my alarm went off two hours later. Shit. Work! At least I had a nine-to-five shift that day – the rare luxury of sociable hours.

The previous evening had been the first time I'd seen Happily Married Girlfriend since our clash over the cash-for-dinner scandal. We put it all behind us, though, along with two bottles of wine, two rounds of cocktails and finally two shots on the house from whichever bar it had been that we were the last to leave.

'I just don't want you to get hurt, that's all,' she'd said when we delicately broached the topic of our previous falling-out.

'I know,' I said, 'but I want you to trust me when I say I am genuinely having fun. If it looks like I'm getting uncontrollably attached to some man who has different motives from me, then, yes, please rein me in. And if you ever think that I'm attracted to older guys because of money, then, seriously, sit me down and lobotomise me. But I think you know that's nothing to do with it. You know I've always gone for older guys. There's something very sexy about a man who's got his shit together; I'm not after their cash. Right now, I'm where I want to be. I don't want to fall in love.'

'So you honestly aren't attached to this Munich Man or that other one, the Breakfast Guy?' she checked. I had very nearly won her round to my line of thinking, very nearly got her to actually believe that what I was doing was not self-damaging. 'And that guy who took you to a spa the other week?' A man had indeed taken me away a few weekends ago, but I could barely even remember his name. 'If you never heard from them again, would you be hurt?'

'Well, yes, but only in the way I would be if a friend disappeared from my life.'

'I think I know where you're coming from now,' said Happily Married Girlfriend. It seemed like we were going to be able to draw a line under this whole thing at last. 'But, on the surface of it, you have to admit, it looks like you're running away from something. Or looking for a rich guy to keep you. So be careful who you tell – especially that story about taking money from that French guy for dinner. For God's sake, keep that to yourself. People judge.'

'Tell me about it,' I said. I relayed the story of the unmasking of my blog and how I didn't think I could ever face Champagne Breakfast Guy again because I was so embarrassed.

'You have a blog?'

'Did.'

'Oh my God!'

'I just wanted to write. I didn't try and make it high profile or anything.'

'How did he find it, then?'

'He told me, via text because I couldn't bear to speak to him, that he'd googled my email address. The name of my

Hotmail account matched the name of my blog page.'

'You hardly used MI6 levels of subterfuge, did you? Surely you can see him again, though. You can laugh about it, can't you?' Happily Married Girlfriend said. There she went again, always trying to coax me into some form of dating continuity.

'No way,' I replied. 'He must think I'm a floozy!' The truth was, I couldn't see Champagne Breakfast Guy again because he knew too much about me. He had read how I'd felt nervous on my first couple of sugar daddy dates, how I had found a new sense of independence through meeting strangers, how I had discovered my sex drive at age 29. He had seen the raw me, not me playing the role of sexy, scarlet-lipped, independent woman, sipping Bollinger or Delamotte or whatever it was in the May Fair Hotel with my La Perla suspenders peeping subtly from beneath my Prada dress. When he rumbled my blog and read about my anxieties, my sexual tastes and my sexual history, it was like he knew me in the way a boyfriend would, and that crushed the mystery.

We were in Wine Wharf in London Bridge, a relaxed bar full of after-work drinkers. We had a meal of hummus, pitta, olives, chips and white wine. Happily Married Girlfriend's little brother was staying with her for the week and he came to join us towards the end of the evening. He was five years younger than us and already a fully qualified doctor. Gosh and here's me getting drunk for the third time this week because I can do my job standing on my head, I thought. I had slowed down my job hunting since joining Sugardaddie. com. I had become defeatist about my chances of moving on to become either a reporter or a more senior producer. It is an impossibly competitive industry and, after several setbacks, I had opted instead to pump my energies into creating a colourful private life.

It was fun to have a fresh-faced 25-year-old male at the

table to question. Tipsy now, I asked him, rather patronisingly, how his love life was. 'Oh, I don't have a love life,' he quipped. 'I have a great sex life, though.' I laughed in delight. Why hadn't I thought of that reply myself?! I had been trying to think of a good comeback like that for months. I would shamelessly usurp it the next time someone annoyingly asked me how my love life was. Of course, I didn't see the irony of being put in my place by a younger man until much later.

But back to me piecing the night together the morning after. What was the screwdriver doing out of the toolbox on my sideboard? I was mystified as to what I could have been doing after I got home.

Then Happily Married Girlfriend emailed me back to suggest that my flatmate might have got the screwdriver out when she was messing around with the burglar alarm. Burglar alarm? What was she talking about? I learned that halfway through the evening I had apparently had a whole telephone conversation with my lodger. It was a new system and I had forgotten to tell her the new code. She'd phoned me with the alarm blaring in the background. At that point, though, I was finishing my second bottle with Happily Married Girlfriend and interrogating her little brother about his sex life. When my lodger realised she couldn't get a word of sense out of me, she called a helpline and they talked her through unscrewing keypads and black boxes. I had no recollection of the phone call. Happily Married Girlfriend was clearly more resistant to memory loss than I was. In any case, I was relieved to have found a reasonable explanation.

♥ ♥ ♥

A few days later, I had recovered enough to meet Munich Man. This was going to be our fourth date.

'Let's go shopping,' read his text message. We met in the usual place, the fifth floor of Harvey Nicks, on a Sunday afternoon. We had a Martini and then he asked me what I wanted to shop for.

I felt self-conscious with him by my side as we walked around the department store looking for things to buy. It was exactly the same feeling I'd had with Greg in New York. What was the right amount of time to browse for? Would he get bored? What was an acceptable value of goods to accept and would it be ungracious to decline a gift? Should I head for the designer counters and act as if I was in the know about the season's must-haves? Or should I modestly look at the lower-end brands to ensure I didn't come across as a grabby little madam? Part of me wished he would just give me his credit card, give me a limit and disappear for a couple of hours.

We walked around aimlessly because I was too polite to make a move towards buying anything. We somehow ended up in the sports department. 'I have to get something from here,' he said, and proceeded into the Adidas concession. 'Do you need anything while we're here, new gym gear, for instance?' Munich Man seemed determined to buy me something.

'No,' I replied. Actually, I could have done with a new gym outfit, but the thought of wearing a £60 T-shirt to go sweating on a dirty gym bench first thing in the morning before I'd showered or brushed my hair seemed totally unjustified to me, no matter whose money was paying for it. My gym clothes, as a rule, are relegated wardrobe items. Instead, I suggested we go and shop for 'something naughty'. That way, at least I knew he'd be getting something out of the shopping trip, too, which would make me feel more at ease.

An hour later, we emerged from the lingerie department with a black and pink lace set, the most fabulous cleavage-enhancing red Wonderbra with two styles of matching G-string, a pair of crotchless pants, which we had sniggered over like naughty schoolchildren, and, best of all, a corset – a proper one, like they wore in Victorian times when they used to faint because they had them done up so tightly.

It had caught my eye as we were queuing by the till. 'Oh, they are beautiful!' I said, feeling the satin fabric as the corset swung gently on the rail.

'A corset!' said Munich Man in wonder. 'They are awfully sexy, aren't they?'

I loved the idea of owning a corset, even though I couldn't think of many occasions when I could wear one. This one was a waist corset; it fitted under the bust and was designed to be worn with something underneath. I imagined it with the cream silk Prada shirt and a pencil skirt. Imagine wearing that to the office to impress The Boss! Or it could go over a crisp white shirt with leather trousers – if I had any leather trousers, that is. I continued to gaze at it. It was a luxury that I would never have considered buying for myself and wouldn't miss having if we left without it.

'Do you want to try it on?' asked Munich Man.

'You must be a 23-inch waist. You can try this one,' said the assistant.

'I'm sure my waist is quite a lot more than 23 inches,' I answered. I noticed that I had neither refused nor agreed to try on the garment.

'Corsets are worn two inches smaller than your actual size,' she said. God, my waist's not 25 inches, either. Not any more. But it was nice to think that she thought I *looked* like I had a 25-inch waist.

Two minutes later, I allowed myself to be led to the tile-floored changing cubicle at the back of the floor, where I was forcibly laced into what felt like a straitjacket. 'Are you sure I don't need the next size up?' I gasped, thinking my cheeks must be going blue.

'No,' she said, 'this is the point of a corset.' What? To break someone's ribs? 'It will give a little, after a couple of wears.'

A couple of wears? I'll have asphyxiated before it gets its second outing, I thought. 'I still think I need the bigger size. The lacing at the back doesn't even come close to joining up the two sides. There's a huge gap.'

'There won't be, don't you worry,' she said, and with that gave another sharp tug that made me think my ribcage would crack.

'Shall I try the 24-inch one?' I squeaked, but the pursed-lipped sales assistant ignored me.

'She looked *amazing*, darling,' she said, as we returned, me flushed, to Munich Man, who was waiting by the till.

'Fantastic,' he enthused, and took the corset from the assistant. Just as he was paying, I grabbed a pair of black patterned hold-ups. They weren't for any of today's outfits but just because I needed a new pair. I didn't think much of it – they were just a normal pair of criss-cross-patterned hold-ups that I could wear under a dress for work.

The store was closing now, and we walked back to his hotel, Munich Man carrying the bags for me. I went into the bathroom to get changed so that we could start the parade of underwear. I opted to begin with the red set. I was wearing red shoes and the cleavage the Wonderbra had honoured me with was magnificent. Munich Man waited in the room, lining up tractor tracks of cocaine. 'What are you doing in there?' he called impatiently, after about ten seconds. I was snapping the labels off – not easy when you don't have scissors – and adjusting my breasts in the bra.

He couldn't wait. He came through the door before I'd managed to fasten the second little hook at the back. He was holding a CD case on which a line of cocaine was laid out. He pushed a rolled up fifty-pound note under my nose and as I snorted it he bent down and kissed my cleavage. I couldn't do all the coke in one go and as I paused, preparing to hoover up the second line, he carried on kissing my breasts. He pulled one bra strap down with his teeth and reached down with his hands, fingering the red satin G-string.

I discreetly dropped the CD case and the note to the floor to free my hands. I unbuttoned his trousers and took off his belt. He was already hard, and huge, as usual. All the time, his face was still buried in the wonderful cleavage created by the red bra. I put my hands on the granite bathroom surface and leaned my head back, making Munich Man trail his tongue from my cleavage up around my neck.

I don't know how long we were in the bathroom for. Cocaine distorts time – or at least lines the size that Munich Man gave me did. He would always do at least two lines to my one, but he always remained rock hard, no matter how much we got through.

'I don't believe you don't take anything to keep going after all that coke,' I teased him yet again later in the evening.

'No, I've already told you I don't. I'd tell you if I did. It's just the company of a beautiful girl that does it,' he said, grinning unnaturally.

The next day was Monday. I had overlooked that fact when I was getting high, strutting around Munich Man's hotel room in various underwear ensembles and getting tangled up in the lacing of the new corset.

I breezed into work in the outfit I'd been wearing the afternoon before, swinging my Harvey Nichols bags. I was friendly enough with one female colleague to have revealed my choice of Internet dating site, and she was always fascinated by my stories. I gave her a peek at the contents of my bags under the desk. She was impressed with the corset. This was not a simple boob tube. This was a handmade, fine-boned, movement-restricting, lead-weight work of art that had cost a lot of money.

Then she picked up the hold-ups. 'Oh, they're just some extras I grabbed for everyday,' I chirped.

She looked at me and raised an eyebrow. 'I don't think you'll be wearing these every day.'

I looked down; she was pointing to the description and the price tag. Out of all the stockings on display, I had managed to pick out a pair of limited-edition crystal-encrusted hold-ups by Wolford. At £180. Months ago, that would have made me feel guilty, but I simply stifled an amused 'oops'. An accidental extravagance like that wasn't such a big deal any more.

Chapter 10

An Unexpected Guest

♥ *November '07*

I loved the way that Munich Man and I could go weeks without there being an expectation that we would see each other and yet it still felt as if we shared a special bond. We didn't kid each other that we had sexual exclusivity, nor even emotional exclusivity, but we had enough respect for and genuine interest in each other to make it feel like we had a private, unique connection. We didn't try to spoil what we had with rules and demands on each other's time. Those were the balls and chains that put me off conventional relationships.

While I loved being free to date other people, I wasn't really interested in one-night hook-ups. I was seeking sex, definitely, but I still wanted continuity – that adds to the excitement. I was looking for a connection, but a low-maintenance connection. Munich Man provided just that.

I planned to wear one of the complete sets of underwear from the Harvey Nicks shopping spree the next time I saw him. I was excited about putting on a suspender belt with real suspenders. I was used to wearing hold-ups, but that's cheating, really. Had I known, however, how long the things would take to get on, I would have given myself *more time*! You have to gather the lace at the top of the stocking and stuff a tiny pinch of the material into the most ridiculously minuscule key-shaped hole. You then have to twist it in such a way that the catch slides into the narrow part of said hole, while being careful not to let the pinch of lace slip out. On the particular garment I was battling with, there was a pretty ribbon over said hole, which made it even more fiddly to direct the ruffle of lace into it. How do girls do this with long, manicured nails, I wondered.

After half an hour, I'd managed to attach all four straps. I sat down, triumphant, and then I realised that I'd put the suspender belt on under the pants instead of over, which totally defeats the object. The idea, I believe, is that you keep them on during sex, so you have to make the pants the most manoeuvrable part of your underwear. Not to mention how time-consuming a trip to the Ladies would be this way. I had to start all over again.

Several 'sorry, nearly there' text messages later, I arrived at the fifth floor of Harvey Nicks. Munich Man was talking to an exotic-looking brunette at the bar.

'Hi,' I said, with a raised eyebrow. Perhaps she was waiting for someone, too, and the pair of them had simply got chatting.

'This is Isabelle,' Munich Man offered. He took one look at my expression and said, 'Ah. You didn't get my voice message?'

I'd spent the last two hours writhing around in every position imaginable battling with a pair of suspenders twice over, so, no I hadn't. 'You left a message?'

'Ah. Well, I wanted to ask you if you minded terribly if Isabelle joined us. We were having a drink earlier and she said she would awfully like to meet you and I thought we could have a little fun. It will be fun, don't you think? You don't mind, do you?'

I blinked, not knowing how to react. Although our evenings were always novel, it would never have crossed my mind that my date would bring another female along, no matter how gallantly he presented the idea. But the hilarity of the situation and all the entertaining stories that I imagined would result were already filling me with a mischievous sense of glee.

Munich Man looked nervous. Because I hadn't been pre-warned by his telephone message, he now had to face my real reaction in person. They were both looking expectantly at me. I could feel them willing me to show a sign of acceptance. They were scrutinising my face for any hint of anger, insult or disgust. They were both sitting on high bar stools and I was standing, so we were eye to eye. I held Munich Man's gaze, giving nothing away. I was sizing up Isabelle out of the corner of my eye. She had huge brown eyes, her pupils heavily dilated. She had a clear, olive complexion and long, thick, light-brown hair with natural golden-blonde streaks. She was more heavily built than me but was wearing a dainty long-sleeved brown dress that gave her an angelic grace. She was pretty in an understated way.

Last time I'd seen Munich Man, in the haze of our cocaine high we had whispered about our fantasies and sexual avenues we would like to explore. I remembered telling him that I had always had a vague fantasy to try a threesome, though I imagined that, having never had the opportunity before, I was unlikely to now, since my friends and the parties I went to seemed to be getting calmer, not crazier. It looked like Munich Man had taken that as a cue for this evening's set-up.

I felt a twitch of nervous excitement. He had organised the fulfilment of a sexual fantasy *for me*. And here it was in front of me as a surprise! I smiled at Munich Man and turned to Isabelle to greet her with a kiss on the cheek. 'No, I don't mind at all.'

We had a glass of champagne and headed for the sushi restaurant on the other side of the fifth floor, as we had on our first date. Again, Munich Man had ruined his appetite by putting half the GDP of Columbia up his nose before eating.

Isabelle was a marine biologist. She was from Spain, the daughter of a foreign dignitary, educated at finishing school and a patron of two charities. A scientist, a journalist and a financier, we were three strong minds and colourful characters. We talked about the rising cost of credit and the jitters this was sending through the banking world (sparked by me asking Munich Man how business was going), the depletion of fishing stocks (sparked by the lack of sushi on the conveyor belt) and whether monogamy is the best form of relationship for modern mankind (sparked by our discussions about what a good idea a website like Sugardaddie.com was). The more wine we drank, the more animated and opinionated we became. It was so brilliantly intellectual, but we all knew that as soon as we got through the sushi, the champagne and the first gram of Munich Man's cocaine, we'd be back at his hotel replacing our sophistication with hedonism.

Which is exactly what we did. We made up a game where we spun a bottle and whoever it pointed to had to challenge a person of their choice to truth or dare. Truth meant they had to answer a question 100 per cent honestly. A dare meant they would be challenged to carry out a task – which was implied to be of a sexual nature.

I had never seen live sex between two people before. And that, if you haven't either, is a much more arousing vision than you might expect. It's surreal, like being lost inside a computer game or in the middle of a theatre set; you don't feel you belong there or should be so close. I looked over at Isabelle. I was fascinated to see how another woman went about sex and how Munich Man reacted. I experimented with Isabelle, too, trying to figure out if I enjoyed it or not. I did, but because of the enlightenment it gave me, not because I felt any greater physical pleasure from the touch of a woman than the touch of a man. I was excited when I kissed her, but not because her lips were softer or she smelled different or her long hair draped over me, but because it gave me an idea of what it's like for a man to kiss a woman. I didn't feel aroused by her, but by the experience.

We wound to an exhausted end at 6 a.m. Once Isabelle and I managed to persuade Munich Man not to call his coke dealer again, we collapsed into three heaps on the king-size bed, Munich Man in the middle. We managed to sleep until 9 a.m., when all three of our alarms went off within around ten seconds of one another, indicating that none of us had trusted the other two to follow through on their word that they would set the alarm for nine.

The alarms were screaming at us that it was time to be sober and live out the day with the rest of the world. Isabelle had to go to a seminar to put forward her argument about cod fishing quotas in the Baltic Sea, Munich Man had to get a flight to Germany for an afternoon meeting and I had to go and read the news.

♥ ♥ ♥

I was dying to open a bottle of wine with someone to whom I could divulge the details of that evening. Only Remaining Single Friend would usually have been just the person to do that with, but, for the time being at least, she was no longer single. She was having a lustful affair with a boy (we called him 'The Boy') she had met at a Hallowe'en party. Hardly surprising, considering she went dressed as a Victorian lady of the night and victim of Jack the Ripper and had asked him for help ripping her fishnet stockings to add to the effect.

I had noticed that since she had begun this passionate

relationship with The Boy she had become much less receptive
to what I tried to tell as entertaining dating stories. Men, I
have noticed, maintain a steady standpoint on life regardless
of their personal lives, but women's moral judgements
fluctuate hugely, and these changes seem to be directly
correlated with the type of relationship they are in.

It goes something like this.

Single girls just looking for fun, like me: they love listening
to my funny stories over a bottle of wine. They encourage me
to tell more. My experiences have made them want to go
Internet dating, too.

Single girls who are looking for a relationship: they enjoy
my funny stories, but they would never engage in the type of
emotionally detached dating I do because the lack of intimate
pillow talk from the men would torture their souls.

Girls in the early throes of a passionate fling: they half-
listen to my funny stories in between checking their phones
for texts. They constantly look for excuses to return to the
topic of how in love they are.

Girls in serious relationships: they find my stories mildly
titillating but wish it wasn't their friend who was telling them.
They regularly ask after the characters from previous dating
stories, as if they expect them to build up to starring roles
rather than remaining walk-on parts.

Married girls who've moved to places like Surrey or Kent:
they find my stories mildly titillating but are secretly
uncomfortable that there is a life full of fun, excitement and
danger out there that they are excluded from. They seem to
prefer the world when it is full of other happy, singing couples
baking cakes.

Married girls with children: as above, but add 'or going to
baby yoga'.

Divorced girls: I only have one friend in this category. I
have given her Internet dating advice.

So, I turned to the less judgemental sex to share the next instalment in my story: the threesome. 'He must have had that planned for weeks and was waiting for the right moment,' was my equally commitment-phobic male friend's response.

He and I had become good friends over the last few years, having established that we had similarly story-worthy dating lives. We were regularly so hung-over after Friday nights that we would share many a Saturday evening watching a DVD and vowing to live a healthier lifestyle in the future.

When I'd first moved to London after university, all my friends were congregated in one area – a rare luxury in the capital. That was before the marriage bug had spread, and I had a whole network of friends on my doorstep, single and forever poised to open wine. It was like living in a year-long episode of *Friends*. Equally Commitment-Phobic Male Friend was one of the few survivors who hadn't moved out to somewhere like Surrey, and so we continued with our regular cork-removing sessions.

I enjoyed getting a male take on my dates, and I had reciprocated with plenty of advice for him over the years. Equally Commitment-Phobic Male Friend's problem was that he attracted clingy, jealous women. The consistency of the pattern was quite remarkable: a girl who slept in her car outside his flat, a girl who hosted a surprise birthday party for him when *they'd only just met*, girls who texted him incessantly, and so on.

'I don't think he engineered it,' I replied. 'He said that she'd only phoned him that day by chance. And she said the same.'

'It takes quite some nerve for a guy to do that, you know.'

'What?'

'Turn up with another girl for a date. Most men would have to beg and plead for that. My God, if I'd tried that with any of my recent dates, I'd have been murdered. No, tortured and then murdered,' Equally Commitment-Phobic Male Friend laughed. 'They would be stubbing out their cigarettes on my chest. You'd find me chopped in bits in bin bags. This guy doesn't know how lucky he is. Or he's doing something I'd like to know about to reel you girls in.'

Chapter 11

Out of love with Online Dating

♥ **January '08**

I can't even begin to count the number of dates I had from the website over those next few months. Most were one-evening wonders that offered nothing more than stimulating dinner conversation and an insight into the mature man's philosophy on love and relationships. Other dates weren't so much one-night wonders as one-night horrors. I met idiots obsessed with their own wealth who knew no other way in which to impress. I met patronising men who seemed to find the idea of a younger woman with no knowledge of the world, no *savoir faire*, attractive. I met married men who, like Date One, hid their status until the actual date. Whenever that happened, I would try to find out as much as I could about what had driven him to join the site, how his relationship with his wife had evolved to this stage. I would greedily digest it all, gleaning as many psychological details as I could. At what point had he fallen out of love with his wife? Had he in fact fallen out of love or had he just lost interest in her? I ——

think I wanted to use what I learned from them in my ongoing painstaking analysis of why I was failing to win the affections of my attached boss.

I met men pretending to be what they weren't, dining in restaurants they couldn't afford. I met a single man in his 60s, larger than life, full of jokes, who simply wanted to find a girl to frequent high-end swinger parties with him (no, I didn't). I met lonely men longing for a life partner and fed up of rejection. I met gullible men who had fallen victim to Sugar Babes who asked for money transfers off the back of various made-up family crises. There were, thankfully, very few who repulsed me and, as far as I can remember, no one who scared me. The worst it ever got, I think, was Eyelash Watcher.

He was 45, lived in Monte Carlo and made monthly trips back to the UK. He had crooked, yellow teeth and was balding. But it wasn't so much his looks that repulsed me as his personality.

We met by Piccadilly Tube. He hadn't arranged a bar or restaurant to go to. One of the things I found so attractive about the idea of someone older and more established was initiative and the ability to take control. When I found myself wandering around the West End in the cold looking for somewhere off the cuff, it felt like I was back to the old world of amateurs.

'You have such lovely long eyelashes,' he said as we sat down in some chain bar that smelled of beer and was filled with 23 year olds and tourists. I felt the skin on the back of my neck crawl. He was sitting uncomfortably close and was edging slowly nearer. His eyes seemed to be glued to me. Of all the compliments to give to someone you've just met, I thought, why would you mention eyelashes? It made me feel I was being scrutinised.

He kept saying things to make him sound young. Ridiculous things like dropping the names of new bands and mentioning how he'd tried 'smoking dope', how he sometimes 'went clubbing'. The obvious façade only exposed a gaping hole of low self-confidence. He asked why I had joined the website. I gave him a short answer, reluctant to reveal much about myself: 'To experiment a little and meet types of people I wouldn't normally meet.'

'Really?' he purred, staring into my eyes intensely. 'What do you want to experiment with? I'd love to do that with you.' I looked away, in a vain attempt to discourage him. 'You're a beautiful girl. Why do you want to meet an older guy?'

I didn't want to reply. Why should I divulge things about myself to someone who was making me feel uncomfortable? I shrugged indifferently. I didn't want to offer him anything of me.

Apparently ignoring the barriers I'd put up, he began to tell me how he'd 'still got stamina' and that he could 'teach me things' if I wanted him to. I cut him short and excused myself to go to the bathroom. From there, I texted a colleague, the one who had spotted the price tag on the Wolford stockings. I knew she was out in the neighbourhood that evening celebrating a birthday, as she'd invited me along. 'On a nightmare date,' said the message. 'Are you still out? Thinking of joining if near.'

She was, thankfully, which meant I just had to sit through Eyelash Watcher finishing his drink and then I was free to go.

'Shall we?' he asked, indicating that we could go to dinner. I said I wasn't feeling well, noticing my improved assertiveness. Months ago, I would have agreed to sit through dinner out of politeness. Most people would. It's startling how we'll go out of our way to please strangers when we wouldn't do the same for people we already know. Yes, I had effectively just stood him up in the middle of a date. But surely that was more decent than to accept the offer of a meal while harbouring feelings of repulsion for him?

He insisted on walking me to a taxi, exuding sleaze the whole way. Wouldn't it be great if he could fly me out to Monte Carlo in the next couple of weeks? I smiled politely, able to endure it now that the end was near.

'Clapham, please,' I lied to the driver. It was best to let Eyelash Watcher believe that I lived on the opposite side of London from where I actually did. As soon as he was safely out of sight, I told the cab driver to stop. I got out and walked to the bar behind Piccadilly where my favourite female colleague was partying her very non-Wolford socks off.

♥ ♥ ♥

Soon, the novelty of the website started to fade. My vexation over my stalled career began to haunt me again. The newsroom seemed to be filling with new faces – younger, keener faces, fresh out of journalism college, striving to be Fiona Bruce, willing to work virtually for free. I had been a journalist for five years and had had a career as a tax accountant before that (yes, my friends think that is hilarious). But it felt like people with far less work and life experience than me were doing the same job. I was doing more presenting and reporting now, which was a start, but it was mainly for multimedia or radio platforms, which is nowhere near as highly regarded in the industry as TV. I didn't necessarily want to be an on-screen journalist, but I did want to feel I was moving up the ranks.

I calmed down my activity on Sugardaddie.com and started to put out feelers to see if I could go freelance, which would hopefully open more doors. I sent off countless CVs and applications and went in to shadow news shifts for corporations outside ITN so that I would be trained to work in different newsrooms. But every time I got a knock-back, I could feel myself turning back to Sugardaddie.com for a quick-fix kick, just as a drug addict slides back into their addiction when things don't go their way.

As well as my work frustrations, I had to cope with my growing crush on The Boss. 'Crush' is a ridiculous word, implying all sorts of teenager-type confusions and helplessness, but there isn't really a word for the grown-up equivalent. 'Infatuation' seemed too strong, 'fancying him' not strong enough, 'lust' too purely sexual and 'in love' too dramatic. He had somehow got inside my head – the only man who really had, even after all those Internet dates. What I mean by that is inside my head enough to occupy thoughts even when out of sight. I let the crush grow, kidding myself that there was a chance of something happening, but then I was constantly disappointed when nothing ever happened, when he said he'd see me at an office function and he wasn't there, or when he said we'd go for lunch and we didn't. It occurred to me that my preoccupation with him was in part what was fuelling my fantasies about the older, powerful man, though I pushed the thought away as quickly as it came.

I was starting to become aware of the real source of my frustrations: my need to move on from the job I was in, and the fact, however loath I was to admit it, that I did actually harbour romantic feelings for someone, despite my insistence that I was truly happy being detached from love. Now that I could see these things, the sugar daddy dating ceased to provide the same escapist release as it had in the beginning. The website may have spiced up my life temporarily, but it wasn't going to get me a new job and it wasn't going to get me the person I really wanted. As soon as I saw it as an activity that masked my frustrations rather than solving them, it started to irritate me.

I grew suddenly impatient with the sheer number of messages and the demanding tone of their senders. Some of these men must think that this is what I *do*, full-time, I thought, exasperated, when I logged on one day. They treat it like a customer services centre, as though I'm obliged to read and reply to every message each and every day. I was looking at a message from a 'BondJames'. He had got in touch with me on a Tuesday to ask if I was free the following Sunday. I replied on the Thursday and said yes, I was free. He'd written: 'You didn't get back to me and I have now made arrangements for Sunday. I thought if you were serious about meeting someone on here you would reply pronto . . . xx' And what exactly is the purpose of the kisses? I thought. A vain attempt to soften his ill-founded aggression?

Another time, I was sent a message on a Saturday afternoon. 'Fancy dinner tonight?' the photo-less member asked. I hadn't logged on that day so didn't get the message until the next day. But before I could reply, I noticed a second one from him, enraged that I had not responded to his offer: 'Well, if you're so rude not to reply then I can't be bothered with you.'

Others would forward the same message over and over again to check I'd got it. It never occurred to them that I might not have logged on during the time in which they'd re-sent the same message six times.

I also hated the way most started messages with: 'Hello Princess/Precious/Sweetheart' before we'd exchanged so much as a cyber-word. They seemed sickeningly false. Similarly, I disliked the ones that read, for example, 'Hi, fancy joining me in California this summer?' because it showed that they cared nothing for building a rapport or testing whether there was a spark.

And I despaired of those perfunctory, unpunctuated stabs in the dark: 'hi care to chat.' No, I don't care to chat because I have a thousand other things to care about! And even if I did have time to waste on those (all the expletives in the world) messenger sites, I'd expect you to at least make the effort to entice me with something – tell me something about yourself or pick up on something from my profile, make a witty remark. If we both think there's an interesting person in there, then let's meet face to face for a glass of wine. Let's not throw away time by 'chatting' with anyone who falls onto our profile pages. In-person meetings have so much more value than hour-long telephone calls, essay-length emails or any form of instant messenger. The Internet should serve as the tool to set up the meeting, not the meeting itself.

Then there were the cold, narcissistic messages, such as this: 'You say in your profile you're bored of younger guys, well I'm bored of my wife. Are you free next week for lunch/ view to some afternoon fun?' I have never thought people should force monogamy on themselves for the sake of it. There are many valid reasons why couples need to stray outside of the conventional structure. But his lack of respect for someone so central to his life and the fact that he was willing to share it with a stranger horrified me. If he really was bored with his wife, he should acknowledge his boredom respectfully, maturely, bravely, and if he had become bored to the point where he had lost respect for her, then perhaps he should seek a separation and stop living a lie.

Then there was TruePoet. I had actually picked him out from a search, which I rarely did. I preferred to respond to people who contacted me, rather than doing the hunting myself. I had added TruePoet to my 'hotlist', which alerts a member that you are interested in them, and he had contacted me.

> Hi, I'm walking in the Highlands at the moment. It's beautiful – I'd love you to see it.
>
> How's your weekend been? Did you manage to get away from the smog of the capital? I live in London but I have to get away every weekend.

Like you, I'm single but looking for something casual
as I enjoy having my own space. x

I looked at his profile, which said he was 47. He worked in
'finance' (the most commonly selected category) and he
enjoyed writing poems and songs in his free time. I replied:
'Scotland sounds great, but I think I'd choose somewhere
warmer for a holiday! What do you write about? And if you
write songs do you play music, too?'

He came back saying, 'I like the cold. It makes me feel
alive. I don't really play an instrument, sadly – just enough
guitar to get my songs down. What do I write about? Well,
maybe it's better to show you. It's maybe too simplistic, and
perhaps not your cup of tea if you're a city girl, LOL. But
sometimes less is more.'

Below was a five-stanza poem entitled 'Wanting'. He wrote
about his longing to touch his beloved; he described her hair
like the breeze that brushed against his cheek, her voice like
the songs he heard in his sleep, her skin like velvet . . . Oh
God, I thought, he's a romantic. This was exactly what I was
not trying to find. As a writer myself, though, I knew how
cruel it would have been to have ignored his proud show of
creativity, so I replied, but with humour so as not to unfairly
lead him on. 'Did you write that while you were there? Are
you trying to woo me by any chance?'

He replied saying he thought that was the point of the
website and sending me another verse, about kisses being
food for the soul. 'I do write about other things,' he wrote.
'My poem "Lust" is very to the point, but it should be.' And
then off he went with another six stanzas – which made me
question his definition of 'to the point' – on all the wonderful
things that made his heart flutter.

It is a typical female trait to respond to male attention out
of politeness or kindness, and it is a typical male trait to

interpret that as positive interest. It's one of those classic Mars and Venus miscommunications. It happens in the workplace, in social situations and in dating. A man is programmed to feel far less guilt than a woman. If a man sees that someone – colleague or love interest – has nothing to offer him, he will simply not respond. A woman, however, is so uncomfortable with dishing out rejection that she will cushion the blow by tagging something like 'but do stay in touch' onto the end. She does it because it makes her feel better not because she means it at all.

That was exactly what I had done when I responded to the poet. My one sentence feigning interest in his poetry, out of kindness, had led him on. He started to deliver new literature into my inbox every day. I didn't quite know how to tell him to stop.

Each time I logged on now, it was with a little less enthusiasm. I had grown intolerant of the many time-wasters and cautious of the delusional souls. One guy who lived in Boston messaged me to ask if I would like to move over there to live with him 'in early fall'. The reason he was actively seeking someone who lived 3,000 miles away was because he liked 'the idea of having a foreign girlfriend – it's exotic'. Surely he wasn't serious?

The meetings themselves had lost their appeal, too. After Eyelash Watcher, I had hesitated to set up other dates. I was less easily impressed now, too. Powerful men I'd previously have put on a pedestal and felt compelled to get to know were starting to seem like normal, fallible human beings – or, even worse, arrogant and detached. I think many of them perceived themselves as having an elevated status because they were paying the way. I chose not to renew my membership.

Chapter 12
Sugar Daddy Detox

♥ **January '08**

Only Remaining Single Friend and I were sitting on opposite ends of my sofa, legs tucked up underneath us, the heating turned up as high as it would go. My boiler was making worryingly loud rumbling noises behind the kitchen door. It was going to blow one of these days, I knew it. On my coffee table, alongside the notebook that I still assiduously filled out with all of my Internet dates' details, were two big mugs of steaming green tea.

It was 7 p.m. on a weekday. I hadn't been up for long. I was on a run of night shifts again, so I'd slept – not very well – through the day. I had to be at work again by 11 p.m. Only Remaining Single Friend wanted to see me – she hadn't said why – but there was no way I could face the buzz of central London. Night shifts turned me into a miserable, skulking hermit. Given the choice, I wouldn't have spoken to anyone for the entire run of them. The days when a thrilling champagne breakfast could assuage the gloom of working nights were definitely over. So I told Only Remaining Single Friend to come to my flat; we could drink tea and eat soup, and I could remain in my dressing gown.

'Do you want to have a proper relationship, then?' Only Remaining Single Friend asked, looking alarmed, after I'd explained I was cancelling my membership of Sugardaddie. com because of my irritation with it and was going to focus more on looking for a new job.

'Oh God, no,' I reassured her. 'I'm just tired of the men on there. Most of them are deluded idiots, or they leave demanding messages or they're serial date-cancellers or they're extreme bullshitters or they're married. And because the novelty's gone, it's beginning to feel like they get more out of it than I do, which makes me feel like I'm providing a service. For free. I didn't used to feel like that. So, new year, new phase, new adventures.'

'You're going to find it strange when you go on a date with someone who expects you to pay half.'

'You mean you pay on a date?!' I was being facetious, of course.

'It's the price of equality. Then I don't feel obliged to sleep with them for a meal ticket.'

'Oh God, can I not do that, either?'

'You're not supposed to on the first date.'

'God, it's all role play, isn't it? Woman mustn't sleep with man because man will think woman isn't worthy. It's bollocks. Everyone assumes that sex means the man got his way and the woman succumbed.'

'Are you going to join a more normal dating site, with people your own age?' asked Only Remaining Single Friend, ignoring my cynicism.

'Oh God, no.'

'Why?'

'Why? Because I can't think of anything worse than dating a load of strangers and trying to force out some chemistry.'

'Erm, what have you been doing for the past year, then?'

'That's totally different,' I snapped. 'The whole point of doing what I've done for the last year is not to have to try to force out some sort of chemistry. It's a different agenda with the types of guys I've dated from that site. We skip the intensity part because lifelong commitment is never part of the equation. It's all about the experience – for them and for me. And they were older – sugar daddies, you know – I didn't expect us to be equals or them to enter into my everyday life.

'There was never any pretence that we were seeking "chemistry",' I said, making air quotes with my fingers and rolling my eyes. 'It's like they were my leisure-time fillers – restaurants and weekends away. There was never any of that crap you get on normal dates where both of you scrutinise each other, assessing whether you can see them as the parent of your future children. If I wanted that, I would have gone on Match.com!'

Rant over. I'd thought Only Remaining Single Friend already understood all that. Of course I didn't want to go on normal dates; I wasn't looking for a normal relationship. She was beginning to sound like Happily Married Girlfriend and it was probably because she was dating someone. Women are so fickle when they change their relationship status.

'It'll do you good to come off that site. You're in danger of losing touch with the real world. If you met a guy tomorrow and he wanted to treat you to a really nice restaurant and he saved up for it, you wouldn't even notice.'

I didn't like hearing it, but Only Remaining Single Friend was right. 'Anyway,' I said, 'What about you? How's The Boy?'

'The Boy is no longer my boy.'

'Oh. Shit. Really? Sorry. When?'

This was obviously why Only Remaining Single Friend had been so keen to come and see me. And I'd just gone on and on about my night shifts and a load of Internet dating messages that had irritated me, when she had far more troubling issues to offload.

Only Remaining Single Friend's recent beau – the one from the Hallowe'en party – whose calling habits she painstakingly analysed every time we shared a bottle of Chardonnay, was now 'a twat'. According to Only Remaining Single Friend, his friends came before her and he spoke on the phone more to them than to her. And they were twats, too. He was inattentive to her, he hadn't met any of her friends – me included. He did exciting things with his friends, but he never wanted to do anything when he was with her other than order a takeaway and have a half-hearted conversation during the ad breaks of whatever he was watching on TV. He never wanted to stay over at her flat; she always had to go to his – and that was a shithole (her words, not mine).

'I don't want to mess around any more. I'm too old to be wasting time with booty calls. That's what it was – that was the only time he ever called.' Her voice was getting louder and higher-pitched and I detected a shaky tearfulness fighting to burst out. 'It's all right for you, getting sex and room service with all these guys in posh hotels. But you know what? I do want to meet someone. Do you know how dirty I felt doing the walk of shame all the way from Balham to north London for the third time in three weeks after I'd given him the best blow job he'd ever had? And then I see you come back from New York head to toe in Prada. What have I got out of him? Nothing!' She was sobbing now. I reached forward and put my hand on her shoulder to calm her, but she flinched. 'Don't,' she warned, indicating that me comforting her would have made her break down completely. 'It makes me think I should do what you do. They may be old and fat and think they can pay their way into bed, but at least you've got something to show for it.'

She stopped and wiped the tears from her eyes. I pulled some tissues from a box on the coffee table and offered them to her. She grabbed them out of my hands. Wow. I hadn't been expecting this. First, I hadn't realised how strongly she felt about wanting to be in a relationship. She'd said she didn't think The Boy would become anything serious, so I'd presumed that, like me, she was happy to take a man for some temporary fun and sexual relief. But perhaps when a woman sleeps with a man she always expects to get something back from it, even if it's just his respect and the triumph of winning his heart. It's justification for allowing herself to be penetrated for a male's pleasure. Prada or a man's pledge of monogamy – perhaps they are equals in a woman's subconscious? I wondered if women had evolved so that they, like men, could only physically partake in sex if they were truly aroused, whether there would be this perpetual cross-cultural underlying inequality of the sexes?

Second, bloody hell: 'They may be old and fat and think they can pay their way into bed, but at least you've got something to show for it'? Did my best friend who knew me better than anyone believe that I hadn't found any of my older, wealthy dates attractive and that I was sleeping with them for designer clothes? Is that what it looked like from the outside? Didn't she understand that I chose to do what I did for the love of experience and adventure?

And third, none of the men I chose to sleep with were fat.

Only Remaining Single Friend had stopped sobbing and was mopping the tears from her red face. 'I don't want a man near me right now,' she squeaked, and then the tears came back.

I comforted her. I told her she didn't mean that and that if she really did want to meet someone, she shouldn't be ashamed about admitting it and maybe she should go on a dating website because that can guarantee – depending on the website – that both parties are looking for a relationship with a direction.

She didn't like that idea. 'You just said that you couldn't think of anything worse than trying to "force out chemistry".'

Damn. I had just said that, hadn't I? 'What about going to a singles event, then?' I suggested. 'Then you get to vet everyone in one go. I'll come with you.'

Hesitantly, she agreed. Gulp. The thought of going to a party full of horny, desperate 30-year-old men was my idea of hell – but this wasn't about me. And, besides, since I'd cancelled my membership of my own choice of website, I needed an awakening to what the real dating scene was like.

♥ ♥ ♥

It can be said that at this point I was highly experienced in talking to male strangers, but when I walked into the singles party with Only Remaining Single Friend, I was at a loss as to how to act. Does a singles party give a girl carte blanche to walk up to any group of men with a bold self-introduction and a handful of business cards? After all, everyone is there to interact, right? Or, given that the implicit reason for us all being there is that we have failed to find a life partner through natural means, do we have to maintain extra cool? We don't want to be labelled desperate, right?

It seemed everyone there shared my concerns. In the first couple of hours, no one spoke to anyone other than the people they'd arrived with. Girls went on the prowl in pairs and men stood with their chests puffed out and their backs to their bar, pretending to be in deep, witty conversations with their mates but really checking out the quality of the female clientele.

The venue – the Embassy nightclub in Mayfair – was dark, loud and so highly air-conditioned that it didn't feel much warmer than the snow-lined streets outside. I was in a backless mini-dress – from a limited-edition collection by Marni, courtesy of Munich Man. It was plenty warm enough for sitting in a nice hotel bar but far too cold for a cavernous nightclub. Only Remaining Single Friend was in skinny jeans and a sexy strappy top. The other girls all seemed to be wearing various different shades of smock dresses with footless tights.

The guys were in just-came-from-the-office suits with their ties loosened. Most were late 20s or early 30s. Instantly, I put my barriers up. They'd be clones of one another, I thought, their expensive Soho salon haircuts the only thing differentiating them from the next fresh-faced, cocky young professional. I didn't imagine any of them had anything interesting to offer me. I was used to dating at least a decade above them, and I felt these guys could never match those experiences. But I was here for Only Remaining Single Friend. She, unlike me, wanted to meet someone – 'meet', of course, meaning 'form a lasting, substantial relationship with, possibly with a view to moving in and having children'.

The party stretched over two floors. We did two full circuits, vodka cranberries in hand, trying to look completely natural and as unlike we were looking for a potential partner as possible.

'It's funny,' I said to Only Remaining Single Friend as I stood at the bar, looking straight ahead so as to avoid all eye contact with any male – heaven forbid anyone might think I was drooling over him – 'on a "normal" night, I'll chat to anyone at the bar. I'll flirt with no shame. But here I'm scared everyone's going to think I'm a desperate madwoman.'

'Me too. Maybe we need more drink.'

I agreed and Only Remaining Single Friend went to the bar to buy a round of doubles while I popped to the loo, where I was greeted by unfriendly faces. As I stood by the hand dryer waiting, I overheard some other girls talking about the excruciating price of the vodkas. 'Yeah, I know,' I chirped, acting on the perfectly natural urge to join in the conversation. The party of three girls whipped their heads around simultaneously, looked my goose-pimpled body up, looked it down all the way to my Louboutins – the ones Greg had bought me in New York – then gave me a look as if I'd just killed their cat. Or stolen their man. But of course, I thought: you don't talk to *girls* at a singles night. They're rivals. Silly me.

A couple of hours later, the atmosphere at the Embassy had transformed from cringeworthy school disco to frenzied, oestrogen-oozing dance floor. Hips were grinding on every corner, women were provocatively shaking their bums in front of men who had now shed their ties and there were scores of vodka tonics being passed over my head. I was worried the red soles of my Louboutins would be ruined by the alcohol-drenched floor, a concern I assure you had never even been on my radar before I joined Sugardaddie.com.

'There's a guy over there who's been staring at you for the last ten minutes,' shouted Only Remaining Single Friend over the whining R'n'B.

'Where?' I looked over and saw a good-looking guy in his early 30s, with a gentle demeanour, standing on his own. He was indeed looking over at me. Instinctively, I looked away.

He walked over confidently and asked me, 'What's your name?' He was every bit as charming as he was handsome. He was a photographer, he said, and wasn't drinking that night because he had just come back from a week-long crazy stag do and had reached alcohol saturation point. Nevertheless he had ventured out to this thing alone, which I had to admire.

'What do you do?' he asked.

'I'm a . . . I'm a . . .' I didn't know what to say. I was so used to making up a profession unrelated to the media so as not to scare off men who were paranoid about their dubious choice of dating site being made into a double-page tabloid splash that it felt strange to give a truthful answer. 'I'm a journalist.'

He was impressed and interested, but I remained uninterested in him, despite myself. Having recently had access to a pool of men who spoiled me with Marni, La Perla and spa weekends without expecting a committed relationship in return, I was immune to feeling flattered by The Photographer's flurry of questions.

'Where's your accent from? I detect hints of northernness.'

'Oh, Cheshire, originally.' I couldn't be bothered. He was taking more of an active interest in me as a person than most of the men from the website, but I remember thinking, there's nothing he can add to my life – what's the point?

No sooner had I formulated that thought, however, than I noted to myself that I had better keep an eye on how that attitude developed, because I was starting to think like one of those arrogant people whom I had always despised – the ones who only give their time and attention to others if they're getting something back.

♥ ♥ ♥

'I am so glad you're off that website,' said Happily Married Girlfriend when I broke the news to her.

'I know you didn't approve, but it's given me unsurpassable life experience – and confidence with men,' I replied in a low voice. We were in Wagamama in Covent Garden, sharing a bench with neighbouring diners so that they were sitting practically on top of us.

'Of course it has,' she trilled, oblivious to my lowered tone. 'You were giving men exactly what they wanted – no-strings fun. Most of the other girls on there were probably Brazilian hookers. Of *course* you were popular.'

'Will you keep your voice down?' I hissed. I could feel myself growing agitated by her view that no relationship was worthy of consideration unless it was based on everlasting devotion and unconditional love. 'It's been good for me. It gave me exactly what I wanted: some fast-paced dating, fun and the experience of meeting wonderful, interesting people. I've had my share of fun, it's over now, but I wouldn't change any of it. So please don't judge what's right for my life by what happens to work in yours.'

'I'm not judging. It's just that I think it was a damaging thing to do.'

'Do I look damaged? I am *enlightened*.'

We paused (much to the disappointment of the couple next to us), knowing the conversation was heading towards an argument.

'So do you have any normal dates set up?' Happily Married Girlfriend asked after a minute, attempting to steer us into safer waters.

But her choice of subject only irritated me further. 'No, I don't have a normal date set up! Why do you assume I'd want to do that? I've come off the site because the novelty of fancy restaurants and cocktail bars has worn off. Simple. That doesn't mean I have to launch myself into Project Find Mr Right.'

'I'm sorry I asked.'

'I'm sorry to snap,' I said, checking myself and speaking more calmly. 'It's just that it bothers me that, as a close friend, you don't seem to get my frame of mind.'

I was annoyed, but maybe there was something in what she was saying. According to Happily Married Girlfriend, my aversion to forming relationships with the opposite sex wasn't a normal outlook to have. 'I just think you're closed to finding anyone,' she told me, 'and I don't know why. What are you shutting yourself off from?'

'I'm not shutting myself off from anything! I don't see the 111 point in going looking for something I don't need when I've got plenty of other things to do with my time.'

Did I want what she had? Deep down, did I want a man to love? On the surface, the thought of a committed relationship filled me with dread and just about brought on an attack of claustrophobia, but, looking deeper, I asked myself, what if there was someone I really adored? Would I then want to connect with him every day and integrate him into my life? I couldn't imagine feeling like that. I couldn't imagine meeting anyone I'd want to give up my free time for.

But my self-questioning was missing something crucial. There was someone who had captivated me all along. I had been repressing my crush on The Boss for way over a year now. If he'd asked me out, I would have dropped anybody else I was seeing. But, no matter how much I flaunted my Prada wardrobe in the office, he was taken. I wanted something I couldn't have, so I was building a world that allowed me to thrive on not getting what I wanted – a world where proclaiming happy singledom and total independence gave me power, an identity and freedom.

By dating sugar daddies whom I could hold at arm's length, I was seeking out an approximation of the figure I really wanted while keeping the door ajar in case the real thing somehow did come my way.

'What other things?' prompted Happily Married Single Friend impatiently, jolting me back into our conversation.

'Sorry?'

'What are these plenty of other things you've got to do with your time now you're not dating? Maybe you should take up a hobby or a class or something.'

'Yeah, I've heard knitting's pretty good at this time of year. But I'm worried the adrenalin might send me over the edge.' She was asking for that. A hobby? How fucking ridiculous. It was yet another sign that she assumed I must be desperately searching for inner happiness in my incomplete, wretched single life. 'No, I'm going to concentrate on finding a new job. I need to get out of where I am. I've been at the same place for four years and I've not moved on at all. I either need to go freelance or I need to get out of the company.'

Happily Married Girlfriend approved and we agreed that all this sugar daddy nonsense had been a way to fill the void caused by the frustration of my slow-moving career. It was probably the first thing we had agreed on since I joined that website.

A few days later I got a text from her: 'Re our conversation the other night would you be interested in v good-looking solvent 33-year-old consultant, was [her husband's name]'s colleague, now back on dating scene after engagement split.'

Happily Married Girlfriend is lovely, really. To me, in a different zone from her monogamous bliss, her unyielding attempts to steer me round to her way of thinking were incredibly irritating, but really she just wanted to help. We often get angry when people try to force their views on us. But they do it because they've found something that works for them, and it's in our nature to assume the same medicine will work on someone else. My sister was exactly the same when she got married – constantly trying to fix me up because she really wanted to help me get a ticket into the exclusive club of coupledom.

Actually, I was guilty of it, too. I had failed to spot how much Only Remaining Single Friend really wanted to be in a relationship, had trivialised her fling with The Boy, had presumed that she wanted nothing more than casual relationships, like me. What sort of friend was I?

Chapter 13

Organic Dating Diet

♥ **March to April '08**

I agreed to give the blind date a try, primarily because I wanted to shut Happily Married Girlfriend up, but also because I had listened to her admonishments, even though it was with irritation. I didn't for one minute think the set-up would end up becoming a 'relationship' – ugh, I could hardly bear the word! – but I was starting to see in myself the negative side effects of my recent experiences. I was becoming alienated from real, more genuine forms of dating. I was becoming less and less receptive to men who paid me attention in the real world. The Photographer from the singles party had gone to the trouble of phoning me – not texting, but phoning. I had a short conversation with him and he asked if I wanted to meet soon for a drink. I said yeah, all blasé, but I had no intention of following it through. I was prejudiced against him. He was a normal man and I assumed them to be mundane. I had met so many colourful characters over the last year, men with exciting, jet-setting lives. I thought of The Photographer as a step back into my old, uninspiring, conventional dating era. The set-up date with the 33-year-old ex-colleague of Happily Married Girlfriend's husband could be the medicine I needed to bring me back to reality.

I was, however, dreading it. I didn't feel a scrap of the excitement I did when I went out to meet older men from Sugardaddie.com. I felt sure the date would be full of hints and clues and silent analysis of what each other's agenda was – something that was refreshingly absent when pursuing a convenience-based alliance.

Oh God, he'll probably expect me to be watching DVDs with him by next Monday, I thought as I pulled on a dress. Then I took off the dress. This is a normal date, stupid. I'm not going to be meeting a well-groomed executive in a tailored suit in a Knightsbridge hotel. And it's a Tuesday night. I should wear jeans, really. What do people wear on normal dates? It was so long since I'd been on one.

I met Set-Up Date in Exchange Square, near Liverpool Street in east London – the same area where I'd met Date One at the 42nd-floor champagne bar. It was one of the most difficult areas for me to get to on public transport. It was a bitterly cold evening and I remember walking across the vast, empty concrete of Exchange Square, seeing a sheet of ice stretch ahead of me. It looked to me like a symbol of the long, uncertain, barren future ahead of me now that I was no longer on a dating website that had, for the past year, provided fail-safe day-to-day excitement.

I entered the pub and the heat hit my cheeks. I felt them flush bright red. Set-Up Date was wearing a white shirt, open at the neck. His suit jacket and tie were in a heap on the chair next to him. He had a glass of house red waiting for me, one of those pub measures that hold a third of a bottle of wine. The stumpy glass looked unenticing, waiting for me on a cardboard drinks mat. I couldn't help comparing it to when I'd met Champagne Breakfast Guy at the May Fair Hotel back in October and he'd had a flute of lightly bubbling rosé

Laurent Perrier waiting for me. Stop it, I told myself. Have an open mind.

'Hiya,' my date chirped. He was chewing gum. He stood up and shook my hand. Shook my hand! How formal.

'It's freezing out there!' I greeted him. I was at ease meeting strangers for first dates after all my experience, but I noticed he was distinctly nervous.

'I can't believe [Happily Married Girlfriend's name] set us up,' he replied, not responding to what I'd said, a dead giveaway that he had pre-prepared his opening line.

'Oh, don't worry, it's a married trait,' I quipped. 'People get a pathological urge to fix all their friends up with each other once they get a ring on their own finger.' He gave a half laugh. I don't think he was prepared for my cynicism.

Set-Up Date wasn't bad-looking, but to me he was a boy, both in terms of looks and mannerisms. As we talked, it felt more like chatting to a colleague than a potential sexual partner – drawing on banal things we had in common to fill the time with idle chat. There was no flirting. Looking back, I don't think I felt safe to flirt because he was my age. To my way of thinking, entering into a rapport with him would put me in danger of being trapped in a union I couldn't easily pop out of. Dating men much older than me and from outside my everyday social circles had provided a safe zone where misunderstandings or character clashes could be put down to the generation gap. But Set-Up Date was my peer – a middle-level business consultant in the City, roughly the same age – so there was nothing to hide behind.

We finished our drinks and he suggested we go to a nearby tapas bar in an indoor market hall. We sat outside the restaurant. We were beside a big patio heater, but it was still cold. I didn't take my coat off and removed my gloves only when the food arrived. I noticed he asked me what wine I wanted to order – something I had never been asked on any of my dates from the website. The men always selected the wine, and always after we had chosen our food. The wine was served in a fingerprint-smeared carafe. It was red and watery and tasted strongly of alcohol. I let him choose most of the dishes – that was what I was used to. He did it awkwardly. I think he was trying not to come across as overly assertive. But I didn't care what he ordered. I don't even like tapas. It's all spicy sausages and greasy potatoes to me. I burned my tongue on a dish that was too hot. The whole evening felt strained. I was right when I'd predicted to Only Remaining Single Friend that 'normal' dating would be about trying to force out chemistry.

At last the bill came. 'Are you happy to split this?' Set-Up Date asked without hesitation. Split it?! He might as well have rubbed the leftover chorizo sausages into my wounds. It seemed such an injustice that I now had to pay for the privilege of learning something I'd already known before I came on this wretched date – that I wouldn't enjoy myself.

Having got used to dining with men who were always content to pick up the bill, I think I had unconsciously drawn the conclusion that the man needed the company of the opposite sex more than the woman did. I hadn't paid on a date for more than a year. It just goes to show how quickly new habits form. I had soon become conditioned to men paying the way. We put down our debit cards side by side on the saucer with the folded paper bill.

One of the attractions of sugar daddy dating is that it draws on traditional gender roles: the man gets to assert his masculinity by demonstrating his greater spending power, deriving pleasure from the thought that he's lifting a burden from his delicate female date; the woman gets to enjoy the feeling that she is being looked after and provided for by this manly, capable being who will relieve her of having to deal with such weighty chores as bills. I had been happily going along with this role play for the past year and was in a state of blissful amnesia about the whole equality aspect of the conventional dating world.

As we walked towards the Tube, he awkwardly reached for my hand. I didn't object; it would have been too harsh a statement to pull it away. It wasn't like I had much sensation in it, anyway – it was numb with cold underneath my leather glove. Next time, he said, we should meet on a weekend and then we could 'let our hair down more'. 'Yes,' I said, 'that would be good,' and I steered the conversation away from a second meeting. It wouldn't be long until I could step onto the Tube, plug in my music and be left alone with my thoughts.

'This is you. I'm getting the bus,' he said as we reached the wide pedestrianised concourse outside Liverpool Street station. He didn't let go of my hand. Uh-oh, I thought, he's going to try to kiss me. The vapours of sausages and cheap Spanish red wafted up to my nose as he leaned in to me. It was easier to kiss him back than to explain why I didn't want to. I had Female Rejection Syndrome again, as I'd had with TruePoet.

I mulled the evening over as I sat on the Metropolitan Line, plugged in to some sad REM song – something I'd never have chosen to listen to while sober. I wondered what on earth was the whole point of finding love. Why would anyone in their right mind put themselves through all this just to search for 'a relationship'? As far as I could see, a relationship was a time-consuming, self-sacrificing chore. Why aim for that when you could keep your independence, go onto a website and find someone to meet two or three times a month for dinner, the theatre and sex? That seemed far less complicated than spending hours worrying over compatibility, I reasoned.

I had found Set-Up Date over-eager to please and nervous. Our conversation was stilted and I got bored talking about my background, my education and my career. Who cared where I'd done my Japanese degree? That was nearly ten years ago. I could have been talking about a fraud case with a real-life suspect, exchanging sexual fantasies, philosophising on the principles behind marriage, reciting islands I'd been to in Asia – these were the kinds of things I'd talked about with Champagne Breakfast Guy, Munich Man, Greg and the others.

As soon as I stepped out of my home Tube station, my phone beeped. I fumbled in my bag, drunkenly spilling half the contents on the pavement, my earphones falling out and getting tangled in the mess. It was a touching text message from Set-Up Date, saying he'd just missed his bus and was walking along the road with his iPod on, smiling about the evening. Oh gosh, the guilt. I replied briefly – nothing misleadingly gushing, but at least I wasn't so heartless as to not respond at all.

I sighed. What was wrong with me? There was nothing not to like about Set-Up Date. He was a sweet, caring, genuine guy with love to give. Maybe Happily Married Girlfriend was right. Maybe I was shutting myself off from something. But what? And why?

♥ ♥ ♥

Right, I thought the next day, with more clarity, Sugar daddy dating is putting me on a different planet, clearly. I can't believe I begrudged going Dutch. What sort of eighteenth-century rationale was I basing that on?

Obviously, it wasn't the money that bothered me. Of course it wasn't. It was being caught off-guard by a situation that didn't fit in with what I'd been used to over the past months.

I couldn't see that then, though. All I could see from the night before was that the longer I stuck to dating men in a different social league from me, men who bought me fine wines, lingerie and first-class airline tickets, the further away from reality I would get and the more I would push perfectly well-meaning men of my own age and status away.

I definitely have to give up dating in such a superficial way, I said to myself. But then considering organic dating was . . . God . . . just painful. I should detox myself of men altogether, stop messing around and sort out the real void in my life. I need to address my career frustration and look for a new job – properly this time.

As well as pulling the plug on men, I decided to have a full emotional, physical and spiritual clear-out. I needed to decide what I really wanted to do. Did I want to carry on working in news? It was depressingly competitive and I hadn't moved up a rung on the ladder for four years. Should I go freelance? A lot of colleagues at my level had done and were now working as news producers in bigger and more high-profile newsrooms. But I knew it was a big step. And did I even want to be a producer? I wanted to be a proper journalist, dodging landmines, doorstepping politicians and hiding secret microphones in my clothes. But I was realising that in broadcast journalism (as opposed to newspapers), roles that required real field research and actively looking for stories were very scarce. Many of my colleagues were leaving the industry altogether because they had realised that it offered little in terms of employer appreciation, decent pay or progression opportunities. And need I even mention the anti-social shift patterns?

I'd always wanted to write; I'd never wanted to sit and edit pictures. Should I look at switching from broadcast to print journalism? Whatever the answer was, men, I knew, should be the least of my worries. My angst about the direction my life was going in didn't have its roots in whether I would find a life partner; it was centred on work.

I went to Bali on a detox holiday. It was a decision made on a whim. I convinced myself I needed sunshine and time on my own to think – and I felt unhealthy from all the cocaine I'd been doing since I'd met Munich Man.

I stopped over in Hong Kong en route to Bali and stayed with a friend with whom I'd studied Japanese at university. She had become a successful recruitment consultant, placing highly specialised banking professionals in executive-level positions in banks across Asia. Her expat friends had similarly impressive jobs and it added to my yearning for change. Being surrounded by all these über-successful people and witnessing their work-hard, play-hard culture made me aspire to become something more important than a multimedia broadcast journalist.

A week's fasting, daily colonic irrigations (!) and hour-long sessions of chanting 'ohm' in the Balinese mountains brought me home rested, motivated, healthy, tanned, thinner than I had been when I was 18 and unable to stomach alcohol for around a month – by far the longest period of my adult life that I've ever gone without.

I got a new job soon after that. I was to manage a brand-new news team on a brand-new news show for Current TV, a small current-affairs channel aimed at young people. I was excited but also apprehensive about leaving the security of a big, established news organisation for a little-known start-up Sky channel. If it all goes wrong though, I thought, I can go freelance. I should have got out of my old job far sooner than I did. The Boss, in part, delayed my departure – my attempts to flirt had become a highlight of my working day.

The new job meant I had to work twelve-hour shifts, from six in the morning till six at night, but I would only work three or four days a week to compensate for the long hours. I still had to work every other weekend, but at least I would never, ever, ever, ever have to work night shifts again – or so I thought.

I started the new job in April. I worked hard. One always does in a new job. This was the new leaf I had turned over. It was very high pressure, especially in the beginning. I had to deliver a new, fresh news bulletin bang on every hour for twelve hours a day. The deadlines were so challenging that I didn't dare stay out beyond 10 p.m. on a school night or drink more than one glass of wine. To be in for 6 a.m., I had to be up at 4.30 a.m. I was not a member of Sugardaddie.com any more. I had no space in my new, more serious life for no-strings sexual antics and endless first dates. My phase of website flings, I decided, was over.

But, in fact, it had hardly even started.

Chapter 14

The Rubber Ball

♥ June to July '08

Early nights and getting up at 4.30 a.m. soon got boring, especially at the height of summer, when the nights were light and the bars were spilling their clientele onto the pavements.

And that was why, as I sat in my garden on a glorious, sunny Thursday afternoon with my three scheduled days off ahead of me, I felt like a caged animal set free. My mind wandered to Munich Man. I hadn't broken my dating detox until now, so there was a big gap in my social calendar that had previously been filled with the excitement of strangers, flirting, sex, swish hotels and spa weekends.

Should I text him, I wondered. I had the day's newspapers out in front of me – all read. I had tried to call my mum – she wasn't in. My sister was at work. Everyone I knew was at work. And, in fact, everyone I knew would be away during the approaching weekend – weddings, hen parties, outings with their husbands and/or kids.

I hesitated because I didn't want to be the one to chase. There is an unfortunate preconception about women: if she chases, she has become an emotional prisoner. That stigma never seems to attach itself to men, who are presumed to be sexually motivated rather than driven by a need for security or emotional closeness.

Munich Man and I had known each other for more than a year by this time, which is probably about as long a shelf life as a sex-based relationship can have. The beauty of genuine emotional relationships is that they can reach imaginative new depths – it's a shame they're so time-consuming. But with Munich Man and me, our thrills and gratification were limited to the culinary delicacies of Knightsbridge restaurants, the pharmaceutical contents of his wallet and our stamina in his hotel room – not unpleasant in themselves, but it inevitably became repetitious.

We had, for the whole year, continued to have mind-blowing sex, which is still – at the time of writing – to be matched in my experience. Though, considering our mindsets were refreshingly free from hidden agendas and our sessions were always fuelled by a cocktail of cocaine, Viagra (I was pretty sure) and room service on his expenses, I shouldn't have expected anything less.

But our dates had become less frequent and more spontaneous, indicating that we had probably put each other on our 'back-up list' of people we called when we had nothing to do, rather than at the forefront of a busy dating agenda. The last time I'd seen Munich Man, I'd woken up and realised I'd lost a pearl earring. He'd said he would take me shopping to buy a new pair for my birthday, which was the following week. That had never happened.

Two months later, he'd phoned out of the blue and asked if I wanted to go to Amsterdam for the weekend to visit one of Europe's biggest swinging clubs, Fun4Two. I was apprehensive but curious, as I seemed to be about everything. Munich Man forwarded me links to and photos from the website and told me it was highly respected and considered the best sex party to go to as a first-timer. The calibre of people was high, the venue was clean and the attitude respectful. I agreed and he booked the flights and reserved a hotel.

Two days before we were due to leave, he cancelled. He was very apologetic, claiming one of his children was going through a difficult time dealing with the divorce. Munich Man had mentioned this the last time I'd seen him, so I believed it was a truthful excuse. I couldn't be annoyed. Obviously he couldn't abandon his children for a swingers' club in Amsterdam. But, I noted, he had made no attempt to rearrange a date since.

Having said that, what was I getting all proud about contacting him for? I wasn't trying to change what we had into anything more serious. Was I? If I wasn't looking for anything more than champagne, cocaine and sex, why did I want to feel wanted by him as well?

I composed at least three different draft texts. 'Hi, how are you, stranger? Do you want to meet for dinner soon?' No, too forgiving. He blew me out, remember. Twice. 'Hey you, aren't we due a meeting soon?' No, too exposed to rejection. I settled on: 'I hear Amsterdam is nice in June. Weren't we supposed to be rescheduling a trip?'

He replied with one of his usual opening lines of apology. 'Sorry for not being in touch, work has been crazy . . .' 'Sorry, I've been out of the country four days a week but it's been too long . . .' 'Sorry, I've been sorting out the divorce, let me make it up to you . . .' I can't recall which one it was that time. Then, his text continued, he had been thinking of me because 'There is a Rubber Ball in London this weekend. You would love it! Are you near a computer?' I was. He gave me a website address for the Skin Two Rubber Ball – an 'erotic party for liberated adults'. The dress code: rubber, PVC, uniform or burlesque.

♥ ♥ ♥

For the second time in my life, I was on time for a date. I got 125 the bus to Camden in north London, where you can buy everything bohemian, from magic mushrooms to handmade jewellery. There are fancy-dress and fetish shops aplenty. I waited for Munich Man by a sizzling Chinese food kiosk at the entrance to the Stables Market. It was raining.

Munich Man was 15 minutes late – not that I minded, since I knew it was usually the other way round. I was waiting calmly under my umbrella when he came hurtling around the corner, eyes wide, hair sticking out, muttering something largely incomprehensible about not being able to park. He was unshaven, dishevelled and looked harassed. He reminded me of the mad professor in *Back to the Future*.

'I'm terribly sorry,' he spluttered. 'Bloody nightmare. The traffic is just awful and there's nowhere to park and the signs – well, they're awfully confusing. You go round one corner and it says one thing . . .' I stopped listening to his words and focused on his gestures. He was wired, I could tell. His pupils were dilated, his jaw was gurning and he was apologising far too much for being only slightly late.

'S'OK,' I said simply.

'Where shall we go first?' He said it so fast his words ran into each other. Already he was looking greedily in every direction as though he wanted to be in every single sex shop at the same time. I noticed he hadn't made proper eye contact with me yet. He had acknowledged me with glazed, slightly bloodshot eyes – the kind you end up with when you've been up until 5 a.m. snorting cocaine – but he hadn't really looked at me in the way you do when you greet someone warmly.

'I saw a shop that looked promising just over there,' I suggested.

'Let's go there. This will be great fun, won't it?' He grabbed my arm and marched us over.

He was wearing a thin, creased, dark-blue suit. As we walked, I noticed it was bobbly with wear. The sleeves were too short. He was wearing a different watch from his usual Rolex, a cheap digital piece of plastic that could have dropped out of a Christmas cracker. The unforgiving light of a Saturday afternoon exposed a raw side of him that I'd never noticed before.

The thought flashed through my mind that maybe this hyperactive bundle of chaos in front of me wasn't the man he said he was. Maybe he didn't have the high-powered job and the country house in Cambridgeshire. Maybe he wasn't the jet-setting fund manager who hopped between Munich and London. Maybe the nights he spent with his Internet Sugar Babes in his swanky hotel room were him living out a fantasy – one he could ill afford. If so, he had carried off the lies very well. The amount of detail he had given me – no one could make that up, could they?

Today, he was a bumbling mess; I almost pitied him. He hadn't admitted to me that he was high on cocaine. If he'd offered me a line and said, 'Hey, let's start early – our secret,' I could have understood that this was a one-off – a kick-start to a day and night of fun. But he was hiding it. Or at least he thought he was; I could see it in his every gesture. What makes someone want to get off his face, alone, on a Saturday afternoon? There must be something about sobriety that he's afraid of, I thought.

We did a circuit of the shops, trying on rubber outfits. It should have been fun, but I had put my barriers up. He was high. How could I connect with him and why should I when he'd deliberately put himself on a different level from me?

The shopping was a consolation, though. The outlandish fashions of Camden are entertainment in themselves. And for a hosiery fetishist like me, it was a delight. I must be the only person in the world who buys outfits to match a groovy pair of patterned tights rather than buying tights to match an outfit. In my bedroom, I have one drawer for stockings and one for tights; soon I'll need another for 'unopened hosiery'. What can you wear with navy tartan tights, really? As Munich Man was looking at studded dog collars, I slipped a pair of brown leopard-print tights and a high-denier, metallic-silver, glitter-seamed pair into the basket. Oh, and some extra-fine fishnet hold-ups with peep toes to show off painted nails. I'd been looking for some like that for *ages*!

We tried on masks, too. I couldn't decide, so we bought two – one was a red Venetian eye-mask with red and gold feathers, the other a full-face white mask with accentuated high cheekbones, feline eyes and a gold feather.

Then I spotted a pair of long opera gloves. Divine. I wasn't thinking about the Rubber Ball. I was thinking about how nice it would look in winter to take off my coat and reveal over-the-elbow gloves. I toyed with a beautiful satin pair, thumbing the shiny material lovingly. Was it cheeky to put those in the basket, too?

'Look!' cried Munich Man. 'Doc Martens! Do you think I can get away with Doc Martens? Are they a good idea? Frightfully chunky. Gosh, Doc Martens – they remind me of . . .' Munich Man was muttering and spluttering away to himself, or maybe to me, I didn't know; it was the usual 100-mph manifestation of his frazzled brain. I shook my head gently to myself and dropped the long gloves into our basket. Munich Man would be too muddled to decipher the receipt.

It took around two hours to choose our outfits. Munich Man went for shiny black PVC cycling shorts, a matching black PVC top, Doc Martens, a top hat and a zebra-print cape, which was labelled 'Sugar Daddy Cape'. We both laughed at that. It was the first time we'd connected that afternoon.

I went for a black PVC dress that laced up at either side and at the back, exposing three strips of flesh where the laces criss-crossed, a purple bobbed wig and . . . well, I already have an impressive assortment of fuck-me boots, so it seemed greedy to get Munich Man to buy another pair, but I did spot a short goose-feather gilet.

We left the chain-smoking Goths of Camden's markets and went for a gin and tonic in a bar overlooking the canal. I was relaxing more now, and Munich Man was beginning to seem less frazzled and actually starting to talk to me rather than voicing a string of garbled thoughts out loud.

'You don't live far from here, do you? We can go to your flat to get ready and go from there,' said Munich Man, sucking the straw in his drink annoyingly loudly.

My flat? I'd never taken a sugar daddy to my flat before. It was audacious of him to suggest it. Not that there's anything wrong with my place. It's a beautiful home. But with sugar daddies there was a tacit agreement that we didn't allow our personal worlds to collide. The man could be ostentatious about his material status, and if that meant showing off his home, so be it. But the woman never exposed her private world. It was supposed to be about hotels and restaurants and breaks in foreign cities, away from normality.

'Don't you need to go back to your hotel and get stuff?'

'I have all my stuff here,' he replied, pointing to our plastic bags.

'What about your car?'

'I can leave it at yours.'

So he wanted to stay. I hadn't had a man to stay since I stopped doing conventional dating. There had been no need to endure the invasion of space. 'Have you not got your hotel room this evening?' I asked. The thought occurred to me again that perhaps bobbly-suited, cheap-watch Munich Man was not based as full-time in the hotel as he would have me believe. What if he didn't live there when he was in London? What if his company put him there only on occasion and the rest of the time he . . . well, maybe he did have a marital home after all?

'But we're here now,' he reasoned. 'We're nearer to yours than my hotel. And besides, it'll be fun getting ready together, won't it?'

What is this guy's obsession with the word 'fun', I wondered, but I answered, 'OK.'

Actually, maybe the challenge of colliding my real life with my sugar daddy escapades would indeed be a 'fun' thing to ride out? My lodger would be in, but, given that she knew all about my exploits, I was sure she would find the situation amusing. She might even turn *The X Factor* off and share a glass of wine with Munich Man and me in our PVC in the living room before we went out.

Munich Man's car was a dirty, battered grey Fiesta, which did nothing to allay my suspicions that his jet-setting executive lifestyle might be a façade. I had found it easier and easier to lie about not being a journalist to men I met on the website. Perhaps Munich Man had also rattled off the same lines so many times that he had become highly convincing. He was parked crookedly on a side street, the nose of the car nuzzled up to within an inch of the vehicle in front, the back end protruding so that passing cars had to slow down to drive past. I could envisage him parking in a fluster just before we met, cramming the car into the tiny space and, in haste, not bothering to straighten it. It was a small miracle he hadn't got a ticket.

He drove erratically, making no excuses for the state of his car, which smelled like a mix of cat wee and incense sticks. I warned my lodger by text that I was bringing a coked-up sugar daddy back to the flat.

♥ ♥ ♥

Later, I was sitting bolt upright in a cab on our way to London Bridge, my face fixed into an artificial smile and my jaw gnawing on fresh air. Munich Man had lined up two enormous piles of his Colombian marching powder before we'd left, and every muscle in my body was tense with the effects of it.

'We're going to run out!' Munich Man spluttered suddenly.

'Of what?'

'Of stuff. I only have one left and we've just done a line from it. We want to have some for later, don't we? It would be frightfully annoying if we ran out. Wouldn't it be frightfully annoying? Yes. I think we should get some more. Do we have time for a detour? Yes, we have time . . .' Munich Man rattled on, answering his own questions for another few sentences. I didn't comment. If he wanted to buy yet another gram, let him. Though, given the shuddering effects of the last dosage, I wasn't sure I wanted any more.

We took a detour to his dealer's house, and Munich Man sent me in! 'I can't be seen like this,' he said. He had a point. The zebra-print cape and shorts combo exposed lily-white bare legs with comically chunky Doc Martens on the end of them. He was wearing eye make-up and a top hat. He looked kind of like a confused wizard who'd forgotten to put his trousers on. I, however, with a long coat over my PVC dress and a pair of high boots, could easily pass as someone dressed for a normal Saturday night out. The purple wig and severe make-up were probably nothing a drug dealer would find out of the ordinary.

Munich Man's dealer greeted me at the door of his flat, holding a cigar and wearing a dressing gown. He looked about 65 and had a thick Greek accent – not at all what I was expecting.

'How are you, my darling?' He didn't recognise me, of course, but it made sense for him to pretend. He ushered me into his porch. I felt conscious of the bright lighting on my theatrically made-up face, the false eyelashes and scarlet lipstick. 'My darling, you will have to tell [Munich Man's name] I don't have any of what he wants. But I have something he will much, much prefer. He will thank me, I promise.' He held up a bag of silvery-grey crystals. MDMA. It was a long time since I'd done that.

I obediently took it from him. After all, I was going to a fetish party. Maybe the additional mind candy would – as Munich Man would say – be fun. 'Same price?' I asked. Not that I cared. Munich Man had shoved me a handful of notes, enough for whatever he had agreed in advance with the dealer.

'Yes, my darling, same price.'

The dealer called me back as I was walking to the waiting taxi. 'And a couple of his favourites. Complimentary, you tell him, my darling,' he said, pressing a plastic bag filled with chunky bright-blue pills into my hand. He laughed and added, 'You tell him I look after him.'

The blue tablets were bigger than my daily vitamin pills, and they were huge. I sneaked a look before getting back into the cab: Viagra! So I'd been right all along.

♥ ♥ ♥

The SeOne club was housed in the old railway arches underneath London Bridge station. The tunnel-like spaces and stone floor remained, giving it an appropriate dungeon-type feel. As I walked in, fresh from the effects of the silvery-grey powder that we'd dabbed our fingers into during the cab journey, I felt as high as my over-the-knee boots.

The four vast rooms were filled. I had no idea so many people were into rubber, PVC and fetish-wear. As we passed from room to room, I felt as if I was walking through a live cabaret. Men and women paraded around in rubber suits, revealing every bump, curve and ripple of muscle. My favourite was a French maid's outfit of stretched black and white rubber. There were men in nothing but dog collars and penis gloves. There were girls with legs up to their armpits in nothing but suspenders and stick-on jewels to cover their nipples and genitals. There were sequin-studded corsets lined in fur and huge feather hats. Some had opted for heavy-duty chains, others for role-play costumes – nurses and policewomen. A handful were in all-over body paint, carrying a token rubber accessory to meet the dress code.

A catwalk ran the length of the first room we entered. Burlesque queens danced their way up and down it. Then came strippers, pole dancers and later a troupe of lesbian dancers.

The next room was set up as a torture garden, with a roped-off path running through it. Models in BDSM costumes were being titillated in cages or bending over a bench and being gently smacked. The night was about exhibitionism and pushing boundaries, not hard-core stuff. Full nudity was not allowed.

The third room was the clubbing room, which was filled with dry ice and tranced-out pill poppers throwing their bare arms in the air and dancing furiously. It was an odd mix of latex meets MC Hammer. Munich Man looked uncomfortable in there, in that way that anyone over 40 looks when there is a possibility they may have to dance and they're not at a wedding.

The fourth and final room was the chill-out zone. That was where we spent most of our time, mingling with the other couples. The atmosphere was young and über-cool, and I think Munich Man felt aware of his age. I did most of the talking. The further the evening took us from our usual sugar daddy role play, the more pathetic I found him to be. Away from the sophistication of Harvey Nichols' fifth-floor cocktail bar, Munich Man seemed at a loss. Either that or he was too wired to speak.

There was one additional room, small and tucked away. It was signposted 'Couples Room'. I signalled to Munich Man that we should go in. I wanted to see. I felt the same sort of excitement as I had when I had experimented with Isabelle; I didn't necessarily have a compelling urge to take part, but rather a thirst to satisfy my curiosity. The floor was lined with cushions on which several couples were sprawled. Some were having sex, others were kissing or feeling each other. I could see two couples grooming each other for group sex. They moved cautiously, as if neither pair was sure just how willing the other couple was to respond to their advances. One girl seemed to be taking the lead, kissing both of the men in turns. There were female bouncers lingering near the entrance to stop voyeurs. The rule seemed to be: if you go in, you join in; you don't just watch.

'Shall we go and sit down?' asked Munich Man. What he meant was, 'Shall we join in?' Fuelled by my fascination, the splendour of my rubber costume, the MDMA and my new feeling of superiority over my blabbering coked-up companion, I agreed. As we approached the pack of writhing bodies, I noticed a haze of steam. We sat down on one of the cushions – away from other couples. This was going to be my first time for public sex; I didn't want the added complication of extra parties getting involved.

I pulled Munich Man down with me, eager to cling to him. It felt as though his body offered some sort of protection from the exposure. He got on top of me and kissed me in his furious way. I couldn't see anything else around me – not the other couples nor the open room – to remind me I was in a public space. The MDMA had removed any anxieties I might have felt and I moved with Munich Man, feeling his hands pressing into my flesh in the gaps in my PVC dress. But the heat and stickiness became too much and we stopped after minutes, getting up quickly. The spell had suddenly been broken and we snapped back to reality.

We headed for the toilets to freshen up. 'I'll wait for you to come back, then I can get the stuff from you before I go in,' Munich Man said.

I was carrying his wallet. Unsurprisingly, his rubber shorts didn't have any pockets. I was carrying a little black patent clutch bag that matched my PVC dress – naturally – so Munich Man had entrusted the evening's supplies of cash and drugs and his BlackBerry to me.

'I won't be long,' I said, knowing he would be eager for me to finish and hand his wallet over to him so he could go and do a line himself.

I went into the cubicle and fished in my bag for the small, flat paper packet of cocaine. Then I stopped. I saw his BlackBerry light up. He had just received a text. I looked down at it. Should I look? Being very protective of my own privacy, I am normally respectful of other people's, but I was starting to feel hostile towards Munich Man. And I had grown suspicious, suspicious that he wasn't who he had been saying he was for all these months.

I sat down on the toilet lid, made sure the door was locked, braced myself and picked up his BlackBerry. 'No, 2nite was not about you pls do not be mad with me u no I need to sort many shit things out I will be bak soon u dont know it all but I cud not see u 2nite one day I will tell u why.' Eloquent, I thought.

I read it twice. It should not have been any surprise. Munich Man and I had never promised each other exclusivity. And I had hardly been looking for that from him. But this text, dramatic and pathetic as it was, was confirmation that I had been Munich Man's Plan B tonight, and that stung. I put the wrap of cocaine back in my purse. I no longer wanted it. I needed to concentrate – because I needed to know more.

I had never used a BlackBerry before. I was also high on MDMA, gin and tonics, cocaine and post-coital hormones, so I had to concentrate hard to figure out how to get to his text messages. I was concentrating so hard my eyesight went blurry. I rested my elbows on my fishnet-clad knees and checked for the third time that the door was locked.

Finally – an icon that looked like an envelope. I selected it and somehow fumbled through to an inbox. The display showed a list of names – all girls. In disbelief, I read as many messages as my racing mind could take in.

'What now?' was one. 'I am thinking I need your hard cock in my pussy lips now,' read another. 'Hey, what are you doing tonight,' chirped a third. I scrolled down. There were several from an unsaved number, all very flirty. I couldn't tell whether they'd been sent before or after a sexual relationship had started. One particularly stood out: 'Do you think I am a pro?' There was another that would have made me smile if I hadn't been so shocked: 'Can you PLEASE respond to my texts?' Well, at least it wasn't just my messages that went ignored!

Then to the sent items: 'I woke up alone this morning'; 'I feel like I need you'; 'Great, I've booked dinner for 8'. Then there was a cryptic text sent to another unsaved number: 'Well, if I MET you I'm sure you would find I can do that.' I had no idea what that meant. There was one I recognised: 'You've been quiet! I've missed you. What are you doing this week?' He had sent me pretty much the same message around a year ago. That, I thought, must be the standard line he used to charm his young fuck buddies.

I went back to the inbox: 'I'm feeling horny and thinking of you.' The next one was from the same number: 'Too far. I'm in Tower Bridge. Can you come to me, baby?' And then came the hardest one to digest: 'Could you kindly transfer some money into my account today, please?'

That one whacked me in the face with the harsh reality that Munich Man was one of those guys who wants as much sex as he can get; he'll try to get it free if he can, but he doesn't mind paying if he has to. Paid for or not, it doesn't mean any more or less to him, and the only thing that distinguishes the two is that one carries the extra satisfaction of being a well-negotiated freebie. I had fallen into the latter category.

Until now, I had only ever viewed sugar daddy dating as an innocent exploration of my own fantasies. But, suddenly, reading that text, I saw it from the men's side. They had their own motivations. In Munich Man's case, it seemed, to get as much sex as he could. And I realised that, since he was more thirsty for sex than I was for personal experience, I could have utilised much more negotiating power. Munich Man would no doubt have been willing to follow the exact same dating pattern but would have paid for it if he'd had to. There were obviously other girls, such as the one in his phone, whom he did pay for sex. For me, he hadn't needed to.

I had no idea how long I had been in the toilets. The drugs had distorted my sense of time passing. I didn't care. The twat could wait. I put his BlackBerry away. I had seen enough. I walked out and tried to smile. 'Sorry, was I ages? There was a queue.'

I waited for him while he went to the Gents for his line. I remembered that tearful evening on my sofa with Only Remaining Single Friend. 'Do you know how dirty I felt when I did the walk of shame home? It makes me think I should do what you do . . . at least you've got something to show for it.' I knew what she meant now.

Munich Man returned and we resumed our tour of the club. He tried to hold my hand, but I brushed him off and walked ahead of him. Far from feeling deflated by my discovery, I felt empowered. Now that this man meant nothing to me, I could let all my inhibitions go. From now on, I thought, this is my night. Why should I go worrying about him feeling out of place in this youthful environment? He clearly considers me nothing more than an accessory to fun, so why the fuck should I raise the quality of my company to anything more than that? I was going to concentrate on my own enjoyment.

As we walked round, I chatted to people, I flirted, I giggled. He was secondary. Where normally I would graciously include him in conversations, I ignored him. The self-assured guy who had wooed me in impressive bars had become more like a little lapdog, following me around. He was nothing more than a 40-something businessman with a weakness for sex, so much so that he – not to mention his wallet – was at the mercy of predatory young women. I was annoyed with myself, too, that I had considered our connection to be anything more profound.

Chapter 15

Seeking Arrangement

♥ **July '08**

A couple of weekends later, I found myself at something of a loose end once again. I had three days off but nowhere to go. The sun was shining and I was full of energy. I love summer, but it does tend to mean that people with partners extricate themselves from the city. They are forever attending weddings together, going on package deals to the Med, taking day trips with their in-laws, going to national parks, festivals or couples-only outings on barge trips through Kent. From a single person's perspective, winter is much more sociable.

I decamped to my lawn, which had turned grey because I'd overdone it with the weed 'n' feed three weeks before and it hadn't rained since. I'm not really the reading-instructions type. I had just scattered the whole box all over and then read the directions afterwards, which informed me that I'd used three times the quantity I was supposed to. Carefully avoiding contact with the chemical-saturated grass, I read the *News of the World*. I came across an article about a prominent businessman being caught out with some 'high-class escorts'. Given my recent discovery of Munich Man's inbox and the snippets of hearsay I'd come across about the men and girls involved in that world, I read on with interest. Apparently, he'd met the girls on a site called SeekingArrangement.com. Curious, I thought. The very title suggested it was based on the model of dating that I had come across unexpectedly on Sugardaddie.com, the one I found myself captivated by but too scared to entertain – the 'pay-as-you-go relationship'.

I logged on to take a look. It was free for girls to register. I had written Munich Man off after the toilet-cubicle revelation at the Rubber Ball; Champagne Breakfast Guy was long gone after he'd stumbled on my online scribblings; and as for organic dating, well, that had turned out to be every bit as boring and cringeworthy as I had anticipated. My recent experiences of cheap red wine, greasy tapas and a raucous singles party still made me shudder.

Given all that, the Internet was beckoning me more and more furiously. The allure of low-maintenance, high-fun dating with someone mature was hard to ignore. Yes, some of the bullshit messages had annoyed me. Yes, the frequent cancellations had irritated me and, OK, I still felt nauseated when I recalled Eyelash Watcher's low, lecherous voice. But, fundamentally, my penchant for the older, wiser, accomplished, emotionally articulate, interesting man hadn't changed. I didn't want to be sitting on my chemical-singed lawn. I wanted to be having a slow summer's evening drink somewhere quaint.

As for the 'seeking arrangement' part, well, I reasoned, all the men I'd met on Sugardaddie.com had placed convenience ahead of compatibility, as I had done, too. Yet, despite the superficiality of our relationships, it had been most enjoyable. In fact, I *wanted* only a limited level of interaction. So, I concluded, I might as well date someone who's prepared to pay for that convenience.

I cast my mind back to when I'd first joined Sugardaddie.

com. I remembered feeling so naughty about my new hobby. I'd kept it more or less secret, telling only a few close friends. I shouldn't have felt so morally dubious about it, really. It was simply a website trying to cater for elite tastes. But you couldn't escape the fact that the pair-matching criteria were based on what some would consider superficialities: prestige and wealth for the men; beauty, youth and dress size for the girls. Any site where a girl can search by salary size goes against everything that we are supposed to think is honourable for the modern independent woman. The idea that attraction can be influenced by wealth is not so much immoral, then, as politically incorrect. That was why I hadn't wanted many people to know about my choice of dating website.

Yet here I was, some 14 months on, joining Seeking Arrangement.com, which was more upfront about introducing people interested in a cash-for-relationship swap, and I didn't feel guilty at all. I used to be shocked and disgusted by men who emailed me with offers of various forms of compensated relationship – shopping trips or a monthly allowance in exchange for my company once a week – but now it seemed logical. Although I'd built a rapport with some of them, with none of the men I'd met through Sugardaddie. com had there ever been any suggestion that we were looking for something long-lasting, nor had there been any pretence of love. So what would be the harm if I accepted money from those types of men?

I had already established from Munich Man's BlackBerry that he was 'supporting' at least one woman. The only reason he hadn't offered me any form of payment was because I had been willing to provide what he wanted for free.

♥ ♥ ♥

Lewis was my first date from SeekingArrangement.com. I didn't go to meet him with the sole intention of negotiating an 'arrangement'; I was motivated by the same principle as always – intrigue and adventure and the joy of a date – it was just that I was now open to the option of there being some sort of allowance involved.

He asked to meet me outside Marylebone Tube station, and then we were to go to his favourite hotel nearby for a drink. I hate meeting outside locations, principally because of safety, but also because it's just not chic to be hanging around on a street corner. He was insistent, however, saying that I'd never find his little boutique hotel on my own.

I waited outside the Tube, my uncomfortable shoes biting into my feet, telling myself that next time I must be more assertive and insist on meeting inside the venue. I saw his number flash up on my phone.

'I'm across the road from you in a dark-blue Jaguar,' he announced. And so he was, standing up, leaning on the open door, his phone glued to his ear, looking for all the world like an Italian mafioso.

'Oh, yes, I can see you. Is your driver going to park?' I was hinting for him to join me in walking to the hotel. I certainly wasn't getting into his car. He didn't move, though, so I walked over to him and he kissed me on the cheek. 'Jump in, my darling, the hotel's around the corner.'

'Do you mind if we walk?'

'Oh, it's fine, darling, I promise you. This is my driver and we are round the corner.'

I raised an eyebrow and gave him a look and he got the message. He gave instructions to his driver in a foreign language – Nepalese, I later learned – and passed him a handful of notes as a tip. Then we walked together to the hotel, tucked away in a little cobbled street. He'd been right – I would never have found it.

Despite his promising photo, Lewis wasn't attractive in the flesh. He was too thin and had a narrow face with pointy features and – ew! – a goatee. He looked like a mixture of Arab and Mediterranean. He showed no signs of greying, but his face was aged.

The hotel visit was a blatant attempt to impress. He obviously knew the staff well and made a point of greeting every single one of them by their first name and asking them specific details about their private lives. 'Are you married yet, Leila? When is the wedding?' 'Have you finished your photography course, Antonio?' He obviously stayed there often, and it was touching how much he knew about the staff; watching them interact, they obviously thought highly of him. But it was a little odd, I thought, to bring a first date there.

The bar reminded me of an old-school gentleman's club. There was no music, just the murmur of hushed male voices. I have since visited that hotel on multiple occasions and I have never seen another female customer. Bookshelves and antique desks displaying leather-bound books cluttered the rooms that made up the bar area. There was a musty smell in the air. Signed souvenirs and photos of staff crowded the walls and sporting memorabilia hung from the ceiling.

We moved on from drinks – rum for him, gin and tonic for me – to a cosy Provençal restaurant not far from the hotel. The sommelier approached us and asked Lewis what style of wine he was looking for. I remember looking up to find quite possibly the most strikingly handsome male human being I have ever seen. I found myself melting in my chair as I fixated on this svelte, upright figure before me, delivering a flawless account of the highlights of the wine list with charm and authority.

My date, however, did not have the same immediately enchanting effect. I found him infuriatingly slow about everything. He talked slowly, he walked slowly and he drank slowly. He would ponder over his next words in the middle of a sentence. I, on the other hand, drink fast, walk fast and my mind works ten times more quickly than I can talk. By the time I'd drunk my first glass of Bouzeron-Aligoté, he was still releasing the bouquet. Yet, as the evening unfolded and the wine flowed warmly through my body, I began to find him calming and surprisingly captivating.

He was a hybrid of Irish, Sicilian, American and English, and his accent had hints of all four. He had once been engaged to a Nepali heiress. They'd lived in a grand house in the tropical Terai region, which borders India, for two years. He'd tried to convert to the Hindu way of life but had found it hard to let go of his Catholic background. They were deeply in love, he said, but her family hated his foreign roots and so it had to end. That was a long time ago, before he'd got married to someone else, but I could tell by the way he told the story that he was still in love with her. Maybe she was his first love, I thought.

He seemed to have had a life full of adventure. When he was a teenager, he'd had a job as a bookmaker and had soon become involved in a powerful criminal circle of match-fixers. How fantastic, I thought. By the time I was on my second glass of wine, I had warmed to him, so much so that I caught myself wondering what he would be like if he were ten years younger and if he shaved off his goatee – and if he stopped making so much fuss about how his food was served. He sent the plates back because they weren't warm enough, and he asked for a fresh bottle of wine to be opened because he said the sommelier – the *gorgeous* sommelier – had not opened it within easy sight of our table.

He had given up his life of travelling when he got married. Nearly all of these super-successful men I met had chosen marriage at some point. So predictable, I thought, as I swirled the Bouzeron-Aligoté in my glass, relaxed but attentive, drawn in by his gentle, soothing voice.

I've met scores of highly independent guys holding highly responsible positions, with jet-setting lifestyles and ferocious drive for success. But these ambitious men have all, at some point, fallen in love with a woman and taken time out to settle down and start a family. These powerful men are no different from anyone else. They still crave love, attention and devotion. Why was I the only person who didn't see the joy of that? Did I have some sort of missing attachment gene? But I had fallen in love before – with The Ex, and exes before him. And I knew I was still capable of it, because I still had romantic daydreams. Romantic daydreams about The Boss. But I would never want to tie myself to married life, to *one person*! Maybe that was why I fell in love with people whom I could only have in my head!

I tuned back in to Lewis. He had tears in his eyes. He was talking about his children. They lived in America, he said sadly. He wished he could see them more and everything he did in his life was somehow for them.

Lewis did something with a gas exploration firm – he seemed deliberately vague when I asked him. He said he wanted to find love again but found it hard. That was why he had turned to the site. 'I know at my age I can't expect someone of your age to be with me. And women of my age, in the same position as me – well, there are not too many around, you know.'

'There are other websites with plenty of women your age looking for what you want.'

'Yes, I know that,' he said dismissively. 'But it would take me years to find someone suitable. This site gives me the next best thing to love. It is full of beautiful girls – like you. I may sound like I'm picky. But if I can afford to be picky, why not?'

'And what would be in it for her?' I probed, daring for the first time to ask someone face to face about an 'arrangement'.

I kept the question in the third person, however; it felt more comfortable to distance myself from the words.

'The things any young girl appreciates,' he answered. 'Help with bills or the odd bit of cash here and there. Trips away, wherever she wants to go. Guidance, experience, from a man who is wise to the world.' He paused. 'But there has to be something special between us, otherwise it becomes something very different.'

We both knew what he meant by 'something very different'.

'I can connect to you, though,' he said. 'How does that sound to you?' We were sitting side by side, and he moved closer to me, so that our shoulders were nearly touching.

I looked at him. I tried to imagine what it would be like to actually go through with it and take him up on his offer. I envisaged going on a weekend away with him. I pictured us holding hands as we walked along the streets of a Mediterranean town. I asked myself whether I could have sex with him. I imagined him lying on top. He seemed too sensitive to be sexual. Would he still have that sad, pensive look about him even when he was raging with randiness? I wondered how much 'the odd bit of cash' would be, how I would ask for it and how I would feel when I had it in my hand.

He neither attracted nor repulsed me. I could see his many qualities. He was self-assured and genteel, and he was obviously a deeply caring person. He had looked hard for genuine love, so hard that now he was willing to give up and take the easy, fast-track way by paying for it.

The concept of paying for a partner is a strange one, but many of the men I met didn't consider it odd. To them, using money to get what they wanted was a matter of course, and they saw absolutely nothing demoralising or second best about paying for someone's company. Most seemed to be so used to getting what they desired by paying their way that they extended those day-to-day tactics to getting a girlfriend. These websites allowed them to find a lover who would agree to be exclusively theirs but would not demand emotional commitment. Unlike a conventional lover, she would be paid not with affection and support but with money.

We got up to leave and he asked jokingly whether I felt comfortable enough to get into his Jaguar with him now. 'Yes,' I said kindly, 'but I really should be going home.' That was when he asked if I wanted to accompany him back to his place. He alluded to our earlier conversation, saying he was 'serious about financial support, you know'. He told me he would be happy to sort out something 'more concrete' and 'more immediate' if I felt 'more comfortable with that'.

No, I said again. This was my first opportunity to negotiate paid dating terms, and what I had learned from it was that I couldn't do it. I couldn't hold his hand in a Mediterranean town, spend the night with him or have sex with him. When I'd set out to meet him, with an open mind about negotiating an allowance, I'd been worried that the experience would leave me feeling degraded. But I found the opposite to be true. I felt that he was the one leaving himself open to exploitation; I was the one with the power. He desperately wanted me to accept his offer. But I knew that if I were to accept I would not be managing his expectations fairly, because he wanted to buy emotional as well as physical closeness.

He gracefully withdrew, said something in Nepalese to his driver and then announced they'd drive me home. I sensed that if I refused the lift it would damage his fragile ego further, and by now I fully trusted him, so I accepted and watched him give another handful of notes to the driver.

♥ ♥ ♥

SeekingArrangement.com was nothing like Sugardaddie. com. I didn't get anywhere near as many messages and the men were more aloof. They often demanded at least five photos before they would consider a meeting. With Sugardaddie.com, we'd meet up after a couple of messages without them having seen any photo other than my twelve-years-out-of-date modelling-days profile picture.

It was a lot more businesslike, too. The messages weren't flirty, they were direct. 'What are you after exactly?' read the first message I received. It scared me. I noticed there were a lot of businessmen from overseas, particularly America, who would typically send messages like 'I'm in London on such-and-such a date, would you be free?' Others indicated the senders were after something longer term: 'A branch of my firm is opening in London. It looks like I will be visiting once a month or more, so am looking for someone to accomp for drinks, theatre, etc. Shall we see if we get on?' I responded to that one. That sounded just the thing I was looking for. But after two or three messages, I heard nothing. I figured I must have been lined up as a back-up in case another girl cancelled. This seemed to be pretty common practice – an indication that the men considered the female members more or less interchangeable.

It doesn't sound at all pleasant, does it? Nevertheless, I remained enthralled and turned on by the idea that these high-flying, powerful, important men were willing to compensate me simply for being their date. I wasn't chasing one of these so-called arrangements solely for financial gain. I was intrigued by the world and the mindset of a man who had so much he could pay for a woman, indulge in her like any other luxury item, relish her like a Rolex or a glass of fine wine. How sexy to feel like cherished, high-quality goods. I had already satisfied my five-star-hotel sexual fantasies. This, I suppose, was my next high. The fact that this new website was even more controversial

148

than the last only made it more exciting.

I had no agenda, no expectations. I was behaving like Date One. I was gripped by a fantasy, led by temptation, but I kept stopping short of carrying it through. My second date followed the same pattern.

He called himself Zeus on the website. We'd only exchanged a few sentences when he suggested meeting up at Notting Hill Gate Tube station. Remembering my vow to meet only in public places from now on, I steered him towards hooking up in a bar. He picked Starbucks. Not exactly what I had in mind, but it was better than waiting for a stranger outside a Tube station.

I arrived on time, unusually, and sat by the window, sipping peppermint tea with a copy of *London Lite*. When he arrived, he was unshaven and dressed in a faded red T-shirt. He looked like a builder. He was short, tubby and had a grubby, lived-in look about him.

He went to order a coffee, but I suggested we go to a bar. The thought of discussing a possible arrangement over a Frappuccino horrified me. Even though I knew within five minutes that I was even less likely to pursue an arrangement with him than with Lewis, I had an inexplicable urge to play-act it out. He said he knew a good place nearby. We headed down a side street and I was expecting him to take me to some funky cocktail bar, but he walked straight into the first pub we came across. It was an old boozer with gambling machines, dog-eared beer mats, miserable red-nosed locals and the stale smell of beer in the air. They served one type of wine, which came from a box. I ordered a beer.

The builder lookalike had met several other girls on SeekingArrangement.com. His first date had been 19, looking to fund her studies. He said she was too young. 'She was very beautiful and all that, but you gotta be able to have a conversation, haven't you?'

Builder Lookalike had a rich Irish accent – his one redeeming quality. But then, working in broadcasting, I rated voices highly, and I'm biased towards Celtic accents, French accents, Russian accents . . . um, this list could get quite long. But, really, who isn't drawn in by an Irish voice?

'She just sat there the whole night and didn't say a thing and then at the end she asked what I could do for her financially. I think she just expected me to magic up a sack of money and hand it over.'

He described his second date as nice but dull. 'When you're doing 90 per cent of all the conversation, it's not gonna work, is it? I mean, if you're gonna have some times together, fun times, and get intimate, there's gotta be a bit of a connection, hasn't there?'

His woes didn't end there. He had arranged to meet a third girl, another student, who lived in Manchester. She said she couldn't afford the train fare to London to meet him. Builder Lookalike sent her the 70-odd pounds for the ticket. 'It was really strange. Y'know, I paid the money into the account like she asked and then I texted her on the day she was travelling. But I didn't hear a thing back. She just disappeared, y'know.'

I felt sorry for him, but at the same time I didn't particularly like him. I asked him what sort of response he got from his profile. 'Oh, I'm inundated,' he said, his Irish accent becoming stronger than ever. 'But that's because there are ten times as many women as men. Obviously, if a man advertises that he's willing to help a girl out financially, he's gonna be in demand. But some of them are pros, y'know. They say, if I meet you on Saturday afternoon in this place or that place, then I want £300 up front. I'm just not into that.'

Finally, I had to ask the question: why had he come to this site and what did he really want from it? He bumbled a little and then gave a long-winded assessment of how he'd lost patience with trying to meet people in the conventional way and so he was looking for 'Y'know, just someone I can see three or four times a month. We can have fun times together, go away and, y'know, if she needs help paying this bill or that bill, I can help her out.'

'So, like an allowance?' I asked.

'Well, not, like, as formal as that, but, y'know, if she wants to go shopping, that won't be a problem. I met this one girl – she was Polish. We sent emails back and forth and what it came down to in the end was that we'd meet a couple of times a month and it came down to, y'know, a thousand pounds a month. Which for a guy is not a lot of money. But for a girl who doesn't earn that much, it's a nice little boost. And if she's gonna have a few laughs and be laughin' and jokin' with him for a few days away, it's not bad, is it?

'I saw her once and she disappeared for weeks,' he continued. 'I couldn't get hold of her. She wouldn't answer her phone. And we'd got an agreement, too. Y'know, I kept my side of the bargain. From what I gave her, we were supposed to meet at least another two or three times that month.'

Builder Lookalike seemed undeterred by his two financial setbacks. He asked if I'd be happy to try out what he'd suggested. Again, I made my excuses and went home. I just couldn't do it. He was fat and unattractive.

But still, I remained absorbed in how this warped world functioned. I had now witnessed at first hand two scenarios of men trying to strike a 'relationship deal'. It was mesmerising to experiment with trading emotions and startling to watch men justifying to themselves paying for female companionship. But, like a cautious child who stares captivated into a swimming pool, I was too afraid to dip a toe in.

Chapter 16
Sealed with a Deal

♥ **August '08**

I was pottering aimlessly around my flat in bare feet and a long summer dress, clutching a glass of rosé. This week's three-day block of rest days fell from Monday to Wednesday. And, yes, it was Monday. Which meant . . . *play time*.

Equally Commitment-Phobic Male Friend rarely came out on a school night and Only Remaining Single Friend was recovering from the weekend, so I logged on to the website to get my stimulation that way. There was a message from an American ad executive, over on business from Chicago. After a couple of emails and exchanges of photos, he asked if I wanted to meet him in his hotel bar. He was staying at the Sheraton Park Tower, one of London's finest hotels, in Knightsbridge. 'Now?' I asked. It was 10 p.m. and I'd put my night creams on.

'I'll send a cab for you. Meet in piano bar,' he replied.

I hesitated, but then I scolded myself. I had the day off tomorrow. And the next day. Hadn't I been complaining that midweek weekends were uneventful? The only thing holding me back was the fact that, thinking I was going to be having a healthy night in, I had eaten two whole cloves of garlic in my stir-fry. I could even smell it on myself.

Quickly, I googled 'rid garlic breath' and, believe it or not, found a Wikipedia entry on that very topic. Lemon juice is good apparently, as is green tea, and you can also chew on fresh mint or parsley. Best of all, though, alcohol helps. I ran to the corner shop to get said items and poured myself another glass of rosé to be on the safe side. I brushed my teeth twice and put my toothbrush in my bag to use later during a visit to the Ladies. Garlic just keeps coming back, no matter how much you brush.

I arrived at the Sheraton's piano bar before American Ad Man – an experience I would not like to repeat. To get to the bar, you have to walk through a large circular reception area with various bars and corridors leading off it and various members of staff casting questioning glances at you. Top hotels are a clichéd escort hangout, or so said my paranoia. I felt several pairs of eyes on me as I walked up to the bar, pulled up a tall, charcoal leather stool and picked up the cocktail list. I looked up nervously, wondering whether I looked out of place. A wink from the pianist fed my fear that I looked as if I was there for 'business'. I wished American Ad Man would hurry up. I texted him to tell him I was at the bar in a red leather coat.

He arrived, very apologetic. He had that admirably American well-groomed look about him: lightly tanned, bright white teeth, chiselled jaw. He looked older than his 49 years but the lines on his face gave him a wise, dependable look. He was sexy.

'Where've you been tonight?' I opened.

'To dinner.' Silence.

'Oh . . . who with?'

'A friend.' Silence.

'Is that an English friend or someone you know from back home?'

'Back home.' Silence.

'Oh.' Silence.

I was drinking a Diamond Martini, which the barman had recommended. It was a Sheraton Park Tower special and apparently the most expensive cocktail in London. He had said it as though 'most expensive' were a good thing! The conversation was so awkward that I drank it in gulps. Eventually, American Ad Man loosened up, but not until I'd referred to the site and asked what he wanted from it – and then, of course, what he wanted from this evening. Wow. I hadn't done this before and could hardly believe what was coming out of my mouth and how experienced I sounded.

Like nearly everyone I had met on this new site, he was puzzled as to why 'a girl like me' had joined. 'Are you sure you don't have a boyfriend?' he asked.

As I had done so many times, to so many men, I explained: I joined because I was bored. Busy but bored. I wanted some excitement, but I didn't want a boyfriend. I'm turned on by the world of BlackBerrys, tailored suits, first-class travel lounges, fine wine lists, five-star service, men with Armani briefcases. That was not the norm in my own life and feeling part of it gave me a strange little buzz. And, of course, I had to add, to set the record straight: 'Let's say that if we can establish some sort of relationship that's mutually beneficial, then . . . well . . . it would make things smoother for both of us.'

There. I had put the notion in his head. I didn't dare embellish any more than that because if I actually pulled this off, I wouldn't know what to do or ask for. I was pedalling blind into alien territory, game for whatever I found.

Once we had got the website questions out of the way, we were both much more relaxed and our conversation flowed easily, in contrast to the stilted chat we'd had when he first arrived. You could almost feel us warming to each other with every minute that passed, like a steadily climbing thermometer. 'I like your attitude,' he kept saying whenever something I said struck a chord with him.

'Let's have one more drink,' I said.

'I like your attitude,' he replied.

When we talked about why I was on the website he liked my attitude. He was an advertising account manager for one of America's largest network channels. He had three teenage children and was contemplating divorce. When we touched on his marriage issues, he liked my attitude. We discussed past partners and the merits of being single versus in a relationship and he liked my attitude. I liked his, too, actually.

'What do you want exactly?' he said suddenly. I knew what he meant.

I squirmed. I had never been brave enough to get this far before. I had only ever played at negotiating, getting a thrill from being so close to something forbidden. 'Well, let's say if you're generous, then I will be too,' I heard myself say.

He half-laughed, sensing that I was uncomfortable talking about specifics. 'I think I can manage to be generous,' he answered, smiling. And that was it. My first negotiated deal.

American Ad Man had a junior suite. The grandeur of the room took me aback. A huge reception area greeted me, with polished wood-panelled walls, high ceilings and a window the full length and width of the exterior wall, giving a spectacular panoramic view of the city. Straight away, he said, 'Well, let's sort you out then, shall we?' He handed me a wedge of £20 notes. 'Count it and see if that's enough,' he said, and with that he considerately walked into the bathroom, out of sight.

I was frozen to the spot, clutching the cash wedge, in mild shock at myself. I leafed through it. One, two, three, four . . . sixteen, seventeen, eighteen . . . twenty-two, twenty-three . . . Eventually, I stopped counting and placed the lot inside my bag. Whatever the final figure was, it was obviously agreeable.

Thumbing through the notes only made me feel uneasy and I was afraid of my admonishing inner voice. It gets very loud sometimes.

We were soon naked. He had a unique way about him – firm, assertive but respectful. He was very well endowed, I noticed immediately. *Brilliant*, I thought, the night just keeps getting better. It never ceases to amaze me how different men can be, not just in size but in shape.

Then he announced he wanted to stop. 'Well, I want to, of course,' he said, 'but I'm going to resist because I like you and I'd like to see you again.'

It was supposed to be a compliment – I think? – but I felt disappointed. I was all revved up. Perhaps he read my dismay, because he proceeded to give me a massage as if offering humble recompense.

Now, I am a massage connoisseur. No price is ever too high and no journey too long for a truly thorough detangling of the muscle network. And what American Ad Man delivered was better than I have ever had in all my experience of Swedish, Thai, shiatsu, osteopathic, cranial osteopathic, naturopathic, super-double-lymphatic or anything else I've gullibly paid for over the years. He kneaded every single lump of stiffened tissue and touched on some muscles in my buttocks I didn't even know were there.

'Honey, you need serious work on your sciatic nerve,' he said.

'My what?'

'Your sciatic nerve, here. It controls all the tension in your lower back and the complete length of the backs of your legs. If you do a lot of running, you'll have a lot of tension here.' Whatever it was he was talking about, I believed him. I could feel my whole leg tingling from the pressure point at the top of my bum cheeks. It felt like I hadn't been touched there for 30 years and desperately needed to be.

American Ad Man reminded me of Greg in New York. He was remarkably interested in me. What did I go for in guys? Where would I live if I could live anywhere? What were my ambitions? He was effectively paying me to give me therapy – both of the physio and psychological sort.

I didn't know whether to stay the night or not. Did he want me to? Was I obliged to? Not having dabbled in this role before, I didn't really know. 'You must have to get up early. I should leave you,' I ventured, testing his reaction. He made it clear he wanted me to stay, if I wanted to, that was. Which I did. And so I slept beside him, occasionally waking to feel an arm around me in the night. I actually liked it, which surprised me, given that I usually need more space than an Apollo shuttle mission.

That was the first time I had accepted hard cash in exchange for intimacy, and it felt far from dishonourable. American Ad Man was more interested in companionship than sex. It was simply that he was the sort of man who was not ashamed of parting with money to get what he wanted when he wanted it, if that was what was required. From our drink at the bar, it had been clear we had a connection and enjoyed each other's company. At that point, where most men would be wondering how to take the night further, American Ad Man saw a cash deposit as a way of securing the continuation of the evening. It didn't detract at all from the fact that we were attracted to each other and enjoyed each other thoroughly.

We arranged to meet again the following Thursday. I booked the Friday off work. I imagined that my having to leave his hotel room at 5.30 a.m. for a 6 a.m. start might breach the terms of our arrangement.

♥ ♥ ♥

'Do you have a friend?' read a text from American Ad Man

the day before we were due to meet. Of course I have friends. What did he want exactly?

His second text clarified: 'I have asked a friend to join us this evening. Would appreciate the company. Do you have a girlfriend?'

Fuck. Did he mean like an escort girlfriend or just someone to innocently accompany us to dinner?! I really am swimming in unfamiliar waters, I thought. The only person I could dream of asking to join me on a date with a man who was paying for my company was Only Remaining Single Friend. Not that I had told her there was any money involved, but she knew that I was on a website with the name Seeking Arrangement.com, so I was sure it wouldn't come as a surprise.

She had been entertaining herself quite regularly, however, with a guy she'd met at the singles party, so I wasn't entirely sure she would want to go on a double blind date.

'Where will we be going?' she texted.

'Drinks at Sheraton Park Tower followed by dinner at One-O-One.'

'Fuck, yeah!'

I texted American Ad Man to say that he was in luck and I did indeed have a friend for his friend. It was a perfect set-up. I was feeling good – not hung-over for a change. I had the day off the next day. My friend was with me, sharing a part of my secret life that no one else had ever seen. She was also on top form. And I was going to stay in his top-floor suite again.

Only Remaining Single Friend and I arrived first, which was a first in itself given our usual record on punctuality. The piano bar was livelier this time and the lighting dimmer. I ordered two Diamond Martinis and asked the bartender to open a tab, which I knew would be taken care of. Only

Remaining Single Friend actually yelped when she saw the

price of the drinks. A guy was sitting to my right and I could feel him glancing over continually. He was visibly plucking up the courage to talk to us. He had a sad and lonely look in his eyes. He was wearing a suit but no tie. The top of his shirt was open and lopsided, as though he had hurled his tie off in his hurry to get to a place where he could wind down. His hair was ruffled, as though he had been clutching at it with stressed hands. It was only 7 p.m., and it looked like he was settling in to spend the evening alone.

'Are you girls on a night out?' he asked at last. He was British and very well-spoken.

'We're meeting some friends shortly,' I answered, politely but not flirtatiously.

'Well, if you would like to join me for a few drinks first, you're welcome,' he said.

I had never realised just how widespread this hotel culture of men picking up girls really was. I wondered what this lone man's story was and why he was here so early on a Thursday evening, desperate for company. Other people's loneliness always makes me sad.

When American Ad Man and The Friend arrived, the man at the bar scuttled off. The Friend was a lawyer and looked much older than American Ad Man. He was heavily built with a red nose and cheeks, a loud voice and a deep and frequent belly laugh. He looked like he was going to be very entertaining company.

One-O-One is a seafood restaurant within the hotel, with a thick menu full of small tapas-style dishes of unusual ingredients cooked up by its celebrity chef. The wine fuelled my confidence and I gently said to American Ad Man, 'Have we got the same deal as last time?' He said we did. His friend, obviously, was not expecting any sort of deal from Only Remaining Single Friend. I had made a point of letting American Ad Man know that Only Remaining Single Friend was not 'on the site' and implied that she was not viewing this as a date in any shape or form, especially not a paid one. American Ad Man assured me that that had never been on the cards. His friend was married and wanted nothing more than to share a lively evening in the company of two British girls.

Only Remaining Single Friend, meanwhile, was too busy being in awe of the restaurant, the service and the menu to suspect anything untoward. 'Are you sure they're paying for this?' she kept asking, worriedly.

The men ordered a disgraceful amount of food. They went through the menu picking at least three things from every page, barely looking at what they were choosing. We had lobster ceviche, crab pastilla with apple jelly and sorbet, quails' eggs and morels, sautéed cods' tongues, red mullet with shellfish and champagne reduction and plenty more. The plates wouldn't all fit on the table and I remember thinking it looked an ugly, greedy scene.

American Ad Man picked up the bill. I heard The Friend ask discreetly, 'You will be able to expense this, right?'

'Probably not, but no worries, buddy.'

We had a brief discussion about where to go next as us girls collected our coats. 'Let's go to Chinawhite!' roared The Friend. 'I have a buddy who's a member. He's there tonight. Come on.'

I didn't really want to go. Clubs are not my thing. I would have preferred to go back to the piano bar and have more drinks and talk where we could hear one another. But we didn't have much choice. The Friend herded Only Remaining Single Friend and me into a cab and we whizzed off to Chinawhite near the West End, where a queue of well-heeled 20-somethings was waiting outside.

The guy who got us into Chinawhite was the most unlikely acquaintance of two American executives. He was standing outside waiting for us, drawing on the very end of a cigarette that looked like it should have been stubbed out ages ago. He was a big, smiling black man, dressed in Rastafarian red, green and gold with a matching knitted hat. He looked no older than 25. 'I thought youse were never gonna get here, like,' he said.

'What did he say?' whispered American Ad Man as we walked down the stairs into the club.

'He was wondering where we'd been. He's Scottish,' I explained. His accent was so strong even I could barely understand him.

The Scottish Rastafarian had been a key witness in a big case that The Friend had won and they had mysteriously stayed in touch. I got the impression The Friend had adopted the Scottish Rastafarian as a reminder of his youth – someone who provided him with an occasional escape from the constraints of his normal life.

I chatted to him while American Ad Man and The Friend went to the bar to order drinks and found myself surprisingly refreshed by his down-to-earth attitude, easy laughter and carefree outlook on life, so different from what I was used to after dating so many sugar daddies.

For some reason, I don't know why, I offered him a line of cocaine. I had started taking it regularly. For years, I had had a take-it-or-leave-it attitude to drugs, only dabbling if the mood of the evening went that way. But ever since my regular hotel encounters with Munich Man, I had begun to associate it with a night out. Every time I'd seen him, he had given me two or three little packets as a parting gift. Damn him! I didn't like the fact that I had got into the habit of carrying cocaine with me everywhere I went. I didn't necessarily take it. I could go for weeks knowing it was in my purse and not touching it, but the fact was it was there, so it was always an option. And I didn't like being without it. I was late for work once because

I realised, while on the Tube, that I'd forgotten to pick it up. It was a Friday and, well, I might need it later. I went back to get it; the prospect of being half an hour late for work didn't deter me in the least.

The Scottish Rastafarian gladly took up my offer. When he came back from the toilets, he seemed agitated and distracted. Only Remaining Single Friend and I tried to engage him in conversation, but he kept putting his head in his hands and shaking it.

'Will you bear with me? I need to sort my head out, like. Yeah, I need to sort my head out for a minute,' he mumbled. He got up and went out for a cigarette. Then he came back and got up again and went for another cigarette. Only Remaining Single Friend went out with him the second time to check he was OK but soon returned without him.

'Erm, he's fucked,' she declared. 'He's talking complete shit and hasn't even lit the cigarette. He keeps telling me how he's in a really bad place at the moment. I don't know, I couldn't understand what he was saying.'

'He was fine ten minutes ago,' I said. And then the penny dropped. I went to the toilets to indulge in the gift that I'd given to the Scottish Rastafarian and found the paper empty. He was obviously not a veteran of taking Class A drugs and hadn't realised that what I'd given him was by no means a single dose. 'Great,' I said out loud.

The Friend had disappeared inside the VIP area, behind a double door. American Ad Man and I tried to go in after him, just for a look around, but were stopped by a female staff member with a Polish accent and a clipboard, telling us that this room was 'by invitation only'. Just as I was disputing my entrance rights, a stunning, petite Asian girl with shocking-pink lip gloss and hair scraped back in a high ponytail walked out. She breezed past me in a haze of perfume and then turned back to look at me as I rattled on about why I should be allowed in. The girl paused and smiled at me, smiled with her whole face. Her skin was flawless and her features perfectly symmetrical. She looked positively doll-like. 'You can join us as guest if you like,' she interjected in a soft voice. She sounded Japanese. The woman policing the door looked really pissed off.

I didn't take her up on her offer, however. American Ad Man was understandably not keen on joining a group of strangers with its own established alpha males. We left shortly after that. The Friend and the Scottish Rastafarian stayed. American Ad Man gave Only Remaining Single Friend money for a cab home and we went back to the peace and quiet of his suite.

We lay on the bed. I regretted my cocktail of drink and drugs, feeling desperately unhealthy. I need a massage, I thought, to get all the coke tension out of my neck. And as if he had read my mind, American Ad Man started massaging me, again asking me intimate questions about my background and my views on random topics. And again, whenever we came close to anything sexual, he used the same line, 'I like you – I don't want to.' I was confused. And disappointed! We eventually fell asleep in an affectionate but loose embrace. I wriggled out of it to get some proper sleep in peace, but every time I stirred I would feel a warm arm reach around me.

In the morning, we walked out of the hotel together. 'Are you happy with our deal?' he said.

'Yes. Are you?'

'Absolutely. I'm in London again in a couple of months. Are you happy to continue with our agreement as and when we see each other? I'm sorry I can't offer more regularity, if that's what you were looking for.'

What he meant by 'regularity' was some form of monthly payment. This man who had given me dinner in one of

London's finest restaurants, massages so good they nearly made me levitate, wonderful company and a fistful of notes was apologising because he couldn't do it more often.

'It works perfectly,' I said. 'I'll see you when you're next over.' And I jumped in a cab home.

Chapter 17

Malaysian Sugar Daddy

♥ September '08

Only Remaining Single Friend and I had gone on a spontaneous shopping-and-cocktails trip to New York. It was the week before her 30th birthday, and having just watched the first *Sex and the City* film, we decided a trip across the pond was an apt way to pre-celebrate.

The riches from my meeting with American Ad Man made the trip a lot easier. Suddenly, I had spare cash in the bank instead of living mostly hand to mouth as I had done throughout my career until now. How liberating it was not to feel guilty about the £350 economy airfare, not to count the extra pennies when it came to deciding whether we wanted to pay the breakfast supplement in the hotel, to know I wouldn't have to stay in for three weeks when I got back . . .

Well, that I definitely didn't do. We stepped off the plane at 10 a.m., exhausted, having done the usual final-night holiday blowout, talking complete crap and toasting our Manhattan bargain-hunting skills in a bar until 2 a.m. and then somehow having managed to crawl onto an early-morning flight and get away with not looking like terrorists.

We both felt dreadful. I had arranged to meet a guy from the website for a coffee that evening, which I had forgotten about. I debated cancelling but that would have been the third time I had backed out. He was visiting from Malaysia and I didn't imagine he would be here for very long. We had talked a few times on the phone. He had a very dry, British sense of humour and had made me laugh. So, as Only Remaining Single Friend headed straight to bed to nurse the effects of three days of excess, two hours of sleep the previous night and the seven-hour flight, I found myself dashing home, showering, make-up-ing, blow-drying and heading out to meet the man who was later to become my Malaysian Sugar Daddy.

I felt dazed, rushing through the pedestrianised cobbled streets of Covent Garden. Just 14 hours before I'd been dashing along the streets of a city on the other side of the Atlantic searching for a cab to take us to JFK. It was that weird, post-long-haul flight feeling where, suddenly faced with familiar surroundings, you start to wonder if the whole experience ever really happened.

Malaysian Sugar Daddy had made his fortune through crop plantations, an inherited family business. He was in the UK visiting family and friends. We had originally arranged to meet in a coffee shop at Seven Dials in Covent Garden. When I arrived, he immediately suggested we go for dinner, leading me to assume that our initial arrangement for a 'quick coffee' was a precautionary measure. That tactic was commonly adopted by men on the site who were wary of wasting a whole dinner date on a girl they didn't find attractive at first sight.

But first, he wanted to quench his nostalgia. 'I miss real ale,' he said emphatically as we walked into a heaving Soho pub. 'I spent a lot of time in London as a young man. There is nowhere else in the world where you can buy bitter like here.'

I liked him instantly. He seemed genuine and fun, and there was something unassuming about him that I found attractive. I felt I could truly be myself within minutes of meeting him.

Once he'd had his real ale fix, we went somewhere nicer – a seafood restaurant called J. Sheekey. It was a pleasant, trendy, cosy place, out of my own price range but modest in comparison to some of my recent dates in grand hotel dining rooms run by celebrity chefs. It was just off St Martin's Lane, where Malaysian Sugar Daddy was staying in the boutique hotel of the same name. I ordered a glass of a nice Chablis. He had water. 'I don't drink so much. Just one is enough for me. Maybe I'll have a whisky later.'

Malaysian Sugar Daddy talked fondly of his work and his employees. He went into great detail about how he made an effort to treat his staff well, house them and keep their families in good health, which apparently was not always the case in his country. 'It's important not to work too hard in life,' he said. 'I never work too hard. If I did, I could earn much more, but I like to make sure I take time out to enjoy life, meditation, friends and my kids.'

'How old are your kids?'

'Both 14. I have twin boys. I am fighting to see them. It's terrible. My ex-wife is trying to stop me seeing them. That fight is a huge part of my life right now.'

I sensed bitterness over his divorce. I didn't ask too much about it, not straight away – those questions could always come later. He had a troubled look in his eyes when he talked about his children and the painful custody battle. He had stayed at home to look after them when they were younger, while his wife went back to work.

'That's quite rare in Malaysian culture, isn't it, for the man to look after the home and children?'

'It is rare anywhere in the world,' he replied with an air of wisdom.

Again, I was uncertain about how and when we would broach the subject of 'an arrangement'. But it turned out I didn't have to venture near the awkward topic. 'I suppose you're wondering why I'm on a site called Seeking Arrangement?' he offered.

'I'm always interested in why members are on there,' I replied.

'I have nothing to hide. I think paying for female company is a natural thing for a man to do – to want something and to pay for it if he has the means to do so. Right now, I am travelling so I want to spend some quality time with someone, see some sights in London, laugh with her, eat with her, maybe even go on holiday with her – but I don't want the bullshit of a regular relationship.'

His Malay accent meant he put the emphasis on 'shit' instead of 'bull' and it amused me. 'What do you mean by bullshit?' I asked

'I like having the freedom to be able to meet more than one person and to spend time on my own sometimes. But if I were to have a normal relationship, that person would demand more and wouldn't respect the time I like to have alone.' He paused, put his fork down slowly and took a sip of water. I noticed he did everything slowly, like Lewis. 'If I behaved the way I want to with a girlfriend, she would shut the door to me. So, I could lie and tell someone I loved her in order for her to spend time with me; but then one day she would find out that was not true. If I have an arrangement with someone, I can ask her to respect my privacy without her becoming offended.'

He put it perfectly. So many of the time-hungry men whom I had met through both websites wanted exactly that but would have struggled to express it so neatly. Some even had trouble accepting in their own heads that that was what they wanted. Most men and women have the conventional model of a relationship so firmly drummed into them that they feel unnecessary guilt at the thought of basing a relationship on anything other than mutual devotion and strict sexual exclusivity.

I admired Malaysian Sugar Daddy's boldness. He had effectively admitted that, yes, he wanted to substitute emotional investment for a financial one. And what's wrong with that, if that's what it says in the contract?

Most men stuttered and stumbled and tried too hard to justify paying for companionship. But, really, the idea was more natural than they realised. These were men in powerful positions, used to getting their own way, used to demanding convenience and the best of all worlds all the time. They wanted the rewards of a devoted girlfriend but they wanted to maintain the freedom, flexibility and extra hours in the day provided by the bachelor lifestyle. Having a woman who would allow both would come at a cost – either in the form of earache or in the form of cash. The astute ones, it seemed to me, opted for cash, but it was amazing how many of them beat themselves up about it.

What I had observed in my very brief experience playing the role of courtesan was that these men were much less uptight when they could see that for the girl in question the money was an added benefit of the relationship, not the prime motivation for it. Simply by being content in their company, I seemed to assuage any guilty feelings they had about the situation. Sports Man, Champagne Breakfast Guy, Builder Lookalike and so many other dates had made it clear that they deplored women who demanded money while the relationship was still at the email stage. I had originally been drawn to these websites because I genuinely wanted to meet attractive, powerful people. I enjoyed flirting with a world above and beyond my realm. Money had not been my original motivation; if it had been, I'm sure I would not have appeared

169

so attractive to the men I met. Money and the other material benefits were just a fortuitous side effect I'd stumbled upon.

'I totally agree,' I told Malaysian Sugar Daddy, returning my thoughts to our conversation. 'Too many people confuse a sexual partner with a life partner. That's why so many women demand too much from men when they begin a sexual relationship.'

'Yes,' he replied, 'I often feel that when I sleep with a woman she weighs me up as a potential partner. Especially in a Muslim country like mine, where women are not sexually liberated. Where I come from, a woman will not sleep with me if she thinks I cannot offer her some sort of long-term commitment.'

'That's not just Malaysia,' I said, trying to emulate his aura of wisdom. 'A woman will never sleep with a man if she thinks there's nothing in it for her.'

'What if she's just crazy about the man?'

'That's still something for her: sexual gratification.'

'I mean truly in love – what if she just wants to be with him all the time?'

I paused. I didn't know about that. However, I made a good effort at an answer by applying my rigid cost-and-effect theory on relationships: 'I think a lot of women looking for a long-term, secure, committed relationship sleep with a man because they consider it the first step on the way to their goal of marriage. It's a universal concept – think of arranged marriages. Even women who don't want all that still expect something from the man they're sleeping with – high sexual gratification or temporary emotional support or financial security.'

'Sex is never free,' he agreed. We paused for a couple of minutes, not uncomfortably. 'So do you want to give the arrangement a try?' he asked at last.

'What would your ideal arrangement be?' I said, unsure of how he would interpret my question.

'Someone I can see several times a year. Someone who can become a close friend and who, I hope, will remain a friend for years to come regardless of how our relationship develops. Maybe we can start with some sort of compensation just for the times when we meet?'

'Well, I don't really have a formula for this, but, yes, that sounds like something we could try,' I responded. I sounded very formal, but I didn't know how to make this anything but. 'And do you want to start the arrangement this evening?'

'Yes, I would like that.' He paused again in that way he had. 'Of course,' he added with a humorous smile, 'if we fall in love, then we will have to reassess.'

'We would,' I said dismissively, 'but I'm not really the falling-in-love type.'

'We'll see. I'll get the bill.'

♥ ♥ ♥

Two days later, Malaysian Sugar Daddy wanted me to meet him again. I was exhausted. I had been working 12-hour shifts all week and still hadn't unpacked from New York. However, he was only in the UK for another week and I had a whole fresh wardrobe from New York to break in, albeit not a Prada one this time.

He asked me to join him for dinner at his sister's home in south-east London. That part of the city is like the other end of the universe for me. I would usually trudge such a distance on various modes of public transport, but since I could now write off the cost of a taxi as a tiny slice of what I would go home with at the end of the evening, I decided to treat myself to a cab. Except I couldn't get one. It was a Sunday night and there was torrential rain. Every minicab office within a three-mile radius was booked up, with a forty-five-minute waiting list. It was a total disaster.

I scolded myself as I hit redial and got an engaged tone for

171

the fifth taxi number I'd dialled. Why am I always so goddamn late? Malaysian Sugar Daddy phoned me for the second time in five minutes. He sounded irritated, as his sister was nearly ready to serve dinner. If only he'd get off the phone and stop telling me to hurry up, I thought, then maybe I'd actually be able to hurry up.

Most people, of course, would have booked the cab in advance, maybe even hours in advance. But, as you may have worked out for yourself by now, planning is something my brain considers an unnecessary, tedious task. It just never learns.

I arrived 45 minutes late. In the time it took me to get out of the cab and to the front door, I managed to get totally drenched. I kicked off my shoes and noticed the wet red suede had turned my feet pink. I didn't want to take off my jacket as it would reveal a red tight-fitting shirt that I suddenly remembered showed quite a generous amount of cleavage. So I greeted the waiting guests with it on, apologetically dripping over everyone as I went around shaking hands, trying to take in a load of Asian-sounding names I had not a hope in hell of remembering. My outfit was, in my opinion, quite low key: skinny jeans and a red fitted shirt with a pair of red heels. But one glance at what the others were wearing – fleeces and jogging bottoms – told me I had overdressed. God knows what they must have thought. God knows how they thought we knew each other. I hoped they wouldn't ask, as we hadn't collaborated on a story.

His sister's friends were nice, but a little dull. 'So, you're a journalist?' asked one of them. I had felt comfortable enough with Malaysian Sugar Daddy to divulge my real job. He wasn't the paranoid type, so I doubted he would freak out. 'Who do you see winning the US elections?'

'Well,' I replied, 'I would have said McCain, but everyone's getting nervous now about his knowledge of the economy.

He's not got much experience there. And his choice of running mate, well, that's really set him back. Did you see the VP debates? Palin was totally ripped to shreds by Joe Biden. She was very good at winking and smiling sweetly for the cameras, but she had nothing noteworthy to say, really. And America can be quite ageist, so that could go against him, too.'

They nodded. I had perhaps been a little over-zealous with my textbook response, but I was desperate to counteract any suspicion that I might be nothing more than a paid-for bimbo. They seemed suitably satisfied, and, of course, there was absolutely no reason for them to think that I was being paid for my company. It was just my paranoia.

After the meal, his sister called her personal driver to instruct him to take Malaysian Sugar Daddy and me back to our respective homes. 'Where do you live?' she asked.

'Erm, well, I'm going to join [Malaysian Sugar Daddy's name] for a drink in town.'

'The car can take you both back to his hotel, then?'

I squirmed, but she hardly batted an eyelid. 'Er, yes, that's very kind of you.' And so we climbed into the back of the car together and were driven to the St Martin's Lane Hotel, no questions asked.

'Don't they think it odd that a girl you've just met is coming back to your hotel? What did you tell them?' I asked Malaysian Sugar Daddy earnestly after we'd been dropped off.

'I don't need to tell them anything. You worry too much about what people think.'

'Yes, but . . . It's clear we don't know each other well. It's clear I'm very much younger and . . .'

'You should be more confident in who you are and what you do. It is none of their business.'

I shut up.

His room was delightful. It was small and cosy, adorned

with elaborate Edwardian furniture. There was a beautiful antique burr-walnut writing desk in the corner, in all its original glory but for the iPod dock on top. In the other three corners were tall brass lamp stands with decorative shades. I sat on the sofa looking at the new bag that I had just bought in New York. It was my new treasure and it looked perfect perched on the arm of the sofa.

Suddenly, I was overcome by a wave of exhaustion. I could barely make conversation. I had had such a hectic week since returning from New York and it seemed to have chosen that moment to catch up with me. I felt cold and helped myself to a brandy from the minibar, hoping it would both warm and invigorate me. I tried to hide my tiredness, but Malaysian Sugar Daddy picked up on it.

'If you want to sleep, just sleep,' he said gently. 'We have tomorrow.' I just managed a smile of appreciation before I collapsed on the bed and fell asleep.

♥ ♥ ♥

Malaysian Sugar Daddy was leaving for home the following Friday. He texted on Thursday and asked if he could see me that evening – his last night. I wasn't quite expecting this level of contact so soon into our arrangement. I had spent Sunday night and the whole of Monday daytime with him. On Tuesday, I was back at work, doing my usual 12-hour shifts starting from 6 a.m. Those hours, even if you are only working four days a week, take their toll. I still hadn't unpacked from New York. Malaysian Sugar Daddy followed up the text with a phone call when I didn't reply. Given the breakneck pace of a broadcast newsroom, I rarely had time to look at, let alone reply to, any texts or calls.

'I'd love to see you tonight,' I said when I finally picked up after a fifth missed call from him, 'but I can't. I have a friend's birthday and I'm up at five again tomorrow.'

'Maybe I could come to your friend's birthday?'

I nearly choked. The thought of having to explain him to the *real* people in my life didn't bear thinking about. 'Erm, well . . . it's kind of a private affair. She's cooking dinner.'

It was a pretty incredible lie, I thought. Who cooks dinner for friends on their own birthday?! However, it really was Only Remaining Single Friend's 30th birthday and there was no way I could not go. For a fleeting moment, I considered throwing a sickie the next day, allowing me to go to her party and see Malaysian Sugar Daddy later. But I didn't want this secondary world to take over from my real one.

'You leave tomorrow evening, right?' I asked. 'Why don't we meet for lunch before you go?'

'You don't expect an arrangement for lunch, do you?'

'Of course not.'

I chose a modest Italian restaurant on Charlotte Street, around the corner from where I worked. I made sure I was on time (for the first time since we'd met). Lunch breaks are a rarity in any newsroom. I had to be super-organised and on top of all my hourly deadlines in the morning to make sure I could go out.

I sensed an awkwardness about Malaysian Sugar Daddy straight away. He hardly spoke. I was asking questions about what he'd done over the past few days. Did he catch up with everyone he wanted to? How were the friends he'd seen last night? How was his hotel? What had he bought for his kids? But each answer was short and he barely made eye contact. I wish they'd hurry up with the food, I thought. The restaurant was painfully quiet. It was only noon, so we were well ahead of the lunchtime rush. I carried on being as chatty as I could, pretending all was normal. Then, suddenly, out of the blue, he blurted out, 'I'm having a bit of a wobbler, really.' In his accent, it would have sounded funny, if he hadn't looked as if he was about to burst into tears, that is.

I didn't need to say anything. In fact, he wasn't even looking at me. He continued, 'I have so much stuff going through my mind right now. My boys, the divorce. I come here and I meet you. I met another girl, too. And here I am meeting you again and I don't know what I'm doing or what I really want. I'm glad I met you, but why? I live thousands of miles away.' He was rambling. 'It's all got a bit too much for me in the last couple of days. That's why I didn't call you. You understand?'

I nodded. Didn't call me? I repeated in my head. I hated to imagine what he thought calling a lot would be.

'I think I am living out what I didn't get to do when I was married. But, at the same time, I miss being married.'

'What do you miss about it?'

'Worshipping somebody. I loved everything about her. Even her smell before she showered. Even if she was sweating with a fever. Everything.' Then he stopped as if he'd suddenly snapped back into reality from a trance.

I tried to probe him about it, but he seemed closed to me now. I asked him if he felt he was in a dilemma about the type of relationship we had. 'No.' I asked him if it was the divorce stress and custody battle. 'That's all part of it.'

I couldn't get much more out of him after that. I certainly didn't ask about the other girl he'd mentioned.

Our food arrived and we ate in silence. I felt uncomfortable, but he hardly seemed to notice. He was somewhere else.

He paid the bill and we walked outside. 'I'm so sorry about this lunch,' he said. 'I know I've been bad company. Please understand.'

'You don't have to apologise,' I smiled. 'You're in a different zone now. You're heading off to the airport in a couple of hours; your mind is bound to be elsewhere. You're starting to think about your normal routine again, back home. It's natural.'

'Thank you for understanding.' He looked like he might cry again. 'I'll walk you back to your office.'

'It's OK,' I said, disguising my alarm. 'It's best I go back alone.' I didn't want him to cross the threshold into my real world. What if he tried to kiss me goodbye in front of the office where people could see?! I had a very proud single status to protect.

I suffered in the afternoon for taking a lunch break. My delivery deadlines were so tight that even getting ten minutes behind would throw the whole afternoon out of synch. I was constantly chasing my tail to make sure we didn't miss a fresh hourly news delivery. I was so busy I soon forgot about Malaysian Sugar Daddy and our awkward lunch.

When I got home that evening, I felt a huge sense of relief that an incredibly pressurised week was over. Malaysian Sugar Daddy was gone, which would mean an end to the thrice-daily texts to respond to, my four-day run of twelve-hour shifts was over for another three days and Only Remaining Single Friend's big thirtieth was out of the way. I celebrated my liberation by going to the gym.

My phone beeped with a text the very second I'd programmed the rowing machine and hit start: 'Hello, beautiful, are you free to talk? I am drunk and feeling melancholic.' It was Malaysian Sugar Daddy from the departure lounge at Heathrow.

To respond or not to respond? I knew that if I did, I'd be listening to the same shit I'd heard at lunch all over again, except this time he was drunk. I felt I owed it to him to call, though. As I dialled, I thought, how ironic: he pays me because he wants a relationship that doesn't require any emotional investment from him, but now he's demanding emotional support from me. Sex had been a very small part of our arrangement over the past ten days; this was what he really needed me for.

I spent around 20 minutes on the phone. I sympathised, but I couldn't truly empathise. I was not qualified to give him advice on his situation: a custody battle over two children and yearning for a lost love. Neither of those was my area of expertise.

I wondered how many other girls, and guys, in genuine relationships were making tedious phone calls to their partners right now, holding the phone at arm's length, listening to their partner's monkey chatter, offering a certain level of sympathy but really wishing they'd just hurry up so they could get on with their own lives. The idea that some people did that and didn't get paid was totally beyond me.

Chapter 18

Hiqlexic

Malaysian Sugar Daddy phoned me regularly from Kuala Lumpur. Too much. But each time, despite my aversion to long telephone chats, I found myself warming to him and actually enjoyed spending time talking into the receiver – very out of character.

We half arranged that I would go to visit him at the end of the year, and each week he would call, pushing me to set a date, which I couldn't do because of work commitments. The channel bosses were due to visit from America and there was a slim chance the news service that I produced would be axed, so I wanted to stick around.

Somewhere in the middle of all this busyness – the series of dates with American Ad Man, the week with Malaysian Sugar Daddy, the trip to New York, the monotonous job with the 6 a.m. starts – I got a touching text from The Photographer. He hadn't given up on me. He had continued to try to woo me ever since that singles party back in February. But unlike most rebuffed men who refuse to hear the word no, he came across as non-intrusive, even sweet:

> Hello Helen, I was just thinking yet again how lovely it
> was to spot you out in the crowd at the event. I know a
> lot of time has passed but if you are less busy maybe we
> could have a drink? You sound like you have such an
> interesting background and I hope you'll find the same
> interest in me. What a lovely day it is today! XX

What a beautifully composed message, I thought. One that
would make most women melt. And after all the guys from
the website whose texts blatantly showed that they had no
idea what they had said to whom, and the freakish Yahoo
Messenger addicts I had come across, The Photographer's
words were like birdsong in my inbox, a reassuring reminder
of how warm it can feel to be thought about.

Yet I just couldn't bring myself to act on it. I had become
desensitised to the prospect of genuine affection. All my
encounters over the past 18 months had been based on
novelty, excitement, sex and, more recently, material gain.
Munich Man, Greg and Champagne Breakfast Guy had
raised the stakes for excitement and novelty. American Ad
Man and Malaysian Sugar Daddy had whetted my appetite
for cash. I didn't have a script for how to handle a man with
more genuine goals in mind. The Photographer was too real
and that intimidated me.

I approached the whole process of using the website
differently now. It was no longer for innocent fun, as it had
been in the early phase of my dating adventures. Of course,
fun and entertainment were still my primary motivation, but
now that I had learned that there were men willing to provide
other rewards – monetary rewards – on top of fun, I added
that trait to my selection criteria.

Comparing the flirty, well-thought-out messages I'd written
to members of Sugardaddie.com in the early stages with the
brusque one-liners I sent now on SeekingArrangement.com,

it was clear how uninterested I had become in the men as individuals. I used to read their profiles and make a reference in my reply to something they had written. Now I just wrote, 'You sound fun, do you fancy meeting?' As much as I still enjoyed putting on my Wolford stockings and sipping champagne in the bars of posh hotels, I was starting to view dates with high-flying powerful executives, which used to fulfil my fantasies, almost as money-making exercises.

I drove myself on because the website still seemed like the perfect way for me to date, given my lack of interest in a serious relationship and my penchant for older men. And occasionally a message would appear to reassure me that there were match-perfect men on the site who shared my sensible, practical approach:

> What sort of casual are you looking for? What sort of help do you like? Have just recently come out of a relationship and was recommended here by a friend. Not looking for the next love of my life, but miss the fun and laughter of a beautiful girl and the intimacy of a relationship.

He had posted a photo to his profile. It was a distant shot showing him on a ski slope, wearing Ray-Bans and an all-in-one ski suit. I asked for a clearer picture. He was handsome. He had a ridiculous, forced Cheshire Cat grin that made him look as if his teeth had been glued together at the back, but he was handsome nevertheless.

I later nicknamed that man Hiqlexic, for reasons I'll explain.

♥ ♥ ♥

I met Hiqlexic for lunch at Zuma in Knightsbridge. I was late, as usual. This time it was because I'd come from having a haircut and, like all hairdressers, she was slow and kept blow-drying the same clusters of hair five times over.

'That's *OK now*. It looks fine. I'm *happy with that*,' I hinted, getting agitated in my seat.

'Just one leetle beet more,' she kept saying in a heavy Spanish accent. 'You will like when eet's done. You will see.' I didn't like, actually. It was too short and I thought I looked like a boy, but I was running too late to complain.

I was looking forward to meeting Hiqlexic. He seemed very upfront and to the point in his emails, and I was pleased to be meeting someone who didn't either forget what messages he had sent to whom or squirm when faced with the rather awkward situation of negotiating some form of relationship in return for money.

'Wine?' he asked straight away. He was well spoken, businesslike. He had lovely eyes, I noticed. He was dark-skinned, perhaps with some Asian blood in him, with a head of hair attempting to turn silver.

'Love one.' I hadn't planned to drink – I had things to do in the afternoon – but my willpower gave way pretty quickly to my nervousness about the situation. If I was going to negotiate this properly, a glass of wine would surely lubricate the discussion.

'What sort of experiences have you had on the site?' I asked. He didn't seem awkward at all and I was reassured by his assertiveness. I was the third person he had met. The first girl couldn't speak much English and the second he thought was too young. She had said she was 25 but apparently looked and acted like she was no older than 20. He had spoken to several others but felt they were all in it for the money. He didn't like how they had started to talk monthly payments over email or on the phone, before they had even met. 'You can't talk about that until you meet someone, because you don't know if you're going to get on. It becomes something else then. There are other websites for that.'

There went that euphemism again. Men seemed to mask their discomfort about paying for a woman by declaring they were seeking genuine attraction and chemistry as well as a sexual relationship. That comforted them – and me – that the transaction was less soulless than hiring an escort. But both parties knew that the two were dangerously close.

Hiqlexic was looking for someone he could meet two to three times a month, for dinner or theatre or drinks, and who would stay overnight with him. It seemed too good to be true.

'I think that site could be a real honey trap,' Hiqlexic told me. 'I'm surprised it isn't more so. There are lots of people in my situation. I don't have the luxury of time to spend getting to know a girl, but I miss intimacy. I can't believe it's not more successful.'

'But it's the stigma attached to it, isn't it?' I said. 'If you tell people you're on a site with the word "arrangement" in its name, there's immediately an element of sleaze associated with it.'

'Well, I could get a normal girlfriend and have my fun that way. I could lie about my feelings like a lot of men do. But I don't want to be that bastard. So, if we decide we like each other and we do meet up as suggested, what do you have in mind?'

I was so glad I'd accepted the glass of wine. 'Well, I'm new to this, so I can only really go on what I know from meeting other people and talking to other people on the site.'

'What would you be happy with?'

'Well, I'd be happy with . . .' I paused. I wasn't bold enough to pluck a figure out of the air, so I resorted to a vague answer. 'Well, I think I'd just like to be able to shop guilt free and have the means to pamper myself a little and afford a few more luxuries in my life.'

'I can certainly help you with that. What's your favourite restaurant in London?'

'Ultimate favourite? Well, I suppose it would have to be Nobu.'

'I'll book a table next week. I'll let you know what day I'm free.'

I still didn't really know what our arrangement was, but I knew there was one at least. I need to be more decisive and assertive, I thought. But then, this is fun, not my career, isn't it?

♥ ♥ ♥

Hiqlexic texted a few days later. Fortunately, he took the reins and settled my uncertainty over the arrangement.

'Good to meet you. I liked you. Now that the awkward part is out of the way, I'd like to take that arrangement forward along the lines you mentioned. Assuming you still do, how about we meet early evening of Thursday 23rd? Shopping as discussed followed by dinner at Nobu. Speak soon, me xx'

I gave him the affirmative, via text, and he asked me where I wanted to shop. I cringed. It seemed so unnatural, meeting deliberately early for dinner so he could honour his side of our arrangement before I spent the night with him. I settled on Selfridges – chic yet not quite as extravagant as Harrods or Harvey Nicks. We had a glass of wine first at an outside table in St Christopher's Place, at the side of the department store.

As soon as I saw him, I thought, oh God, you're not as good-looking as I remember. I think, though, that that was a psychological reaction to the fact that I was committed to continuing the night through to the morning – if I accepted the shopping trip. My encounters with American Ad Man and Malaysian Sugar Daddy had both been spontaneous and we had come to our arrangement after an evening feeling comfortable in each other's company. If I had seen Hiqlexic in the street, he would definitely have captured my attention, yet because I had a side of a deal to honour, I felt the voluntary element of desire had been removed.

'Your hair looks different,' he said. That was a typical remark for Hiqlexic, I would discover. He would never give a compliment or a criticism but simply make a statement of fact.

'Not really,' I replied. 'I just styled it differently.' Actually, I hadn't done anything out of the ordinary, it was just that the last time we had met for lunch, I had come straight from the moron hairdresser who'd chopped it too short and blow-dried it flat so I looked like I'd had a pudding basin rammed onto my head.

'Are you ready to shop?' he asked cheerfully.

I wasn't ready to shop at all. I felt awkward. And I felt overdressed because we were en route to dinner. And I felt as if I was hoarding material goods for all they were worth just to fill some kind of quota. And I didn't know Hiqlexic at all. A shopping trip can give away a lot about personal tastes and characteristics (dreaminess and bumping into the sharp ends of clothes rails, in my case), so, strolling around with a stranger holding my hand, I felt somehow as if my privacy was being invaded.

'Look,' I said at last, after we'd aimlessly circled the ground floor twice and I'd picked out some miracle anti-wrinkle cream that I've never considered even sampling before due to the price tag, 'I bet the last thing you want right now is to be dragged around a department store. I think they do some form of gift vouchers here. Why don't you just make up whatever you see fit that way?'

I worded it delicately. I still felt awkward about setting a figure. I had put the ball in his court and that made me feel more comfortable. Hiqlexic agreed and disappeared to the customer-services counter while I hung back, stroking the touchable fabrics of the clothes on the nearby rails, pretending to browse.

'This will keep you in shoes for a short while, but not for life,' he said when he returned, handing me a little black box containing a bright-yellow, shiny Selfridges gift card. I had no idea how much money was on it, but that added to the excitement. I trusted him enough to believe he would honour our agreement generously, but I had also learned enough about his character by now to predict that he would not have been unnecessarily lavish.

♥ ♥ ♥

I felt much more relaxed when we arrived at Nobu. I was glad the arrangement had been settled. My bright-yellow store card was safely tucked into my purse. Tomorrow, on the way home, I would go and see how much was on it and spend it with glee.

This was my second visit to Nobu on Park Lane and my fourth Nobu experience; I'd also been to the New York branch and the one in Mayfair. I loved the buzz of the place. Hiqlexic disagreed. 'I always feel a bit like I'm in a posh McDonald's,' he said. 'It's brightly lit and I feel they try and usher you in and out as quickly as they can.'

The menu in Nobu is pages and pages long, but he made his decision in 30 seconds: black cod with miso. I took my time to sift through, wondering if the same tuna sashimi I'd had at the New York branch with Greg would be on this menu. That had been delicious. I don't know how long I had my gaze fixed on the menu, but when I looked up Hiqlexic was staring at me intensely. It was quite uncomfortable. I remembered now that he had also ordered noticeably quickly on our lunch date at Zuma and had watched me intensely then, too.

'I've decided,' I bluffed, clamping the menu shut. I didn't want to feel his watchful eye on me any longer. When the waiter came, I pointed at the first things I saw that sounded edible. I ended up with two pieces of lettuce and a tiny bowl of liquid tofu sprinkled with dried fish flakes.

Over dinner, or rather over my snack, I asked him about his relationship that had recently ended. It had lasted nine months. She'd moved into his flat after five months, which to me was unfathomable.

'It was fine until we went on holiday together for the first time. Then she completely changed.'

'In what way?'

'When we got back, she suddenly started talking about our future and having a family. Incessantly. That was all she spoke about. I can't commit to those things now. I travel to New York one week, Sydney another and Singapore the next. There's a lot of time in hotels. I may even have to do a few years abroad in the not too distant future. But she wanted a concrete plan that involved moving out of London at some point.'

'How old was she?'

'Thirty-seven. I can't expect a regular girl to put up with my lifestyle, I suppose.'

'And if you want a relationship on your own terms, I suppose the noble thing to do is join a website that allows you to set the boundaries?' I added, putting words in his mouth.

'It's not that I want a relationship on my terms. It's just that if I have to cancel a date because I am at the office until eleven at night, it's genuinely because I'm at the office until eleven at night. I'm not cheating. Most girls won't accept that.'

I think Hiqlexic was more nervous than I'd initially judged him to be. He was terse, answering questions briefly and then stopping, as if that was his bit done. He wouldn't expand with

187

another connected thought or ask me a follow-up question. But part of me was relieved by the lack of questions because I had concealed the fact that I was a journalist and that cut out a huge chunk of what I could talk about – direction, ambition, conversations with a colleague, frustrations with managers, observations on the industry, career history. His lack of interest in my everyday life was a good thing as far as I was concerned.

On the website, I had totally removed any reference to the fact that I was a journalist and it had had a notably positive effect. Not only had I received more messages, but I no longer received jokes such as, 'Are you going to do a big exposé on me? LOL.' When other members asked what I did, I said I created video content for websites, which wasn't strictly untrue, given that all of my news output went on the Internet. Scarily, the more times I said it, the more naturally it came out. And more scarily, I started to believe it myself sometimes.

When it comes to people I hardly know, I've always preferred to be the one asking questions, rather than talking about myself (this is not a courtesy I bestow on those who know me well, who find it hard to get a word in). Because of that, my fake profession only ever put me in difficulty once. That was on a date with a web programmer who started asking me lots of awkward questions about HTML. I wriggled out of it by faking a need to go to the toilet, thus creating a break in the conversation and giving me a chance to change the subject.

Hiqlexic was a partner in a very large European law firm. As we talked, I got more of a sense of his no-nonsense character and his constant forward planning. He seemed to be the kind of person who was always trying to get to a destination but never relished the process of getting there. He had already asked me which day I could be free the following week and had made two references to planning a trip during the next month.

'I don't know how much time I can take off work,' I told him. 'I've just had a week off to go to New York.'

'With another arrangement?' he asked.

'No! With a friend, a shopping trip.' It was the truth, of course, but I realised that Hiqlexic didn't quite trust me yet. It also concerned me that he wanted our thrice-monthly arrangement to be exclusive, which I was under the impression was not the norm.

'You get three days off in a row each week, don't you?' he asked me.

'Yes, but with the twelve-hour days I do, I need those three days to catch up on –'

'Look, I do fifteen-hour days most days. I'm offering you a trip anywhere you want to go. Where do you want to go?'

'Somewhere hot.'

'Well, that's hard at this time of year in three days. It is doable. South Africa is eight hours and we can get a bed on the flight each way, but we'll only have thirty-six hours actually there. Dubai is only five hours, but I know the flights are daytime only, so we wouldn't be able to get a bed in-flight. We may as well go somewhere that allows us to sleep on the flight to maximise time. The Caribbean isn't even that far, but there's a time difference and that would mess us up for three days.'

'Aren't they all a bit far away?'

'And your point is?' He screwed up his face as if I were putting a ridiculous obstacle in the way. He wasn't interested in discussion. He was talking in order to decide on a destination, not for the pleasure of sharing a wonderful and exciting travel plan. 'Leave it with me. I'll get my secretary to investigate options. What are your days off then? Thursday to Sunday?'

'It changes each week. I work on a rota.'

'Give me the dates you have off three weeks from now and I'll organise it.' He meant it, too. He sat with his hand poised over his diary, waiting for me to get mine out.

'In three weeks' time, I have the Wednesday to the Saturday off.'

'Consider it done.'

When we got up to leave, I noticed how light-headed I was. It was understandable given that my ordering technique had left me with two mouthfuls of tofu and three of lettuce. When we got back to his flat, on The Strand, I knocked a plant over and soil went all over his über-modern wooden floor.

'Oh, shit! Sorry!'

Hiqlexic neither laughed nor seemed angry. He simply picked up the plant and swept up the mess. It was a simple chore he had to complete to move on to the next task in hand, which was camomile tea.

Owning one paving stone on The Strand would probably mortgage most people to the hilt, so I wouldn't like to imagine the figures behind Hiqlexic's flat. His entrance hall was about the size of my office, and the hallway leading to the numerous bedrooms was about the width of the M6. His living room was lined with books, from top to bottom. Books, books everywhere. History books, economics books, autobiographies, philosophy books, a book that offered an analysis of cognitive behavioural therapy, another claiming to be the definitive work on sixteenth-century kabuki theatre.

'Have you read all of those?' I asked him.

'Some more than once. I'm a fast reader. It's terribly annoying.'

'Annoying?'

'Well, because I travel so much. I can't carry the amount of books I'd read in a few days. I've taken to buying the most boring and obscure ones I can find because that slows me down. I'm reading this at the moment.' He held up *Ethnicity and Territory in the Former Soviet Union: Regions in Conflict.* 'Basically, the more boring the better.'

His bedroom was as awe-inspiring as the rest of the flat. But I noticed immediately his windows had no blinds. Great. I am a very sensitive sleeper and this did not bode well for my melatonin levels.

'Doesn't the light bother you in the morning?' I hinted.

'I only sleep for four or four and a half hours a night. I'm normally up before it's light.'

I sighed inwardly. Tomorrow was my day off, but why change the habit of the week and sleep beyond 5 a.m.?

I got my own back, though – not deliberately – by causing a commotion in the middle of the night. I got up to use his bathroom. The light switches resembled the control panel of a 747 and I didn't know which one to press. Too complicated, I thought in my half-slumber, I'll just fumble in the dark. I felt my way around the shiny granite to the toilet, which started to flush automatically when I hovered over it and wouldn't stop. The next challenge was the tap, which looked like the control panel of Concorde! There were about ten red flashing digital buttons in front of me. The first two didn't do anything. The third triggered a furious high-pressure jet of water, which hit the sink and my hands so hard it sprayed everything within a two-metre radius, including my face. I tried to turn it off, but every button I pressed made the water come out faster or hotter until the whole goddamn time machine of a bathroom was filled with steam. It was 3 a.m. and Hiqlexic looked like he was deep in REM sleep. I didn't know what to do. Add to this the fact that I am, without contact lenses, so short-sighted that I can't even see my own belly button in focus. So I couldn't see, I couldn't turn off the taps and it was getting unbearably hot.

191

I had to go and wake him. 'Sorry, but I can't figure out your taps. They won't stop,' I whispered as delicately as I possibly could. He didn't flinch. He simply opened his eyes, got up calmly, fully alert, and walked to the bathroom.

'Oh, well done. You managed to turn on the steam room.' Again, he seemed neither amused nor cross. He pushed a button, the water subsided, he returned to bed, shut his eyes and went back to sleep.

As I got dressed to leave the following morning, he watched me with that same intense stare he had had when I'd looked up from the menu the night before. I was so eager to escape his gaze that I put my hold-ups on inside out, which meant they didn't grip my legs and were falling down to my ankles as I walked out of his football-pitch pad and onto The Strand.

♥ ♥ ♥

Only Remaining Single Friend emailed me at work the next day to ask how my date was. I replied:

> Feel sick. He barely let me look at the menu. I ate two pieces of lettuce and drank two bottles of wine and knocked over a very expensive yucca tree. He snores and he's got this too-cool-for-school bathroom. His taps look like they've come out of a modern-art exhibition. Tried to use them when visited loo in middle of night and couldn't turn them off! So complicated. All electronic and shit. Had to wake him up to turn taps off. Total disaster. Are you free tomorrow?

Only Remaining Single Friend found it so funny she forwarded it on to all her colleagues. Gosh, if only they knew the full story, I thought! I met her a few days later to discuss the disastrous date in detail.

'He sounds like he's one of those prodigies with no social skills,' she said.

'The guy could devour *War and Peace* in a day. And it's not just the books, either. He read the *FT* in about 15 minutes, front to back, everything.'

'He must have just scanned it, right? Read headlines and little bits?'

'I'm telling you, he read every word in ten minutes and then started talking in depth about things he'd read, the fors, the againsts. He digested it all.'

'He's probably got an IQ of about 500.'

'Highest I've ever come across. He retains everything. The American elections came up in conversation and he knew every single one of the forty-three past presidents, the years they came to power and every bill each one brought in. He could quote the whole lot. He probably knows their dates of birth, too.'

'Are you sure it's true? Was he bluffing?'

'No. I checked everything he told me afterwards. I'm a journalist, aren't I?! But, you know, he has no . . . compassion. He takes everything literally. He can't pick up humour. And he states the blindingly obvious sometimes. Like, when I came out of the shower with my hair wrapped in a towel, he said, "Oh, you have a towel on your head." And he plans incessantly. His life is an auto-saving spreadsheet.'

'You know what that is? That's low EQ – emotional intelligence.'

'Sky-high IQ. Zero EQ.'

'Sounds like something an astronaut would say.'

'Maybe we could abbreviate it. High IQ . . . low EQ. Oh, fuck, what does that spell?'

We had to write it down. It read 'HIQ LEQ'. 'Hmmmm. He's Hick Leck. I shall call him Hick Leck.'

'Brilliant,' laughed Only Remaining Single Friend. 'He's

Hiqlexic – a total boffin with no social skills.'

'Oh my God! Hiqlexic – like dyslexic, only with emotions!'

We squealed in delight at our ingeniousness and ordered another bottle of wine.

Chapter 19

Gentle Persuasion

♥ **October '08**

I received a curious message on SeekingArrangement.com a few days later: 'Hi babe, how's this site for you? I make this account with my boyfriend. We are looking for meet couple. I have many photos. Message me if you would like meet me and my boyfriend.'

It was from a girl. I hadn't even known you could message members of the same sex. I looked at her email address and profile name and detected the distant ringing of a bell. I looked again and said the name aloud in my head: MissPenelope. Yes, she was the girl who'd contacted me over a year ago, when I was on Sugardaddie.com. The one who'd told me that she knew a site where she could get £10,000 a month. I remembered clearly.

I replied straight away. It was too deliciously intriguing. I wondered if she knew that she had contacted me before. I had the same photo (the 13-year-old one), but this was a different website. We exchanged several emails and then photos, and a week later she suggested the two of us meet for coffee to see if we got on. I noticed that my messages to her were more responsive than those I sent to men. I replied promptly and worded them carefully. Usually, while I would be flirty and playful, I was constantly changing the time and date to meet. I didn't make a conscious decision to adopt a more professional tone with her, but it was something I found myself doing – perhaps a sign of how much more delicate negotiations with the same sex are.

Could I do lunch on Friday, she asked. That would be hard, I said, as my work schedule was very tight. I didn't want to risk committing to a daytime meeting in case a big story broke and I had to cancel. Standing up a woman seemed like it would have more serious consequences than having to suddenly change plans with a man. I could manage an early-evening coffee, though, after work. We agreed to meet in Starbucks, a dangerously close three minutes from my office.

During the last hour of my working day, I grew nervous. I was going to meet a girl! I made absolutely sure I wasn't late. I freshened up in the Ladies before leaving the office, ensuring that every hair was combed, every eyelash declogged of mascara clumps, every nail filed, that my shoes were clean and one earring hadn't fallen out again. Women notice these things. If this is what guys feel like when they go on dates, I thought, I'm even more glad to be a woman.

A petite, Asian-looking girl was waiting in the entrance to the Tottenham Court Road Starbucks, oblivious to the crowds of people she was standing in the way of. Her long black hair was falling loosely over her face and into her eyes. Even without make-up, she was stunningly beautiful. As we greeted each other, I thought there was something familiar about her.

'It's Helen, right?' she asked. I could tell straight away that she was Japanese. She was in jeans, a casual T-shirt and trainers, yet she looked incredibly glamorous. She liked me instantly. 'You're *perfect*. He will love you,' she said, and she gave a little giggle.

We sat down. I asked if she was Japanese. She looked taken aback that I had guessed. I told her I'd studied Japanese at university and had lived there for two years. She was delighted and made me say something in Japanese.

'*Nihongo mou wasurechatta*,' I said, in a very rusty accent. It means, 'I've totally forgotten my Japanese.'

She squealed and clapped her hands and told me I was '*jouzu*', which strictly means 'you're good' but in practice means, 'I have to tell you that you're good, but I don't really think that you're that good – it's just that I have to say something polite.' If she'd genuinely thought my sentence was a good attempt at her language, she would have said I was '*umai*'.

We talked about Japan and the food we missed. She'd come to London to study five years ago but felt she could never go back to live in Japan because she was considered too Western. It sounded a familiar story. We moved on to what we did now. Her, nothing. Me, well, I said something about video production but made it sound as little like the feared beast of journalism as I possibly could. I didn't want to ask too much about him – The Sugar Daddy – for fear of being perceived as a threat, though I found out that he was a Parisian financial adviser, aged 58.

'Did you meet on the site?'

'No, no. An introduction. Through another girl. But it's the same world.'

I didn't exactly know what she meant, but I sensed it was better not to ask too many questions. I would learn more in time, I was sure. But that snippet served to fascinate me even more. Her boyfriend seemed to be a sugar daddy in the truest sense: they had a long-term relationship; he housed her in a flat and stayed with her occasionally; she didn't work but joined him as and when he could fit her into his complex life. It all sounded so very, well, French.

I couldn't wait to meet him. I couldn't wait to get a glimpse of the dynamic of their relationship and see how it worked. It was a murky but chic world that I was drawn to despite myself. I am dabbling in this out of curiosity – *journalistic* curiosity – I liked to tell myself. I didn't want to abandon my career for a life like MissPenelope's, but I did like the idea of experimenting with it. The dichotomy of a world that was so glamorous on the outside but was more than likely riddled with sordidness, eye-popping tales and secret lives intrigued me.

'He's in town tonight, actually,' MissPenelope told me. 'We're staying at Claridge's. Are you free to join us for drinks after dinner?'

'Tonight?'

'Is that problem?' she asked, blinking, an innocent look on her face that would make most men give in to any wish she expressed. I noticed she let the occasional mistake slip through the net but overall her English was impressively flawless.

I wasn't sure I wanted to go ahead and meet them as a couple. I was aware that I was venturing deeper and deeper into my fantasies as the weeks went by. I had arranged to meet MissPenelope for coffee simply because I couldn't resist the intrigue. The next step was further than I had prepared myself to go.

You've accepted money from American Ad Man, you've negotiated some sort of monthly shopping allowance with Hiqlexic and you're half planning to go to visit Malaysian Sugar Daddy, said my inner voice. You have to draw the line. And, more to the point, you have to work tomorrow morning at 6 a.m. I hoped I hadn't said any of that out loud.

'Tonight's a little awkward,' I said to MissPenelope. 'I have to be up so early tomorrow and I've been out nearly every evening this week.' I didn't want to put her off completely, because this might be something I'd return to. I just wasn't ready right now.

'Just come for two hours,' she pressed, with an irresistible little giggle. I wished I was as good a flirt as she was. I imagined she got everything she wanted from men.

'I'd prefer to come when I'm feeling more lively and when I don't have to be up so early, so I can relax properly. Plus, it's a bit embarrassing, but I have my period,' I lied.

'We don't care. I just want him to meet you. I know that he would love you. He tips very generously. Think about it. I have to go now to get ready for dinner.'

I could tell that she knew she was going to get her own way. I wished I had that quiet confidence. Or rather I wished I had her ability to get people to do exactly what she wanted, which was why she had that confidence in the first place. We got up to leave.

'You really suit hats, don't you?' she observed as I pulled on my matching hat, scarf, coat and gloves and we walked towards the exit. She was looking at my face closely, like a flirtatious man would.

'I love hats,' I replied. 'Hats and shoes, they're my weakness – I have loads.'

'Oh!' she trilled, delighting in the topic of conversation. 'For me, it's dresses. Evening dresses. I love them and can't stop buying them.'

'The thing about evening dresses is that I find I just never get the opportunity to wear them.'

She paused in the street, looked at me and purred, 'Oh, you will. With us.'

♥ ♥ ♥

I went home, looking forward to a much-needed early night and an even more essential trip to the supermarket. I don't think I'd seen a home-cooked vegetable for two weeks. I was at the checkout when a text came through from MissPenelope: 'Helen-Chan, [The Sugar Daddy] has arrive today. He would

be happy to know you. Please join us for talking. He will give
you the tip. Please see us from 10. X'

Shit. I didn't want temptation. I wanted to be left to have
an early night without the uneasy thought that I could be
missing out! Sometimes I scold myself that I am nothing more
than an incurable opportunist with an addiction to taking
risks.

I remembered how I'd felt before meeting American Ad
Man. I had hesitated then, hadn't I? But my spontaneity had
led to something great. I remembered meeting Malaysian
Sugar Daddy after my flight back from New York. I was
exhausted then, but living up to my promise had also led to
something fantastic. And then there was her use of the word
'tip'. That was also undeniably a motivating factor.

An hour and a half later, I was in a cab, which was
becoming quite a habit. I had always got the Tube everywhere,
but since my recent multiple cash-flow boosts, it was always
cabs after dark.

The Sugar Daddy had a suite at Claridge's, a five-star hotel
with a boutique feel in Mayfair. When I entered their room,
it felt like I was walking into a public library. The reception
room was like the lobby of a small hotel. The bathroom was
so long you could hardly see the end of it, and it contained
more pots of cream than the ground floor of Selfridges.

She opened the door in a dressing gown. Her hair was tied
up in a loose, swinging ponytail, and now, with a fully made-
up face, she looked even more familiar. I had definitely come
across this woman before.

They offered me a glass of champagne and I gladly
accepted, welcoming the instant invigorating effects. This
was a delicate situation. Not only was I aware that I had to be
up and at work for 6 a.m. the next day, I also realised that
now they'd got me here they would probably try to persuade
me to have more fun than just a chat. Added to that, as I

spoke to The Sugar Daddy, I was conscious that I had to be careful not to ignore MissPenelope. I know how women are.

He was striking. Although he looked all of his 58 years, his sex appeal and presence were startling. He had a rich Mediterranean glow about him and a full head of thick black hair, delicate features and a pair of big D&G glasses framing piercing blue eyes. I would have guessed he was Italian, not French. Talking of which, his accent was as hypnotic as he was.

'Tell us about your fantasies,' he said. 'What sort of things would you like to try that you haven't before?'

I tried to hide my extreme shyness, answering, 'Oh, they'll come out in time. I'm more interested in yours.'

'We have many, many new fantasies all the time. Life is about trying them.'

'Have you tried everything you've wanted to?' I asked.

'One can never do that,' laughed The Sugar Daddy. 'There is always something else. When you try everything, that is when life is over.'

'What is your latest inspiration?'

'We are working on one fantasy at the moment,' he replied thoughtfully, as if he were voicing his ideas for a colour scheme for a room, 'with a pre-op transvestite.' He paused and reached for the Dom Pérignon. 'It's just that I don't know how it would work. And also we just can't find an attractive one. They're all ghastly. Aren't they, sweetie?' He leaned over and affectionately brushed MissPenelope's face.

'Oh, yes, we have to keep looking,' she said, smiling sweetly. She was sitting upright with her legs crossed, her head to one side, looking at me with an amorous gaze.

'What about men?' I asked. 'Have you asked men to join you as well as women?'

'Oh, yes,' The Sugar Daddy said, with a dismissive flick of his hand. 'For her birthday, I got a man to join us, a friend of

mine. I wanted to give her a real good time.'

MissPenelope giggled, raising her hand to cover her mouth and dropping her head coyly, as if trying to hide the fact that she was doing something so untoward as laughing. It was a typical Japanese gesture. Maybe that was why she looked familiar.

'A friend of yours?' I repeated. 'Wasn't that a little awkward?'

'Oh, no, he is like us. In fact, we must introduce you to him some time. I think you will like him.' If The Sugar Daddy's friends are of his calibre, I thought, I definitely wouldn't be averse to that idea.

MissPenelope jumped up and suddenly declared, 'I'm going to try my new dress on.'

Ten long minutes later, she emerged in a slinky black number that clung to her toned body. It was totally backless, with a plunging neckline that draped perfectly over her breasts. That was it! She was the girl from Chinawhite, the one who'd offered to help me get into the VIP lounge by inviting me to join her group. The girl who'd *flirted* with me!

'He bought me this, but I haven't worn it. I wanted to wear it to dinner tonight but he was so hungry he couldn't wait for me to change.' She giggled again. 'Do you like it?'

'I love it.' I got up and went over to stroke the shiny black satin. 'You have such a lovely figure,' I said, and I placed my hand gently on her. I could sense her delight. We talked a little more about the dress and our figures and then I thought I had better go. I'd specified a chat-only first-time meeting, and I was sticking to my story that I had my period. I had to actually be at my desk six hours from now.

He helped me with my coat at the door. 'Let me compensate you for your travel expenses.' He reached into his pocket and carelessly drew out an assortment of foreign notes. 'I'm afraid all I have is euros. I do apologise.' He handed me a 500-euro note. Travel expenses? I thought. He must think I arrived by helicopter! It looked like monopoly money. Maybe it was monopoly money. The thought made me realise what an insecure world this could have been if I'd relied on these encounters as my main source of income. If the note had been a fake, there would have been nothing at all I could have done about it.

Chapter 20
Val d'Isère

Hiqlexic had made a number of suggestions for our planned break. Each option was presented to me in an email, meticulously planned out, with flight times, how long that would give us to sleep, an approximation of how many hours we'd have at our destination and a weather report.

Skiing seemed to be the best option – no night flight, little time difference and, I thought, plenty of activity in case we found that we couldn't stand each other. A day on a beach can feel like a long time to spend with someone if you can't find anything to say to them.

We flew to Lyon BA club class, and a huge black car with black windows, black leather seats and a minibar drove us the three-hour journey to Val d'Isère.

I find you can sometimes learn more about someone from simply accompanying them as they go about a routine chore than you can by actually sitting and talking with them. I had had lunch, two dinners and two overnight stays with Hiqlexic so far, yet I found I became more enlightened about his character as a result of the six hours of travel to the French Alps.

I was late turning up to the Heathrow Express terminal at Paddington. And I was late because Hiqlexic had phoned so many times before I left home to ask if I'd left yet. The first time I actually picked up.

'Have you left yet?'

'No, I'm just finishing off packing.'

'But you're meeting me in an hour.'

'I know. I'll be there in an hour.'

I picked up the second time, too.

'Have you left yet?'

'No, I'm just gathering a few last things and making sure everything's turned off and cleared up in my flat.'

'But you're meeting me in 50 minutes.'

'I know. I'll be there in 50 minutes. It takes me 25 minutes to get to Paddington.'

The third time, I did not answer, nor did I the fourth time, but the fifth and sixth missed calls came in quick succession, so I presumed there must be something urgent. I called back.

'Just checking you've left.'

'NO. I'm. Leaving. NOW!'

Then, believe it or not, he phoned again to check I had my passport. By then, I was late and it was his fault.

Nonetheless, we got on the Heathrow-bound train with plenty of time to spare. Immediately he started mapping out our plans. 'The train takes 15 minutes. We'll be at the airport by 4.45, check-in by 4.55, we'll be clear of security by 5.10, we'll get to the executive lounge by . . .'

I stopped listening and took out the G2 section of *The Guardian*, which I had extracted before throwing the rest of the paper away earlier that morning.

'Oh Lord, you don't read *The Guardian*, do you?'

'I try to read a selection of papers.'

'I didn't have you down as a left-wing socialist, but each to their own,' he sneered sarcastically.

Sugar Daddy Diaries

'What would you recommend?'

'I don't read a paper. They're propaganda. The media exists solely to scare us and it prints what it wants us all to believe.'

I felt myself becoming riled. As a journalist, I was quick to defend the integrity of my profession. 'The media doesn't do that at all. The media merely reflects an agenda that's already set by the public's interest. You don't read a paper at all?'

'I read the *FT*. I get the financial news. That's all I need.'

I shut up because I knew I couldn't win. I don't imagine anyone could ever win with Hiqlexic. He was impossibly opinionated and stubborn.

Yet, at the same time, he was consistently and annoyingly chirpy, avoiding silence at all costs and choosing to fill it with small talk. I never did get to read the G2 because whenever there was a pause in conversation he restarted it. Sometimes he'd make a ridiculous statement of the obvious – 'Oh, the stewardesses have all tied their scarves in the same way' – sometimes he would choose to break the silence with more merrily recited forward planning: 'We should land by 8.30 p.m. local time, be at the car by 8.50 local time . . .' Or he'd talk at me, quoting some historical nugget from his book or spouting reams of scientific facts. 'This author's take on the credit crunch is that housing bubbles in the West were deliberately created to mask the damage inflicted by companies shifting production abroad. That's actually ridiculous, because if you look at the history of the world's successful economies the boom-and-bust pattern is an essential component.' And then he'd go off on a spiel full of unfathomable economic jargon.

We arrived at our chalet late into the night. It was beautiful, spacious and warm. 'Righty-ho,' he virtually sang. 'Let's get unpacking.' I felt like I was on a school trip.

'Oh, I'll leave mine,' I replied casually. 'We'll have to pack it all up again by Saturday lunchtime.'

'Oh, I see. You're the untidy type,' he stated. I don't to this day know whether that was meant as a scathing admonishment or whether it was just innocent tactlessness. I ignored him.

♥ ♥ ♥

Due to Hiqlexic's preternaturally efficient body clock, he would always wake at around four. Luckily, because of the plus-one-hour time difference in France, on our first morning he didn't actually jump out of bed until five, giving me a pleasant one-hour lie-in.

'It's a great day for skiing,' I said at breakfast, feeling genuinely enthusiastic now that I was fed and caffeined. 'I can't wait to get out there.'

'You've had no bread.' Hiqlexic looked alarmed.

'No, I don't really eat bread.'

'You need carbs.'

'I've had plenty. I've had a big bowl of muesli and lots of fruit.'

'You can't ski all day on fruit. You need bread.'

'I don't want any bread.'

'When you ski, you burn an average of 500 calories per hour. You have very little fat, so your body will be expending more calories to keep your vital organs warm. You *need* to eat some bread.' He looked over at the buffet as if silently ordering me to get up and do as I was told.

'I don't *want* to eat any bread!'

I could feel adrenalin surging through my body and my temper had gone into standby mode. I was ready to fight. I was going to assert my right to choose my own diet no matter what he fucking said. He went deadly silent, clearly enraged that I hadn't heeded his wish. I was furious and we walked in silence to the boot-hire shop.

The glorious sunshine we'd awoken to stayed, and the blue skies over the powdery white snow, on what was the start of the best ski season in Europe in more than a decade, soon put us both in a good mood again.

Hiqlexic was a much better skier than me, but he insisted on staying by my side. 'I don't mind if you want to go off and do some black runs while I stay on the blues and reds,' I suggested. 'I'll meet you at the bottom.'

'No, no,' he chirped. 'We'll lose each other. Best we stay together. You'll be warmed up enough to do a black by the end of the day, won't you?'

'We'll see,' I said. Trying to explain a broken leg to friends and family who had no idea I'd actually gone skiing would have been difficult.

Hiqlexic was a total contradiction. He carried my poles for me, opened every door and helped me with my boots, yet he'd sneer if I fell, roll his eyes when I needed to stop to defog my glasses and get irritated if I had to stop to go to the toilet.

He is very obliging, I thought to myself, rubbing more wind protector into my cheeks in the mirror on one of my contentious toilet stops, if he's doing something that's his own idea.

There was nothing personable about him – a defining characteristic of low EQ. He looked at everything logically. There wasn't a hint of emotion or humour in anything he did. He was precise, punctual, driven – a true high achiever – but he didn't know how to acknowledge his emotions. That was probably why he viewed intimacy as something that could be bought.

At night, he would literally cling on to me as if I were a teddy bear and whisper, 'Thank you for being here.' Physical neediness seems to be common in high-powered men. I had learned from Greg, American Ad Man and many other dates that no matter how well these high-achieving males conveyed an image of unflappable collectedness in their professions, once naked and out of their tailored suits they begged not for sex, but for affection, acceptance and reassurance.

Hiqlexic was an only child who had been sent to several international boarding schools. His father had been stationed in the Middle East as part of the British military and had married an Egyptian woman, Hiqlexic's mother. I wondered whether Hiqlexic had felt like the outsider as a child, desperate for approval. Maybe his way of fighting back from his childhood angst was to achieve, achieve, achieve. He was fiercely competitive. Every fall in the snow was not a hilarious mishap but an infuriating error of judgement on which he had to perform a post-mortem. 'I think the lump of powdered snow came up at such an angle that it caught the inside of my ski just as I was at the 45-degree midpoint of my turn, which knocked my skis, so the tip of my right crossed over my left at about two-thirds of the length of it, and that disrupted my body weight. Terribly annoying.'

Three hours later, he was still beating himself up: 'I really shouldn't have fallen on that slope back there. It was a very easy slope. I must concentrate more.' I told him he should actually just relax more, but he didn't even acknowledge my comment.

All of our activities were meticulously timed. At the bottom of the chairlift, Hiqlexic would look at his watch. Then he would look at it at the top and then again at the bottom. He worked out the time we had spent in the lift and the time it took to ski down, allowing for an estimated amount of time spent tightening boots and adjusting glove linings. Once he'd done all the calculations, he would pipe up with the ratio of how long it had taken to get up in the lift to how long it had taken to get down and how that compared to the previous lift.

When we were going up in the lifts, he wasn't sitting doing quiet calculations. Oh, no. Such was his aversion to silence that he'd strike with another one of his statements of the blindingly obvious. 'Those people are having a race,' he'd say, pointing to where some people were having a race. 'Someone's dropped his pole,' he'd tell me, indicating someone who had dropped his pole. Sometimes, if he couldn't think of anything to say to break a silence, he would make a funny face or stick his tongue out in a desperate attempt to fill the void with some form of interaction, no matter how ridiculous. When we got off the lift and began to ski down the mountain, he would declare '*Allons-y!*' in sing-song French just to fill the air with words.

He had this awful habit, too, of telling me what to do just as I was about to do it. He would say, 'Turn left when we get off the lift,' even if the only possible way to turn was left. And he would make up non-existent arguments for himself to win.

That one is easier explained by example: one afternoon, when we reached the bottom of the mountain, there was no queue for the lift to take us back up again. He said, 'You see? I told you this would be the better lift to use.' But there hadn't been even a hint of disagreement over which lift we were going to take. Generally, I just followed him around the mountain. Somehow, he had created a competition in his head, and he was now declaring himself the winner.

Everywhere we went, we arrived ten minutes ahead of schedule. To me, that was torture. Being early seems such an unnecessary waste of perfectly good time! I simply can't bear the thought of cutting anything short in the pointless pursuit of over-punctuality. Also, I hadn't worn a watch for ten years and estimated the passage of time by intuition – not that I'd ever advocate that method.

After Val d'Isère, I expected never to hear from Hiqlexic again. Surely since I'd felt so irritated by his anally retentive ways he must have felt the same in reverse? We'll probably just not contact each other again, I thought. A relationship based on a shopping allowance is only ever going to be short lived. Maybe he'd meet someone via natural means. He was, after all, a very good-looking, eligible bachelor.

For a whole week, I didn't hear from him, and then, out of the blue, I got a text, as though everything were completely normal: 'Hey, how are you? Free to meet next week? What day would suit? Me xx'

I replied, letting him know which days I was free. Yes, 'Why?' is indeed a very good question. I was still excited by the idea of a monthly arrangement, I suppose, even though we hadn't dared to dictate what that would be in concrete terms yet. I was happy with weekly dinner dates, I told myself, I just didn't know if I could do another three days away with him.

And so, over the next couple of months, our relationship settled into a routine. I saw him roughly three times a month and we went for dinner or to the theatre, or sometimes he would cook a meal in his enormous kitchen. I grew used to his highly organised routines and he grew on me to an extent. He was affectionate and genuinely concerned with people's welfare (note welfare, not emotions). I realised he was an incredibly vulnerable, sensitive man who craved the tender words of a woman. He wasn't actually a nasty or vindictive person at heart; it was just that he had no ability whatsoever to see the world from another person's point of view.

After the first month, we became less awkward about defining our arrangement. He didn't like to refer to it as 'an arrangement', he said. It was too clinical. He liked to think of it as a shopping allowance because he had given one to his ex-girlfriend. We settled in the end on a monthly Selfridges gift card. Neither of us had done this sort of thing before, and a plastic card felt less dirty than cash.

You can imagine, though, that, getting a new yellow card

to put in my purse every four weeks, I ended up with stacks of the things. I'd find them lying around my flat, in the pocket of different coats, in the glove compartment of my car, and I had no way of telling how much money was left on each one.

After three months, I had bought everything I liked in the store. Not wanting to blow it all on clothes, I tried to spend the money as wisely as I could. I switched my massages and beauty treatments to the Selfridges salon. I met friends there for drinks and lunch and treated them. I bought a set of crockery (since I drop so many plates). All my gifts for birthdays, weddings and christenings came from Selfridges.

But, of course, I was paying top whack for everything. I soon twigged that if I had the choice of spending the proceeds from the arrangement on the high street, my new secondary income would go a lot further. I didn't know how to broach the subject. Then Decléor – my favourite skincare range – closed its Selfridges counter and moved to Harrods. That was the last straw. I told Hiqlexic that if he didn't mind terribly, I would prefer cash.

Chapter 21

Happy Moonlighting

♥ *December '08*

Of course, I didn't tell any of my friends about my new fortunes. Given the reaction my simply being on Sugardaddie. com had got, imagine how they'd have responded to the news that I'd moved up the ladder of amorality and was now using a site where the exchange of cash or gifts was a prerequisite of any relationship. Only Remaining Single Friend knew bits – she knew I was on the site – but she didn't know about the negotiations involved.

Female friends in relationships, I had learned, were best kept completely in the dark about my dating habits. They found it near impossible to understand that another woman's genuine motivation for meeting men could be fun or sex. They thought there should be something else – which was ironic given that that was exactly what I was looking for now: something else, something to compensate me for all the bother.

Because of that, Happily Married Girlfriend – gorgeous, lovely, well-meaning Happily Married Girlfriend – asked after Set-Up Date nearly a whole year on from when she'd tried to fix us up. I suspected that because I hadn't revealed anything about my complicated romantic life to her recently, she must have thought it was so uneventful that Set-Up Date was still potentially relevant and worthy of discussion.

'Why didn't you like him?' she demanded accusingly over a two-for-one credit-crunch-busting meal deal at Pizza Express one evening.

'I don't not like him,' I said. 'I just don't like him.'

'You don't know him!' she shrieked.

'There just wasn't a spark,' I insisted. I couldn't believe I was being made to feel guilty about telling a friend I wasn't going to date her husband's ex-colleague whom he hadn't even seen himself for more than a year.

'You should have an open mind. Get to know him. You could get to really like him. He's a really nice guy. Why don't you just see him one more time and see how you feel?'

I don't know why people always say 'He's a really nice guy' as though it's a powerfully convincing argument for dating someone. It's hardly the most compelling advertising slogan, is it? I also don't know why people presume that one's sole goal in life is to find someone they 'really like'. Failing that, force yourself to see them again and again until you convince yourself that you 'can get to really like them'. Anyone would think we were some pathetic species whose organs will shrivel slowly and painfully unless we find a mate with whom we can fuse our beings by the time we hit 30. Come to think of it, there's a parasitic fish worm, Diplozoon paradoxum, that has almost exactly that problem (I wrote about it once). But I like to think we are higher up the food chain than one of those.

'I'm too busy to date someone that I'm not really into,' I replied. 'It was lovely of you to introduce me, but I have other stuff going on. I have to prioritise.'

'What are you so busy with?'

I paused. What am I busy with?! A full-time job with twelve-hour shifts four days a week; a documentary on niche

Internet dating sites that I volunteered to do in my 'spare' working hours since I thought it would be good show-reel material if I ever got round to going freelance; a slightly obsessive four-times-a-week gym habit; a milder but still slightly obsessive urge to keep my flat in a nice clean state; dates from the website; emails and phone calls preceding meetings with dates from the website; Hiqlexic (there was always a demanding text or fifteen missed calls from him); weekly phone calls from Malaysian Sugar Daddy repeatedly asking me when I was going to visit him; my diary notes on dating sugar daddies; a social life; and, oh, a long list of things to buy to complete my winter wardrobe (boots, mainly – none of my 57 pairs of shoes were good on ice – and a decent coat – it had got far too cold for the red leather Prada one).

Maybe I should get a cleaner. I could afford one now, after all. Or maybe something else had to go. Job? That was the dullest of all the above. Maybe I should go freelance now, while I had my Hiqlexics, American Ad Men and MissPenelopes as a sort of financial safety net? Would my moral code allow me to do that? Little did I know that this hypothetical question was soon to be put to the test.

'Well, what are you busy with?'

'Oh,' I brought my mind back to the table and Happily Married Girlfriend. 'You know, life admin.'

'Don't tell me you're using that dating website again,' she said knowingly (though not that knowingly – she thought I was still on Sugardaddie.com).

'Not as often as I used to. Just when I'm bored.'

'But I thought you said you are always busy?'

'You can be busy and bored. They're not opposites.'

'If your time is that precious, why spend it on those types of men? They're players. And bullshitters. Most of them are probably married and they date multiple women because they think they can buy them.'

'That makes it all the more exciting,' I taunted her. 'Why meet the same stale date over and over when I can get fresh ones whenever I want? Look, I don't want someone phoning me every day and planning all my weekends between now and next Christmas.'

'I just don't want you to get hurt. Or one day wake up and regret all this. Don't you want to meet someone who looks out for you, who you can learn about and who will really love who you are?' continued my concerned friend.

'Nope.'

Her idea of the situation is muddled anyway, I thought. I'll never bring her round. She thought all these men wanted was fun and a short-lived high. Actually, it was me who wanted that. Around half the men I'd met on Sugardaddie.com and SeekingArrangement.com genuinely wanted to find a partner but were either too busy or travelled too much to attract one. Many of them had tried other means to find love, failed and so now they were having a go at paying for it. It was just a new approach. OK, there was Munich Man, but he was an exception to any rule.

'Well, if you do want fun, why don't you find it with nice, *normal* people, through a *normal* platform.' I hated the way she emphasised the word 'normal', as if normal equated to morally right. 'What about your new job? Isn't there anyone interesting? Or all your friends? Couldn't they set you up with someone?'

'Ha!' I nearly choked on my dough-balls. 'My colleagues are, like, 12. And I've met all my friends' friends. And all their friends' friends' dogs' friends. Believe me, there's a reason why I and five million other adults in this country turn to the Internet to date,' I told her, quoting a figure I'd researched for my dating documentary at work that day.

♥ ♥ ♥

Since escaping Claridge's with Monopoly-money paranoia, I hadn't heard from MissPenelope and The Sugar Daddy. I assumed they had decided not to pursue their proposal any further than our fully clothed chat. Maybe I was too pure for them, I thought. Maybe I had disappointed them by not allowing myself to be corrupted.

Then just after I'd stopped thinking about them, I got a text from MissPenelope to inform me that The Sugar Daddy was back in London and 'we would be pleased to meet you. We are at the Claridge's again. Can you come 9 p.m.?'

What a delicious text. An exclusive hotel, a marble reception, a man in white gloves manning the lift, another glass of Dom Pérignon, The Sugar Daddy's purring Parisian accent, MissPenelope's expensive evening gowns, 500-euro notes. How naughty. How could I resist?

The time clashed with a work event, though – the long-awaited visit by my two bosses from America. They wanted to discuss 'the future of the news operation', which really didn't look that bright. We had a team dinner booked. I couldn't drop out. But The Sugar Daddy was here for one evening only. I doubted they'd wait another six weeks for me.

I texted back, saying, 'I have a meeting this evening which may run over, is it OK if I come a little later?'

Look how polite that text was! Had I been replying to a man, it would have been, '9 is tricky can we make it 10?'

She texted back, 'As you wish. Bring some things you may like to play with. And some music u like.'

It was an odd instruction. Things to play with? I couldn't imagine my limited collection of sex toys adding anything to what had sounded like their extensive sexual experiments.

In my bag, as I flew out the door, late as usual, to meet my newsroom colleagues in a restaurant on Charlotte Street in Fitzrovia were: purse; phone; make-up bag; spare pair of stockings in case the ones I was wearing laddered; black fluffy handcuffs, which Munich Man had bought to clip onto his wrists when we went to the Rubber Ball and which I had not used since; another small male sex accessory that I'd bought years ago when in a relationship but had never taken out of its packet; my toothbrush to use after dinner; and three CDs. The Sugar Daddy may have been able to afford suites in fancy hotels, but he obviously didn't travel with an iPod.

'That's a big purse!' exclaimed my American boss as we all settled in at the restaurant. He was, of course, referring to my bag. 'What do you women carry in there?'

'Oh, you know, girl stuff.'

This was the first time I'd actually met my two bosses, though we'd had plenty of painfully drawn-out and totally futile transatlantic conference calls. Over tapas, we discussed the news operation and ways we could make it more appealing to young viewers.

'I think we were a bit slow in breaking the story about the UN considering renewing its sanctions against Laurent Nkunda in the Congo. We need to be first to break stories like that,' said American Boss.

'Well, I don't think the story was actually that important. It wasn't even a UN decision – it was just an announcement that they were considering renewing the sanctions. I think that day our viewers were more interested in the case of Kyle Doyle and his Facebook status update about his sickie that ended up being forwarded around the world. I don't think we should aim to be too broad in what we cover.'

I was getting cross. We're a young person's channel, I thought. Why would we want to go all international affairs? I didn't want someone telling me how to set the agenda of the news desk that I ran quite happily day-to-day, thank you very much.

'We want to be an online platform that people come to to find out what's going on in the world.'

Name me an online news outlet that doesn't, I thought, glad that my bosses lived abroad. My mind wandered to the stockings and handcuffs in my bag and what on earth the rest of my night would entail.

'Are you coming for drinks, Helen?' he asked after we'd finished the meal and a smaller group was going on to a bar.

'I have to go and make an appearance at a friend's birthday drinks, I'm afraid. I'd love to join you, but I'll be in trouble if I miss it.'

'Well, if you have to go . . . We'll see you Monday. We'll sit down and outlay how we can progress on defining a news agenda that works with our brand and tells people that we are a cross-spectrum one-stop shop for all genres of news. Let's take a couple hours to brainstorm, and we can give the channel an appropriate direction.'

He's so fucking American, I thought. 'Yes, sounds a brilliant plan. See you *on* Monday.' I emphasised the preposition because it annoys me that Americans miss them out.

I escaped into a black cab and instructed the driver to take me to Brook Street in Mayfair. As I sat in the back checking my phone, I felt a shudder of excitement go through me. And that was what it was all about. I wasn't going there for the 'tip', as MissPenelope called it. Well, I did enjoy the extra luxuries, the freedom to shop, not feeling guilty every time I ate out, but those were relatively small perks. The real thrill was the secret. It was switching from professional journalist to hotel-hopping paramour, just because I could.

I popped to the Ladies before getting into the lift. I checked my stockings for ladders, brushed my teeth and tidied up my hair, which I still hated, by the way, because of the recent disastrous haircut, and which I now noticed was also lopsided as well as being too short.

The Sugar Daddy had a different suite. This one had a larger hallway, decorated in rich blues and golds, with an elaborate brass mirror as the centre point. The sitting room opened off it with sky-high ceilings and heavy bold curtains draped to the floor. MissPenelope was sitting on an Edwardian wood-framed sofa in another black dress, her shoes kicked off and her legs curled underneath her, swirling a glass of golden Pouilly-Fumé.

'Sit down,' they both said gushingly, and MissPenelope released her trademark giggle, covering her mouth with her hand. I literally sank into probably the most comfortable cushion I have ever sat on. It was hard to believe I was going to be paid for this.

We chatted. It was much more relaxed than our initial meeting. They wanted to order food. I told them I had eaten.

'Oh, darling, we waited,' MissPenelope pouted.

'I'm sorry, I thought you would have gone ahead without me. I'll have a dessert with you.'

She giggled and said, with cringeworthy innuendo, 'Don't worry, we'll be having plenty of dessert later.'

I had a fruit platter and they had steaks. It arrived within minutes of ordering. A timid waiter from room service laid out a large, polished-wood table and we moved to the dining area. The Sugar Daddy ate two mouthfuls of his fillet.

'That is enough. I don't like to overeat, it is very important for the digestion to eat little and often.'

MissPenelope shrugged and finished hers and half of his. 'I don't care about that. I like to eat!'

We talked about food, languages we spoke, liposuction, the credit crunch, the fetishes of Japanese businessmen and shopping. Then we moved back from the dining table to the sofas.

I am so remarkably suited to this, I thought as I sank into

the soft sofa cushions again, feeling a surge of euphoria from the wine. I am blessed with all the right qualities to enjoy my spot of moonlighting. I love meeting people, I'm fascinated by their stories, I enjoy sex, I prefer older men, wealth and power turn me on, love doesn't interest me, I thrive on doing the forbidden. And I love to write about it all afterwards.

I swung my legs over The Sugar Daddy's knee and we kissed. He was passionate, strong and assertive. MissPenelope refilled our glasses and joined us. She pushed her lips into our kiss, her long dark hair falling all over us. She was more sensual than Isabelle had been when I'd found myself in the unplanned threesome with Munich Man. Her skin was cool and soft and she was sweet-smelling. I let them both undress me, together. There was a notable physical contrast between the manliness and assertiveness of The Sugar Daddy and the gentleness of MissPenelope. I didn't feel attracted to her as such, more mesmerised by her. She was a real-life paid mistress. I was in awe of her, as if she were a celebrity.

As in my first threesome, I was spurred on by the novelty, but this was an entirely different experience from the coke-fuelled session with Isabelle and Munich Man. This couple were passionate and sensual, fuelled by desire. They focused all their attention on me, rather than on each other. I was in the middle of them both. It was clear MissPenelope was engaging because she was desperate to. It wasn't just an opportunity to spice up a sexual experience, as had been the case when Isabelle and I kissed with Munich Man.

'Well, I have to be up tomorrow,' said The Sugar Daddy as we lounged around chatting much later. It was the early hours of the morning, and I took that as my cue to leave. I was beginning to feel drowsy anyway. 'I must give you your travel expenses,' he added. 'I'm afraid, again, I only have euros. I apologise. Is this OK?'

Chapter 22

American Ad Man and His Crazy Crew

♥ **January '09**

For the first time in my adult life, I hadn't had to worry about money at Christmas. I loved going home that year and producing as big a pile of presents as others had produced for me. I was no longer the poor journalist daughter – the one who was still struggling to get her career going, the one who never had any money. And in the run-up to Christmas, I could afford to go to all the nights out, and buy the drinks, and get cabs home. I invested in a proper warm coat, a full-length black sheepskin one, which I had tailored to fit me. Then I bought matching, quality leather boots – not my usual made-in-China variety that women's magazines warn me will give me crippling bunions by the time I'm 40. I spent more on that coat than I ever had on one single item. It made me feel positively regal whenever I put it on.

My boiler broke down just after New Year. It was the third time in a year. I was finally able to replace it instead of paying to drag on its sorry life for a few months longer. What would have stressed me out a few months ago now hardly made me blink. Did I ever feel guilty about how I'd suddenly elevated myself to this new zone of financial comfort? Not at all. I didn't consider myself to be doing anything wrong. I certainly wasn't hurting anyone.

Shortly after the boiler incident, American Ad Man got in touch to inform me he was 'stopping by' London, for two nights only. I was delighted. I had thought several times about those two nights at the Sheraton Park Tower and had been wondering if he would ever choose to get in touch again. I thought he might have had a reality check about paying out extortionate amounts of money to give a girl dinner and a massage, or perhaps have met another girl he preferred.

He had spent the last seven days on a sailing trip off the Canary Islands with a group of ten other men, or so his brief email told me. They would all arrive en masse on Friday evening for a final weekend in London before heading back en masse to Chicago. He didn't want to subject me to an alpha-male dinner but asked if I would like to join them for drinks at the Lanesborough Hotel at 10 p.m.

I was happy with that. I had work to do on my documentary, so the later the time the better. The Lanesborough is a stunning Georgian building at Hyde Park Corner. It is grander than any other hotel in London. Every guest gets a butler. The interior smells of wood, so thick is the rich oak panelling that lines the walls from top to bottom. The wide entrance corridor, clad in marble, stretched ahead of me, giving a true feeling of stately importance. I got there before him and waited in the marble reception area with my sheepskin coat on. How familiar, I thought, recalling the first time I had met him, when I'd had to wait for him in the bar of the Sheraton with my lethal Martini, under the knowing gaze of the pianist.

I saw a convoy of black cars arrive outside. A flurry of doormen moved towards them and an entourage of grey-suited, inebriated middle-aged men, oozing charisma, stepped into the lobby. In the middle was American Ad Man.

'I recognise that hat!' he boomed, and bounded over to greet me in a hearty embrace. 'Come on, there's a whole bunch of us in the bar already.'

Before I could utter anything in reply, I was being led by the arm into the midst of the group of men. It was like being swept away by a tornado. In front, behind and to each side of me was a burly male figure, all moving fast and furiously towards their destination – the Library Bar.

There I became even more disorientated. The men were milling about in every direction, all summoning waiters and sommeliers, each exuding an aura of importance. It was chaos. Some were demanding tables, others were demanding drinks, someone else wanted to know if 'this pathetic piece of paper' was the full wine list. American Ad Man introduced me to about five people simultaneously. Everyone had a one-syllable name and told me in a deep and heavily accented voice that he was from Chicago. 'I'm Bill, I'm from Chicago.' 'Pleased to meet you. I'm Ted. I'm from Chicago.' 'I'm Matt and I know [American Ad Man's name] from Chicago.' They all shook my hand firmly but seemed to lose interest by the time I got to the bit where I said, 'Hi, I'm Helen.' Their eyes were everywhere, looking for staff, giving new orders. I felt like I had just stepped onto the set of *The Godfather*.

They were all drunk. I tried to ask where they'd been that night and why they were all on a trip together, but no one could give me a coherent answer. They were sitting down, then standing up, then a waitress delivered drinks, then she took them away because they were wrong. It was total pandemonium and the room was filled with the cacophony of their deep, slurring voices.

I got enough information to work out that they all had a mutual friend who had his own yacht. To beat the January blues, they'd decided to get together and organise a sailing trip, factoring in a stopover in London on the way home.

'Jed – the guy with the yacht – isn't here. He met a girl where we were having dinner and I think he's "occupied".'

'I see,' I said, wondering what sort of girl he had met to get so closely acquainted with so quickly. Someone like MissPenelope? 'And where was dinner?'

'Le Gavroche.'

'Oh, the French place in the basement, with all the animal sculptures on the tables?' Le Gavroche was another flamboyant haute-cuisine hangout in Mayfair. I had been there with Hiqlexic.

With the men were two average-looking girls with streaky make-up. They were sitting down at a table, looking really pissed off, or just bored maybe.

'Helen, this is Natalie and Erica,' offered American Ad Man.

The two girls, who looked much younger than me, half-heartedly raised their hands and gave me pathetic featherweight handshakes, as if they were really putting themselves out. 'Hi,' they said shortly, barely even making eye contact and certainly making no effort to remove the permanent scowls from their faces.

I had no idea where Natalie and Erica had come from or who they were with, but the presence of two other girls at least made me feel less self-conscious about being on the arm of American Ad Man. The guys had only been in the country for a few hours and I was wary about how I would be received as a female intruder in the group.

American Ad Man told me that Natalie and Erica were from Sweden and Estonia respectively. They had both joined the party on the yacht to accompany one of the men – the oldest one, Sam. Sam looked way beyond retirement age. He had a stern, no-nonsense look about him and within five

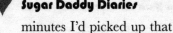

minutes I'd picked up that he was the natural leader of the group.

One by one, everyone started to sit down. At one point, we could even have passed as a normal, civilised group of friends having a drink. Sam sat between the two girls, who looked a bit scrawny up close. They still seemed bored and still hadn't said a word, but occasionally one of them would take Sam's hand, as if she had just reminded herself to make some token gesture of affection. I noticed the other men paid them no attention at all.

The calm did not last long. After about twenty minutes had passed and several unsatisfactory rounds of drinks had been sent back, four of the men started complaining that there were no women in the bar. They asked me if I knew where they could go to meet women. It was approaching midnight. I suggested the Met Bar in the Metropolitan Hotel, the Mandarin Oriental, the bar at the Sanderson or the top floor of the Hilton at Park Lane. If they could bear pumping music, they could try to bribe their way into the members-only Kingly Club. Or if they preferred younger ladies, they could go to Chinawhite.

They were gone as quickly as they had arrived, leaving me alone with American Ad Man. He beamed. 'Quite a crazy crew, hey? I'm beat from spending a week with them.'

'Crazy is an understatement,' I laughed. 'How have you been?' And we picked up exactly where we'd left off.

The next morning, as we walked into breakfast, we bumped into several of the mafia-like crew, giving off the same vibe of importance and chaos as they had the night before but this time sober. 'Can you toast this more? It's not done enough,' I heard one voice say above the breakfast chatter. 'Can I get fresh lemon with this tea?' yelled another.

We joined two of the guys at a table. I recognised one of

them from the night before but not the other, not that it mattered. He followed the same formula: 'Hi, I'm Jed, from Chicago.'

'Jed's the guy with the yacht,' said American Ad Man proudly.

'Oh, it's your yacht?!' I said excitedly. I'd never met anyone with their own yacht. I asked him loads of questions. Could he skipper it himself? Did he have to employ a full-time crew? Where would it go now that he was heading back to the US? He seemed unimpressed and gave monosyllabic answers. He wasn't really interested in me. I suspected that, in his world of private yachts and luxury hotels, he had come across a lot of young, fascinated girls asking stupid questions over breakfast.

'What do you do?' I asked, after enough time had passed since we'd discussed his personal yacht that it wouldn't seem like a loaded question.

'Jed makes amazing feats of engineering happen,' American Ad Man chipped in. I suspect he answered on Jed's behalf because he knew the answer required more than one syllable. 'Jed designs bridges and tunnels under the sea and water systems for remote villages. What's that project you just finished, Jed? He built a big steel bridge over some part of the Alps . . .'

'Not the Alps. The Himalayas!' said Jed. More syllables, I noted. This was promising. Then he actually managed some sentences. 'It was in India. We built a bridge to link two towns that it used to take four hours to travel between. It's going to be one of the busiest routes in the world. We were the only ones who could get the cranes and the gear into the mountains.' He gave a gleeful smile and went back to munching, with his mouth open, on his retoasted toast.

Just then, Sam arrived at the table with a tall, thin woman in her 50s by his side. She looked well groomed but tired.

'This is my wife. She's just flown in,' he announced.

All the men around the table immediately put down their forks and spoons and pieces of toast and stood up. 'Hello, Mrs [her surname],' they all said, and shook her hand, one by one, paying her the utmost respect. Obviously, the girls from the night before were nowhere to be seen.

American Ad Man and I went back to his room. He had an hour to pack before the swarm of men were to leave to fly back to the States. I lay on the bed and watched him fold shirts into a small bag.

'That must have been a bit awkward just now,' I said, 'when Sam's wife arrived and she saw me sitting amongst all you guys for breakfast. She must be a little suspicious of you all.'

'Nah,' said American Ad Man, 'they have an understanding. She's experienced enough to know that men are men, and men will be like boys when they are away on a trip together.'

I fell silent. I had just witnessed that woman commanding instant respect from a virtually uncontrollable group of self-important alpha males, and she'd done it simply by virtue of her status as a wife. It was quite a contrast to how they'd greeted me and how they'd blanked the other girls. Yet with her role as wife, there seemed to come, according to American Ad Man at least, a tacit expectation that she would turn a blind eye to any unsavoury antics when her husband and his friends were away from home.

'And how's your marriage?' I asked.

He paused now, stepping away from his folding and packing and directing his full attention to his answer: 'We're living more unhappily ever after by the day.'

'Oh. Sorry.'

'I just can't connect with her as a human being. We don't have any dialogue.'

'Why's that?'

'She's spoiled. She's quite a well-known figure in America. She had a very privileged upbringing.'

My journalistic ears pricked up and I asked, trying not to sound too excited, 'What sort of well-known figure?'

'Her father is a very famous actor. She grew up with a lot of public attention and was surrounded by a lot of money. It's hard for someone not to be affected by that.'

'Which actor?'

He laughed. He wasn't going to give.

'Do you still love her?'

'Yes. I love her still. But I'm not in love. Oh, I don't want to talk about it. Going back to family life tomorrow, you know? What about you? You still don't have a boyfriend?'

'Oh, no, no, no!'

'I thought I'd come back to London this time and you'd tell me you were happily shacked up with someone and wouldn't want to see me.'

I laughed. 'What would I want a relationship for?!'

'I like your attitude.' I had forgotten about his favourite phrase. 'Why not?'

'Don't need one, I guess. I've got lots going on in my life and, well, it's a lot of hassle, isn't it?'

'Hassle? Wow. You're ice-cold, honey.'

'No, what I mean is . . .' I tried to think how to phrase this without sounding cynical. Every time I answered this question, it came across as flippant, and I really didn't mean to be. 'It's . . . well, you give up a lot for a relationship. A lot of time, compromises and part of your personality. Even your opinions and values end up adapting to those of the other person. What I mean by hassle is having to synchronise calendars, giving up a Saturday afternoon, having to meet his family. I just don't want that. But equally I know that you only get what you put in, so I don't expect to get the rewards of a relationship either. So when my boiler broke the other week, there was no handyman boyfriend to call. I got on a stepladder with a screwdriver and tried to fix the stupid thing myself.'

He laughed. 'You want a boyfriend for HVAC?'

'HVAC?'

'Yeah, you know: heating, ventilation and air con.'

'We don't need air con in the UK. Haven't you noticed? We call that DIY.'

He looked puzzled. 'What does that mean?'

'Do-it-yourself.'

He roared with laughter. 'Very funny. In your case, it is. How did you just think that up so quick? You're funny.'

'I didn't make it up. That's what we actually call it here: do-it-yourself. It's jobs around the house – things that require screwdrivers.'

'DIY? You British are so funny sometimes.' He paused to laugh for a good half a minute and then went back into serious mode. 'Do you want to know what I think about what you said?'

'Tell me.'

'I don't necessarily disagree with you. But what I think about those things you describe, the DVC . . .'

'It's DIY.'

'Whatever – the phone calls, the meeting in-laws. They are things that I suspect you would find, if you had a connection with someone, would not be an interference in your life at all.'

'Oh, but they would! It's the days when you need to be 100 per cent focused on something: you have a deadline, you have emails to send, you want to have dinner with a friend, but they want to cook a meal with you; or you want to start a new hobby and they mock you; or they've had an awful day and they need your time and attention, but what do you do if you just can't give that at that moment? That's what I mean by compromise.'

'That's called multiplexing.'

'Multiplexing?'

'Yes. You know, managing lots of stuff.'

'We say multitasking.'

'You British are so funny.' He chuckled again. 'I have a very dense life. I have children, a wife, a company, management issues, staff problems. All the time, I'm juggling things. Those relationship things are just something else – it's just part of my life and my schedule.'

'But think how much more you could do if you didn't have to deal with that stuff! You'd have more time to do what you want to do.'

'But I want to do those things. It's my life, and everything I have to do is part of the full package.'

'You obviously think routine is a small price to pay for what you get in return. I think it's a huge price. But that's why you're a businessman and I'm a . . . I'm a . . . I'm . . . not going to make you late. Won't they be waiting for you downstairs?'

He made a call to one of his crew. Their cars were waiting outside the hotel to take them to the airport for their flight back to Chicago.

We walked down to the lobby where the other guys were gathering, dressed in power suits, creating a general atmosphere of high-profile chaos. 'Where's the goddamn driver?' one of them was saying. 'Dave, did you get concierge to send the luggage ahead of us?' nagged another.

'Have a safe flight,' I said to American Ad Man as I kissed him on the cheek.

'I'll be back in a few weeks. So don't go getting any boyfriends just for your DVC.'

'DIY. It's DIY.'

I decided not to get a cab. It was a beautiful, crisp, sunny day and I felt really awake. There is no drug that gives a

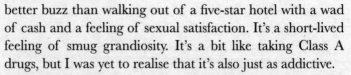

better buzz than walking out of a five-star hotel with a wad of cash and a feeling of sexual satisfaction. It's a short-lived feeling of smug grandiosity. It's a bit like taking Class A drugs, but I was yet to realise that it's also just as addictive.

I walked towards Hyde Park, planning on taking a walk, but then, feeling flush, redirected towards Knightsbridge and popped into Harvey Nicks. Using beautiful, crisp, uncreased £50 notes, I bought several overpriced luxury items I didn't need at all.

Chapter 23

Redundant

It was a Monday morning. I had spent the night with Hiqlexic in his flat on the Strand. I was starting to see more of him than usual. He was between jobs, having been headhunted by one humungous law firm from another. He had around six weeks of gardening leave with nothing to do other than phone me fifteen times a day, read a few more world-history epics and use up his air miles before his company account expired.

Next week, he told me, he was going to the States for three weeks to visit a host of old friends. He was starting in LA, followed by a visit to old school friends in Santa Fe and he might, if he had time, squeeze in some skiing in Aspen. And then he would go to Washington on his way home to visit old colleagues. Phew, I thought. I would get some respite for three weeks. Maybe I could fit in my trip to Kuala Lumpur while he was away? I had postponed my visit to Malaysian Sugar Daddy twice already because of a shake-up of programming taking place at work.

I am a bad sleeper away from my own bed, so I woke up

groggy and thinking of soya lattes. I set off for work, wearing a pair of flats and carrying my heels in a small yellow Selfridges bag. Hiqlexic had handed it to me in horror when he saw that I was shoving my pavement-soiled heels loose into my handbag along with my purse, make-up bag, phone and an apple. 'You're going to eat that apple?' he'd said, aghast. 'You can't put your shoes in the same bag!' Honestly, it was like something my mum would say.

I was sleepy and dazed as I wandered towards Tottenham Court Road. I sensed I was late but wasn't sure how late. As I have already mentioned, I don't wear a watch and, considering I was carrying two bags and a Starbucks coffee and had gloves on, rummaging for my phone to check the time was out of the question. I got to work at 9.15, with half my coffee left. There was an email waiting for me, 'inviting' me to go to a meeting with HR to discuss 'the future business plans of the company, which could affect [my] employment'.

Oh. Right.

The 'invitation' was for 9 a.m. I didn't know what to do first: finish my coffee, log on or wander at today's markedly slow pace towards HR. This wasn't entirely out of the blue. When the bosses had been over from America we'd discussed programming. With a new year had come a new schedule, and it didn't feature the hourly three-minute news bulletin any more.

We had been told in December that the decision 'could affect our employment' but 'not to worry' because the channel was putting together a number of pilot programmes and, as of 1 January, we would be working temporarily with the brainstorming team to thrash out new programming ideas 'until the long-term programming strategies of the company became clear'. That was why my daily start time had changed from six to nine, which, naturally, I didn't consider a bad thing.

It was a bit odd, though, to put a team of broadcast journalists and video editors on a brainstorming team. I'd never done anything like that in my life. I had no idea what 'mission-critical core competencies' were and I thought 'turnkey solutions' was the name of a locksmith.

The HR officer looked pained as she told me, 'We sadly have no positions within the new business plan to accommodate your skill set.' They had a whole list of employees to deal out the death sentence to that day and I was first on it.

I don't know why, but I found myself fighting back a smirk. Not because I was pleased – not at all. It was one of those inexplicable reflex reactions to bad news, like when someone says they've had an accident and you can't help the corners of your mouth turning up. On the other hand, part of that extremely unwelcome urge to smile probably did stem from a touch of excitement. Now I would *have* to go freelance. With that came nervousness, too. I couldn't help running through all the little securities I was being forced to give up on the spot: a salary, colleagues, a travel card, a reason to get dressed in the morning, an answer to the 'What do you do?' question at parties, health insurance, my favourite organic sandwich shop, use of a printer.

As I walked downstairs, one of my colleagues was on the way up.

'This is it, isn't it?'

What could I say? It wasn't really my place to confirm her fate on the stairs. But I couldn't lie. 'Well, at least they let us know at a decent time in the morning,' I replied. 'The day's still young.'

We both laughed. What else was there to do?

Half an hour later, my email was disconnected and my pass deactivated. That really pissed me off, because it meant that when I got to the security, carrying two cardboard boxes filled with notebooks, two spare pairs of shoes, a forgotten-about bag of Boots toiletries, two unopened packets of rice crackers and a pair of sunglasses that I thought I had lost, the guy took my name and asked why I didn't have an up-to-date pass. How fucking humiliating.

I went to Starbucks again and texted the girl I'd met on the stairs to join me. She arrived five minutes later, also with a cardboard box, which I noticed was half the size of my two. We sat with our lattes and made jokes about what we would do now.

'I could always sell my shoe collection,' I began.

'I could sell my car!' she joked.

'Oh God, that would save me a salary in parking fines alone!' I continued. That was all we could do: laugh to prevent the reality setting in.

Two more colleagues joined us. They too had just been 'invited' to HR's office. As soon as we considered it a reasonable time for lunch (11.30 a.m.), we moved to somewhere licensed, and that afternoon the four of us got through about half the previous year's yield of Californian Colombard Chardonnay.

Tomorrow, I assured myself, I will draw up a plan as to how I'm going to make money from here on in as a free-agent journalist.

At some point, I texted Hiqlexic to tell him the news. He texted back within seconds, as he always did: 'Now you can join me next week in the States.' I was irritated. It was so typical of him. All he could ever think about were the practical implications of any situation, never the emotional side of things. I had just been made redundant. Who gave a fuck about being his companion in the US next week? What about my life next week, next month, in six months' time?

He wasn't strictly the cause of my irritation, however. During that afternoon, as the messages of condolence came in via text, emails to my iPhone and comments on my

Facebook status, I noticed that I felt annoyed with everyone. That seemed to be my predominant emotion over the redundancy. It wasn't the situation that upset me – that was plain economics and I had seen it coming for a while (kind of); it was people's reactions that bothered me. They all seemed so insincere.

'Poor you.' 'Isn't it terrible?' Nothing seemed to have any depth to it. It wasn't their fault, of course. What can one write to one's redundant friend to make them feel better? Only those in the same position can really understand. But still, I couldn't help feeling annoyed by all the messages of support. I felt they trivialised the situation by implying that it could be helped by a simple text. I remembered feeling the same about sympathy cards when my father had died several years ago. Although they were well meant, they'd seemed like a pathetic attempt to fill a huge crater with a bucket of soil.

Working in the unpredictable media industry, I had come up against the prospect of redundancy on average around once every 18 months in my career. But I had always escaped *le chop* until now. And it wasn't until now that I realised exactly what I'd be losing. I'd get by, I knew that. I could freelance in other newsrooms and, thanks to all my sugar daddies last year, I had savings to fall back on. But it wasn't losing the salary that really smarted, it was the blow to my pride and my sense of myself. A career reflects who you are, defines your daily routine, determines what you think about when you get up and when you go to sleep. To have someone tell you you are no longer needed is quite the knock-back, even if the decision is based purely on economics.

Only Remaining Single Friend phoned me straight away when she saw my Facebook status. She offered to take me on a crazy blowout later in the week, at her expense, so that I could let my hair down. Happily Married Girlfriend phoned, too, very concerned. She invited me round to dinner and offered to set me up with another of her husband's friends.

I didn't have time to do either of those things, however, because both Hiqlexic and Malaysian Sugar Daddy put in aggressive claims for my time. When Malaysian Sugar Daddy learned that work commitments no longer prevented me from booking my trip to see him, he was delighted. 'Well, you can stay with me for longer now. Three weeks. One month. Hopefully six months.' I detected a smile in his voice, so I hoped he was joking.

He pestered me to look at flights. I told him I would get things organised that week and would hopefully visit him the week after. Hurry up, he told me, because if I could get there by Saturday he was visiting the jungles of the state of Kelantan on the east coast, and it would be great if I could come.

Hiqlexic, however, had other ideas.

Chapter 24

Aspen

Hiqlexic saw my redundancy as nothing more than a timely and fortuitous event that meant I could be his skiing buddy on the Aspen leg of his US trip. And now that it looked like I might have to depend on being a paid paramour for a regular income, I felt obliged to accept. But I couldn't put my trip to Malaysia off again. And I wanted to go there more than I wanted to go skiing. But then I wanted to go skiing, too . . .

But you've just been made *redundant*, I told myself. You should say no to both trips, have a reality check, stop playing around on a dating website and look for some freelance work.

And that was what the voice of reason was still howling in my ear as I skied down the slopes of Aspen six days later. I had booked the earliest flight I could to Denver, which was a day later than when Hiqlexic had wanted me to get there. 'Why didn't you take the BA flight to Detroit and then get an internal transfer direct to Aspen?' he'd said to me down the phone from his Santa Fe hotel room. He sounded irritated. In fact, the reason I hadn't taken that route was that I'd been looking for a flight that could take me on to Malaysia afterwards. Obviously, I couldn't tell him that because he didn't know I was going to Kuala Lumpur.

Meanwhile, I was making similar excuses to Malaysian Sugar Daddy. 'But if you don't get here for another two weeks, you'll miss the jungle trip. We'll stay in a fantastic place and see all kinds of wildlife. And if we have time, I'd like to take you to a beautiful island called Penang for a few days.' I couldn't tell him that I had a ski trip to squeeze in before coming to visit him because I didn't want him to guess that I had another sugar daddy.

I had told them both that the delay was because I was creating leads for freelance work for when I got back. There was the added complication that Hiqlexic didn't know I was a journalist. Oh, and also that Malaysian Sugar Daddy booked me a flight from London to Kuala Lumpur, when in fact I needed one from Denver. The final twist was that I had to take (and hide) summer clothes to a ski resort and ski gear to a 35-degrees-in-the-shade climate.

What am I doing?! I scolded myself as I skied down the beautiful Aspen slopes in Colorado. I've lost my job, I've come skiing with one guy and I'm going to Malaysia to visit another next week, with just an hour's touchdown in Frankfurt to separate the trips – neither of which I've funded myself. I am getting out of control. I need to be in the UK launching my new career. I need to be making phone calls. At this rate, *this* is going to be my new career – a paid holiday companion for rich men.

I had messages on my phone from concerned friends and ex-colleagues offering me advice on making contacts as a freelancer. Nobody knew where I was, except my lodger and Only Remaining Single Friend. I felt such a fraud. I had Malaysian Sugar Daddy texting me to call him when I was free; meanwhile, I had Hiqlexic chirping '*Allons-y*' in my ear every five minutes.

The resort was the most picturesque ski setting I had ever experienced. Everything was so vivid I felt like I was skiing inside a computer simulation. The air was clear, the snow was crystal white and the trees were a deep, rich shade of green, in perfectly straight lines along the slopes. But, despite the beautiful scenery, the good food, the spas in the evening and the best Californian wines, I couldn't enjoy myself.

My head was clouded by my redundancy. Whenever Hiqlexic wasn't talking at me, telling me some trivial fact or making an annoyingly jolly statement of the obvious, my mind wandered to what the fuck I was going to do when I got back from my month-long free holiday. I must have come across as worryingly withdrawn.

Although Hiqlexic knew about my redundancy, he seemed totally oblivious to the emotional turmoil that goes with losing a job, and I couldn't talk to him about it. At first, that irritated me, but then I reflected that, in fairness to him, because I had hidden my real profession from him he probably didn't know how ambitious I really was and how much my work mattered to me.

Malaysian Sugar Daddy had also seen my redundancy as the opportunity he'd been waiting for. At last, I would have the time and freedom to visit him. But then, I reminded myself, this was the only reaction I could expect. These were not truly relationships in which we offered each other mutual emotional support. These were relationships with defined boundaries. With Hiqlexic, I bolstered his ego and brought some light femininity into his intense, corporate world. I couldn't expect a sympathetic ear or some considered guidance. No, my rewards were money, meals and holidays. That had been my choice.

♥ ♥ ♥

It never stopped surprising me that, as a top-of-his-game, successful lawyer, Hiqlexic was pathetic when faced with being alone. He came and talked to me in the shower, he looked over my shoulder while I texted, he talked at me when I was trying to read a newspaper, he mauled me through the night, not releasing me from his arms as he slept, no matter how much I tried to wriggle free, and if he was ever ready before me, instead of sitting and waiting patiently he would come and watch me intensely as I applied mascara in the bathroom mirror. He stared at me in the way that had startled me when I'd looked up from the menu in Nobu on our early dinner date. It was invasive.

'I think I need to get my boots adjusted again,' he said one hour into our second day on the slopes.

'Again? Didn't they do it properly last night? I thought they heated them up to mould them to the shape of your feet.' The previous night, we'd spent two hours in a shop while he chose a pair of new ski boots, even though he already had two pairs in his luggage. I waited patiently as he got them professionally fitted. They stuck in pieces of foam, they had him standing on a ski simulator, they got out a thousand screwdrivers and they measured his feet eight times. I thought we were going to be there all night.

'I think they need just a millimetre of elevation on the outside of my heels.'

'You can go back this evening, can't you? As long as you can ski today, they'll be OK until tomorrow,' I replied.

'No, I need to go now.'

'OK. Shall I meet you for lunch somewhere, then?'

'You won't come with me?'

I screamed inwardly. Why on earth did he need me to go and accompany him while he got his boots fitted again? I wanted desperately to stay on the slopes and enjoy the sun and the open air. But Hiqlexic wouldn't entertain the idea of going alone. I had to trudge along with him and sit inside the poky little ski shop sweating in my many thermal layers.

Unbelievably, he still wasn't happy with his boots. A good few ski runs before the last lift closed for the evening, he announced, 'I need to get them adjusted again.'

'Again?!'

'Yes. We'll be at the top by 3.45. We can ski down by 4.10. We can change by 4.20 and be in the shop by 4.30.'

In my head, I said, 'What do you want me to do – hold your fucking hand?' Out loud, I said, 'I quite fancy doing a few more runs. Can't we stay on the slopes and you can go later? Say around half six?'

'It closes then.'

'Well, six.'

'Let's compromise. We can go at five.'

I was utterly amazed by this small victory. Then I remembered I had booked a slot in the spa. 'Oh. I have a massage at half past five. You don't need me, though, do you?'

'Can't you change it? I'd like you to come with me. I may need your opinion.'

'Change it?'

'Yes.'

'I'll see,' I said. I had no intention whatsoever of rearranging my massage.

Luckily, I couldn't change it anyway, and, even more luckily, he would have had to pay if I'd cancelled. That meant I had a blissful hour of peace on the massage table while he went alone to his precious ski shop. Then I had another whole wonderful, harmonious, soothing, beautiful 15 minutes of private time before he got back.

As I floated out of the treatment room, the lady at the desk stopped me. 'Ma'am, your boyfriend came in 15 minutes ago and said you had to be somewhere by 6.30.'

'Did he, now?'

'He asked for the treatment to end early. That's against our policy unless it's an urgent matter. I took the liberty of not disturbing you. I do hope that's OK, ma'am.'

My jaw dropped. The audacity of him! I tried not to show my seething contempt. I simply rolled my eyes and replied, 'He wanted me to go with him to get his *boots* fixed! I'd rather watch paint dry. Believe me, I am *so* glad you didn't interrupt my treatment.'

I said it in jest, hoping I'd elicit some sort of human reaction. I wanted her to humour me, I wanted her to roll her eyes, laugh and say, 'Tell me about it. *Men*, hey?' But she didn't. She looked startled by my blunt British humour and replied with a poker face, 'As you wish, ma'am.'

Suddenly, I felt like bursting into tears. What I desperately needed right then was a human connection, a friend, someone on my wavelength. Hiqlexic was at my side 24–7, yet I'd never felt lonelier. I craved the company of my friends and my normal life. I wanted to ski and fall over and laugh. I wanted to go for a drink at the end of the day and stumble back to my room at midnight singing – still in my ski boots. I wanted to eat with my fingers. I wanted someone to tell me something funny. I wanted to sleep undisturbed until past dawn. And I wanted my job back.

♥ ♥ ♥

Hiqlexic arrived back from the boot shop in good spirits. He had bought himself another hat, another pair of shades and some technically advanced sweat-absorbing inner soles for his boots. To my relief, he didn't seem to begrudge the fact that I hadn't accompanied him.

'What do you fancy eating tonight?' he asked.

'Anything, really. Maybe we should get the shuttle bus into town and just wander.'

'We need a plan,' he said, looking at me with disdain. I'd obviously made an outrageous suggestion.

'Dare to be adventurous.' I was deliberately provoking him, but he didn't have the emotional intelligence to pick up on my tone.

The differences in our characters manifested themselves at every opportunity, and my preference for spontaneity over planning was one of them. At the top of the ski lift, he would have to look at a map even if we knew which run we were doing. I preferred to ski blind and enjoy the surprise of where we ended up – even if it was a nursery slope. Between ski lifts, he would pick up his skis and spend several laborious minutes strapping them together methodically and arranging all his kit so he could carry it comfortably. I would simply gather up my skis, poles and gloves in a big bundle and attempt to carry it as far as I could before something dropped to the floor or I poked myself in the eye.

'Let's have a look at this guide to the town and decide,' he said finally. He simply could not do anything without at least some semblance of a plan. We settled in the end on a true American-style diner. The portions were piled high, the tables were red and white check. They served thick milkshakes, burgers and fries, mounds of chicken wings and corn on the cob, and the waitresses called the men 'sonny'.

Being in the US, we somehow got onto the subject of the sub-prime mortgage market and the number of 'foreclosures', as the Americans call repossessions. Hiqlexic became more and more opinionated. He said that anyone who had defaulted on their mortgage – and the same applied in the UK – was completely at fault and deserved to have their home taken away.

'That's a little harsh,' I suggested calmly. 'No one could predict the collapse of lending on the scale it happened. Particularly the types of people it affected. I don't expect many of them were well versed in economics. If a bank approves a loan and tells them it's within their means to afford the repayments, of course they'll believe that.'

'No. It shows they are thick.'

'What?'

'Anyone who accepts a 100 per cent loan is stupid. Common sense should tell them that if the value of the property drops even by a fraction they'll go into negative equity.'

'But we're talking about many uneducated people who haven't had the privileges that we have.'

'In this day and age, where information is rife, that's their own fault. These people, who are now being bailed out by the government because they were stupid enough to accept a high-interest loan they couldn't afford, are now costing me – the honest taxpayer – millions of pounds. I pay 40 per cent on virtually everything I earn, and now my taxes are having to subsidise imbeciles.'

I wasn't shocked by his opinion. It was a function of his total inability to understand anyone's perspective other than his own. I wasn't shocked, I was disgusted and I wanted to do battle with him. I wanted to wrestle him down so that I could ram a compassion pill down into his empty soul.

It was pointless, though. Each time I attempted to make a point, he knocked me down with a hard fact or a chunk of history. I had no hope of competing. He brought in the history of the benefits system to try to demonstrate how state bailouts have been ineffective in the past. He dropped the name of this Bill and that Act and the politicians who'd pushed for them.

'Do you think these people who defaulted on their loans should be put out onto the street?' I demanded.

'Yes, they should. I should not have to work 15-hour days to earn a wage to hand to the government so they can give it to people who are too lazy to earn a living.'

He was living up to his name – an enormous IQ and an ability to retain a dictionary's worth of information, but not even a dot on the emotional intelligence scale. His world was black and white.

I desperately disagreed with him, but I couldn't compete with his arguments. I told him we were debating a social and moral principle and that it was unfair of him to base his arguments on historical facts when he knew full well I couldn't produce reams of history off the top of my head to support my view.

'So you want me to give you a concession?' He screwed his face into a ferret-like frown and shrugged at me as if to say, 'Don't be so ridiculous.' 'Many of my friends say things like that, but if I consider someone an equal I won't insult them by making allowances. This is history. If you want to disagree with my point, then you should research your facts.'

As with so many arguments, anger stems not from what you are arguing about but from how you argue. Our disagreement was now less about our political viewpoints than how we were interacting personally. I felt like he was revelling in the satisfaction of putting me down. It suddenly dawned on me that this was why he was paying me to be his companion. It wasn't conversation and laughter and intimacy he was seeking; he wanted someone at his side on whom he could impress his intellectual mightiness.

As we walked to the shuttle bus, he piped up again, hammering home one of the same points he had made twenty minutes ago. I don't get angry very often, but in that particular moment every drop of bottled-up rage seemed to spill over. Every part of me was insulted on every level.

'Is this what you want?!' I exploded when we were on the bus. 'Is this why you've flown me out here? Is this what you want from me? Someone to put down and humiliate for your own intellectual satisfaction? Is that how you get your kicks?

Is that the "arrangement" we have?!' The other passengers turned to look, but I didn't care.

'You have absolutely no ability to connect with another human being on their level,' I continued. 'You have to create a hierarchy, with you always at the top. Is that why you say you can't connect with women?' I was so mad now, I was looking for raw nerves to singe. I didn't care about the consequences. I didn't care what the other passengers made of it, because in that moment I felt nothing but rage. I would have left him there and then. I would have ordered a taxi and gone straight to the airport and booked the next flight home, regardless of cost. I would have abandoned all my belongings, all my luggage, in the chalet. Because in that moment, nothing – absolutely nothing – was more valuable than my independence and getting away from feeling like I was nothing but a boost to his ego.

It was the first time in all my experiences of being paid for company that I had ever felt degraded. Hiqlexic didn't say anything. He just stared ahead.

He reminded me of every reason why I didn't want to be in a relationship. He was constantly trying to change me, reminding me of things I had said, and when, and why he thought those things were wrong. He was always suggesting I do things differently: 'Why do you always order fish not meat?' 'Why don't you hang your towel up?' 'Why are you reading this book and not that book?' 'Why are you putting yet more cream on your face?' (The altitude made the air very dry and I soaked my face in Decléor.) Hiqlexic was living confirmation of my deep-rooted fear that relationships are constrictive, claustrophobic and spirit-deflating. I vowed to myself that I would never, ever, ever, ever get into one again.

We walked back to the chalet in silence. I had no more rage left inside me, but I was breathless with emotion.

He held the door open for me and entered in his usual

slow, controlled manner. He put the keys down, hung up his coat and took his phone out of his pocket. Always the same bloody routine, I thought.

He walked over to the breakfast bar and leaned against it. 'There's something you need to know about me,' he said calmly.

'What?' I almost spat.

'I am not well liked in what I do. I demand minute attention to detail and I drive people crazy with small demands and making sure I am briefed on every aspect of my work. I don't have many friends, either, because I don't have good social skills. That's not what I pretend to be good at.' He paused. 'But that is why I am so good at what I do, and that is why I am where I am. When people realise that, they tend to like me. Everyone who has worked with me for a significant amount of time has stayed in touch and respects me enormously. The ones who don't understand the way I am are the ones who don't understand the way I work.'

'Perhaps if your success comes at the cost of your personal qualities, you should try to learn to adopt a personality that you can keep separate from your work,' I replied.

'I work 15-hour days and most weekends. It makes little difference to me what I am like outside of the office. If you knew more about me, you would know that is why I am one of the best at what I do.'

We left it there. I didn't abandon all my things and get a cab to the airport, and I didn't fly home early. But I did go to bed angry. And I did make a note to remember this if I was ever tempted to get into a relationship.

Chapter 25
Malaysia

♥ **February '09**

From Colorado, I went straight to Kuala Lumpur. I arrived in the middle of the night. Malaysian Sugar Daddy's driver was waiting in the arrivals hall with a big sign: 'Miss Helen'. Malaysian Sugar Daddy was still away in the jungle. He was due back the following morning. I was so glad. Not only did it mean I could hide my ski luggage, but it also meant I could sleep starfish with a bed to myself. I had endured 21 hours of flying, all the way from Denver via Frankfurt. Malaysian Sugar Daddy was under the impression I'd been on a 12-hour flight from London. His housekeeper waited up specially to greet me. She prepared some fruit, a jug of iced water and some herbal tea.

I slept so deeply. After six days of being woken up at dawn by a chirping, anally retentive Hiqlexic, it was bliss. I relished every inch of space, both physical and mental. I stretched out in the bed and when I woke in the morning I got out my laptop and, without getting out of bed, started writing my diary, eating the rest of the fruit and deliberately letting the juices drip everywhere just because there was no one there to tell me what to do.

I hadn't been there long when I heard the door. Malaysian Sugar Daddy had arrived back early. He had caught a night train from Kelantan. I could hear him creeping around. I emerged from the doorway of my room.

'Hi.'

He turned, looked at me and smiled. 'Your hair's shorter.'

'Yeah,' I smiled back. It was good to see him. I walked over and went to kiss him on the lips.

'Oh, we can't do that here,' he said, stepping back. 'My housekeeper and driver are here and they know my children.'

'Oops,' I said. It was a stark contrast from Hiqlexic, who would grab my hand at any moment he could.

We spent the first day doing nothing. I sat on the roof terrace greedily soaking up and breathing in sunshine. My skin hadn't seen a single ray since the end of summer, other than on the ski slopes, of course, and it doesn't count if the temperature is minus ten. Malaysian Sugar Daddy told me his staff were laughing at me. They couldn't understand why someone would deliberately position themselves in the sun when they spent all their time avoiding it.

We visited some historic shrines near to his home and walked and talked. He was easy company. He talked about his children. He hadn't seen them for several months, which upset him deeply.

The next three days passed in a similar way. We did nothing in particular but absorb each other's company, pottering, visiting the local market, finding somewhere different to go for lunch each day, dropping in to visit Malaysian Sugar Daddy's friends. He didn't seem at all worried about what they might think of him entertaining a blonde stranger for a week and then taking her to a tropical island for five days.

It was wonderful being with someone who was content to be quiet. He had an inner calm and a dreaminess about him.

We spent several hours each day sitting quietly in his huge lounge area, reading or tapping away on our laptops. Malaysian Sugar Daddy only needed to work during the rubber harvest season. So for ten months of the year he was a man who lunched and fielded the odd phone call in Malay.

Without Hiqlexic invading my every thought, I finally had time to digest the fact that I was unemployed. Now that I had a chance to think constructively about it, I was beginning to feel more positive. Finally, this is the kick I need to make me go freelance, I told myself. And it means I can make time for some print journalism as well as broadcast.

'You can stay here for as long as you like,' said Malaysian Sugar Daddy one day when I brought it up. 'You have your own room. You don't have to pay for anything.'

It was a kind gesture and I could tell he meant it as such, but I didn't even entertain the idea. I was already feeling guilty for being away and not having done anything about my unemployed status yet. 'As much as I would love to, I need to get back. I need to sort out some work.'

'What will you do?'

'I'll go freelance. I've wanted to do that for the last year, anyway. Longer.'

'I have two friends who are journalists. One is a network newsreader and the other an investigative reporter. I could organise a dinner party here one evening and you could meet them both. It could be useful for you.'

Malaysian Sugar Daddy did many helpful things like that. The more I got to know him, the more I learned how selfless he was.

After three days, we travelled to Penang Island, a beautiful place off the west coast of Peninsular Malaysia. The rainy season was just ending, so in a way my redundancy had been perfectly timed. He had several friends based there whom he wanted me to meet.

Malaysian Sugar Daddy's list of connections was getting more impressive by the day. Friends who had crept into conversation – in an unostentatious way – included a former general in the US army and a human-rights lawyer who had made his name fighting a case against the Indian government. This particular evening he introduced me to a prominent artist and his beautiful but stony-faced wife.

The artist had prints of his work all around his house. The originals, I presumed, he had sold. That was probably how he had afforded this place. His wooden house was the most impressive modern build I had ever been in. It was elevated several feet from the floor to keep it cool. From the outside, you could see the Portuguese influence. On the inside, it was Scandinavian in design with wooden floors, gaps in the stairs, huge rooms running into each other and no hallways. There was a swimming pool that ran half indoors and half outdoors and a master suite annexed from the rest of the house, with separate his 'n' hers walk-in wardrobes.

'Do you want some of this?' the artist asked, passing me a pipe filled with weed, which he and his wife were sharing.

'No, thanks.' That is one drug I've never enjoyed. All the dinner guests were passing around joints and pipes, but I stuck with my Scotch, the only alcohol he had.

In many Asian countries it is the custom to drink – and in their case smoke – as much as you can before eating. The meal is served at the end of the night and is the host's way of saying they want to bring the evening to an end but they will provide a meal to send you to sleep with. I was getting used to this now, but I had had a few evenings of being more drunk than I would have liked and feeling as if my stomach might eat itself.

The second night was a stark contrast. We met another set of his friends in a dark and dirty back-street bar in the centre of George Town, Penang Island's capital city. We sat on uncomfortable metal chairs on a dog-eared laminate floor around a dirty bar. The place served only beer, local liquor and Pringles. We met two of his friends – a novelist who was on his eighth book and his wife, who fostered homeless children on the island. Several months later, when I became a fully fledged freelancer, she became a valuable source for one of my stories.

The writer accompanied us back to the hotel at the end of the evening and his wife went home. He and Malaysian Sugar Daddy wanted to share a single-malt Scotch and a joint. Malaysian Sugar Daddy left me alone in the lobby bar with the writer while he went to the room to roll one. I asked him eagerly about his writing. He was living out my ambition. Over a Talisker, he told me all about his efforts to become a published writer, how it had threatened his marriage, how he had overcome rejection and how he had researched one of his books by joining a group of Tamil Tiger rebels in Sri Lanka.

For the remaining three days of our trip, we headed for the luxurious resorts and beautiful beaches in the north of the island. We stayed in an exquisite hotel, and I had never received better service. We couldn't sit still without someone coming to us offering water, a clean towel or a parasol.

'Don't worry, the sunshine's not going to go away,' Malaysian Sugar Daddy laughed when I nearly had a heart attack at the prospect of being shaded by a big umbrella.

'If you lived in a country that gets five days of sun a year, you would say no to one of those, too!'

We arranged the parasol so that it left him entirely in the shade and me entirely in the sun. I smiled because it was such a change from the inflexibility of Hiqlexic; Malaysian Sugar Daddy just accepted compromise. It was rare for us to be together for long stretches, anyway. Most of the time, we would dip in and out of each other's company. It meant I had plenty of time alone to read, write my diary, swim, use the gym and form my new career plan.

How amazing it is, I thought, that two people can make you feel and behave so differently. Hiqlexic made me uptight and irritable and I was constantly fighting for my space. I felt inadequate in his company, with him constantly lording his knowledge of world history and whatever else over me. Malaysian Sugar Daddy, on the other hand, fed my mind. He talked about philosophy and great writers and society and culture and what it means to be happy. For all the encyclopaedias that Hiqlexic had swallowed, he never once inspired me, sparked a positive emotion in me or made me laugh. I learned plenty of facts from him, but nothing about life itself.

Much of the time Malaysian Sugar Daddy and I spent together, he would be smoking a joint; I would occasionally have a drag to check whether I had changed and did like the effects after all (I hadn't and I didn't) and then we would lounge around and philosophise about relationships and the concept of prostitution. We were both fascinated by the subject and we liked to explore the idea of how closely linked our relationship was to the age-old profession.

'I've used escorts in the past,' he confessed. 'But it is very different. You spend two hours with them, it's expensive and you are left with an empty feeling afterwards. I want to be with someone I enjoy spending time with. Yes, someone I can have sex with, but someone who . . . I want us to be friends for years to come.'

'The danger with an arrangement, though, is you can never be sure of someone's motivation for being with you.'

'Would you have come here, if I hadn't offered to enter into an arrangement with you?'

It was a direct question and I wasn't expecting it. 'Yes,' I said, because I think I would have. I'd thought the same when

255

I'd visited Greg in New York. The Prada clothes had been a bonus, but I hadn't expected it. I had changed since then, though. I was less naive, two years older and less wide-eyed.

'I know that,' Malaysian Sugar Daddy replied. 'I am confident of that. So there is no danger of confusing your motivation,' he went on. 'If I choose to sell use of my body, I should be allowed to. If a woman chooses to sell use of her body, she should be allowed to. If a man is paying for that, it doesn't mean there can't be affection, too.'

'Why did you use escorts? Was it for sex or for affection?'

'I was not the typical customer. All the girls I met really liked me. They told me they saw a lot of arrogant men and they didn't normally meet people as respectful as I was.' He paused. 'All women are someone's daughter. They choose to do what they do and there is a person in there we have to respect.'

'Not all choose, though,' I said.

'That's a bullshit argument.' Again he emphasised the wrong syllable and again it made me smile.

'What about trafficking victims?'

'Of course, that happens. But it is far rarer than society wants us to believe. They use exaggerated statistics of the number of prostitutes who are forced into what they do to support their argument against it.'

'It doesn't mean that things like trafficking and sex slavery can be ignored.'

'No, but I am talking about something a world away. I am talking about the escort who is brought up in an affluent society and chooses to sell her body. Society should not reprimand her for that. I once met an escort who simply loved sex. She said to me, "I just have to have sex every day!"'

Malaysian Sugar Daddy was insistent on us trying some MDMA. A friend of his had given him a phone number for some dealer who sold it near to our resort. I didn't really want any. I'd decided that my drug-taking days were over. I'd banished them soon after banishing Munich Man. But because I'd done cocaine with Malaysian Sugar Daddy once, on his trip to London, he saw me as his naughty drug-experimentation partner. In fact, I'd introduced him to coke. He had never taken any until he met me. He said he wanted to try it and I happened to have some with me and that was it. Now he loved the stuff.

'I have never done MDMA before,' he told me excitedly after he'd made his call. 'It's only a short cab journey away.'

I groaned inwardly. I didn't want to give up an afternoon on the beach to sit in a non-air-conditioned, bumpy rickshaw to go and meet a dodgy local dealer to buy drugs I didn't even want. 'I'm trying not to do any drugs at the moment,' I said.

'If you don't want to, don't. If you change your mind later, that's OK, too. But I want to. You can stay here. I will get a cab and be back in one or two hours.'

Malaysian Sugar Daddy's attitude was very much live and let live. He didn't expect me to accompany him on every errand. And if I didn't want to join him in something he wanted to do, he wouldn't try to persuade me, but it wouldn't put him off his own plans, either. We were two independent minds and we seemed to be able to work in harmony without ever forcing the other to do anything. I was so grateful for that.

Later, after he had returned with his package, we sat on the balcony of our beach cottage overlooking the ocean and drank a bottle of absolutely awful sparkling wine. Malaysian Sugar Daddy sprinkled some of the MDMA powder into his glass and, despite my earlier attempt at willpower, I agreed to join him. It's no fun being sober with a high person, after all.

Again, our conversation turned to the morality of prostitution. Malaysian Sugar Daddy posed the question of whether all women are inherently prostitutes.

'I think most people only ever do anything if they can see some sort of reward,' I responded. 'People only stay in relationships because there's some gain to be had. Think of people in stale marriages or strained relationships. They stay because it still gives them something – financial stability or a secure home life.'

We went on and on, but we never once incorporated the topic of love into our theories. It just never crossed our minds. Yes, we agreed, all relationships are variations of 'arrangements' and isn't it ridiculous, then, that modern cultures still condemn prostitution? Malaysian Sugar Daddy said he thought that was a symptom of repression.

'If men and women were truly equal, prostitution would be legal,' he said. 'For ever, women have used sex for power. The one thing a man can't guarantee himself, no matter how powerful, wealthy or well connected he is, is consensual sex. Women hold back as a means of keeping authority – sometimes as punishment. And if some women choose to sell it, it takes power away from the others.'

At the hotel we were staying at, we had noticed another couple. He was over 50, fairly plump but by no means repulsive. She looked mid-20s and had beautiful, long, flowing black hair and the body of a dancer. We had commented on them before, speculating as to whether she was some sort of high-class escort. Now that I was on the periphery of this world myself, I had started to notice just how prevalent these types of scenes are.

Malaysian Sugar Daddy brought the couple into our debate. 'Would you spend the week with someone who you weren't necessarily attracted to, but who wasn't offensive, if he were to pay you, say, ten thousand pounds?'

'Don't know,' I answered. For me, attraction had been how I justified accepting store cards, cash and shopping trips.

'If I slept with someone I wasn't attracted to in some way, whether it was emotionally or physically, I think I'd feel compromised.'

'Why? If he wasn't offensive and the sex was pleasant? It is society's taboo ingrained in you that makes you think that.'

'The main thing stopping me would be what other people would think, rather than because I would feel bad about it,' I answered.

'Exactly. And I don't know why society disapproves so much. It has existed for years and years. It is like any job. In any job, we have to pretend to like people, to be nice to people we don't like, play politics. Sleeping with someone for an income is the same as any job. Yes, she will have good and bad experiences, but anyone can have a bad day at the office.'

He was almost making me feel like I wanted to try it. I thought for a brief moment that that would be an easier way of making money than having to spend four whole days at a time in a ski chalet with a man who drove me insane. But then, I had never considered that what I was doing was 'for money'. It was for adventure. Wasn't it?

I poured more of the awful sparkling wine. Malaysian Sugar Daddy was deep in thought. 'Once,' he continued, 'I hired one of the top escorts of Europe. I wanted to experience it. I saved for it. Later, I found out she was a superstar of the escort world. She was known as *the* whore of Europe. I booked her through one of the top agencies.'

'What was it called?' I interrupted. This sounded like a good story I could follow up at a later date now that I was a freelance journalist – was going to be one anyway, when I got back.

He told me the name and said, 'I asked if she could join me for one week. The woman on the phone said, "You do know that her daily rate is six thousand euros?" I didn't know that. But I said OK. This was not something I could really afford to do at the time. I was nervous. I told the hotel to give her a grand welcome at the airport. When she arrived, she said that she had received the most over-the-top welcome she had ever had. And this girl travelled around the world doing this all the time. They gave her flowers, they picked her up in a limousine, they offered her champagne in the car. She said she was expecting me to be some kind of star.'

'What was she like?' I probed.

'She was attractive. But I wouldn't say stunning. She was very tall, about six foot, and she insisted on wearing these huge heels, so she towered above me. She knew exactly how to charm men, she knew exactly how to sit. I asked her to take her make-up off because she was wearing too much. She hated that. She said no, but I said I wanted her to.'

'And did she?'

'Eventually. I asked her to, so she had to.'

'And what was she like as the week went on? Did you like her?'

He paused again, as if he wasn't sure. 'It was just an experience. I am glad I got the chance to do it. She was not someone I would see again. Not like you.'

He looked at me amorously and I could tell the MDMA was taking effect. 'When we had sex, she was completely all over me, arms, legs wrapped around me, slurping. I was taken aback. It was too much. She was thirsty for sex and I didn't know how to handle it.'

I felt that same mix of shock, excitement and curiosity that I had when I'd met Sports Man way back at the start of all this and he'd told me about the girl who'd asked him to 'sponsor' her – only now the level of taboo I was dancing around was much greater than it had been back then.

Malaysian Sugar Daddy grew more sentimental as the evening went on. He kept telling me how glad he was that I was there with him, how he felt I would be a lifelong friend. I was more controlled. I hadn't taken as much of the powder as him.

I too was starting to feel a deep affection for Malaysian Sugar Daddy, but it didn't translate into a sexual appetite for him. His mind and his insights made me wildly attracted to him but there was very little physical contact between us. He wasn't tactile, nor did I ever feel an overwhelming urge to be tactile with him. I was in love with his mind, not his body. When we did have sex, we lacked the affection of lovers. When we awoke in the morning, we were like polite strangers: 'Shall we go to breakfast?' 'Are you hungry now?' 'How did you sleep?' There was always a degree of formality between us, as if there were parts of us we still wanted to keep private.

At his home in Kuala Lumpur, we slept in separate rooms. The theoretical reason was that he had servants in the house and he didn't want them to know we were more than friends, but in truth we were both relieved to have that distance. He brought me tea in the morning and sat on my bed reading the paper, while I tapped away on my laptop. We often joked about how, if we ever became a couple, we would keep separate rooms. He said he couldn't stand the thought of sharing a bathroom with a woman. I said I slept better alone. It suited us, but, looking back, it was probably a sign that we were never destined to be lovers – just compatible acquaintances whose paths crossed for a brief period of our lives to bring us both a rich learning experience.

On my last evening before heading back to London, Malaysian Sugar Daddy handed me an envelope containing his side of our arrangement. He didn't say a word as he placed it in my hand. On the front, he'd written 'With love'. I opened it. It was full of fifty-pound notes.

I was drying my hair at the time. Some friends were coming

to dinner. I don't think it had anything to do with Malaysian Sugar Daddy wanting me to meet them. There were always people calling in unannounced. Bevies of his friends would arrive at his immaculate home with just a few minutes' notice, all expecting to be fed and entertained. It seemed to be a very *mi casa es tu casa* culture.

Malaysian Sugar Daddy's cook had put on a huge buffet of various curries and noodle dishes and laid it out at one end of his long lounge. We ate standing up and there was constant toing and froing to the buffet table. No one stayed still for long enough to have a conversation with anyone. That seemed to be the way it was all the time. They simply enjoyed being in each other's company and there didn't seem to be any need for conversation of any particular depth.

My flight was leaving early the next morning and I knew I had just a few hours left. I remember suddenly feeling a pang of love for Malaysian Sugar Daddy and a very slight sensation of tearfulness. I had enjoyed spending time with him more than I'd imagined I would. I loved hearing what he had to say. I would miss that. I was leaving tomorrow to fly halfway around the world, to face the reality of being jobless.

Could this really be me actually feeling attached to a man? A man who wasn't a fantasy, like The Boss. These were feelings for a man I could have. But then, I thought, no, you can't have him, stupid. Because he lives in Kuala Lumpur! Maybe I could stay? I could just not turn up for my flight in the morning. I could easily afford another ticket any time I wanted. Or maybe I didn't have to go back at all. I could live like a queen with my own bedroom, maid and driver. I could stay here and see sunshine every day and train to be a yoga teacher or something.

I took in the mix of Malay and English chatter around me and I knew that I didn't belong there. If we really did fall for each other, I couldn't stay. I'd hate it after a while. He couldn't move to the UK – he had his sons and his business. All these thoughts were going around in my head in a delirium, and every time I looked at Malaysian Sugar Daddy I felt my heart rise a centimetre nearer to my throat.

No, I had to fly back to London in the morning. I had a new career to start. And a lot of questions to answer about how I had just managed to afford a month away after being made redundant.

Chapter 26

My New Life

♥ **April to May '09**

When I got back from Malaysia, Hiqlexic insisted on seeing me as soon as possible.

I couldn't understand it. After the bickering on holiday and the shuttle bus outburst, surely he too felt that we were totally incompatible? Could he really be that desperate for female company? Or was it that his social skills were so poor that he actually thought that the tension and arguments between us were normal? When I did meet him, he held me tightly and repeated how much he'd missed me over and over. It baffled me. He was a good-looking guy. Surely he didn't need me as much as he thought he did?

Hiqlexic had started his new job and was working breathtakingly long hours. He would get up at 5.30 a.m. and would rarely be home before 10 p.m. He was a member of three different gyms – one near his flat, one next to his office and another in the City, where he often had meetings. He went twice daily. I continued to see him on a weekly or fortnightly basis, usually for a late dinner. We always went to a famously extravagant restaurant – Le Caprice, The Square,

Maze – but he treated the experience as though he were popping in to a takeaway on his way home from a long day, hurrying through a main course and a soft drink, constantly checking his BlackBerry and always keen to finish up and get home.

I too had thrown myself into my new line of work, becoming so engrossed in my new self-employed status that I didn't really distinguish between my personal life and my working life. Pursuing less TV and more print journalism, I felt for the first time in my life that I was doing what I really wanted to do.

When I'd trained to be a journalist it was because I'd wanted to chase exciting stories, find things that other people hadn't, and I'd wanted to write. I didn't want to sit with headphones on all day editing pictures. Branching out into TV journalism had been an unplanned change of direction. Now I wanted to get back on course again.

But getting into print journalism when I'd spent seven years on a video and radio desk was hard. Most freelancers, I learned, develop an area of expertise – something that interests them or of which they have particular experience or knowledge. I thought hard. Dating seemed a pretty good place to start.

I began by getting short articles on dating events into the smaller London papers, off the back of my dating documentary. That led to bigger pieces. Given my brushes with money and sex, and the philosophising I had done with men who had either paid for my company or admitted to paying regularly for other women's company, I was keen to explore the issues and arguments surrounding prostitution. So I started to write about the sex industry, with a positive slant wherever possible.

Malaysian Sugar Daddy knew all about what I did, but I didn't want to tell Hiqlexic or American Ad Man or any other new dates that I was trying to forge a career as a writer on dating trends and the sex industry. Nor did I want to tell my curious friends and colleagues the real reason why I'd chosen to specialise in the topic of sex. Nor could I tell the editors of the papers I pitched my stories to why I felt so well placed to write these pieces. It was quite a challenge to avoid such a huge area of conversation, especially considering how passionate I had become about my new career.

It could be very awkward, too. Take one of my earliest articles – for *The Guardian*, about a cookery class for singles. Obviously, Hiqlexic had no idea I had written it, because he had no idea that I was a journalist, let alone a journalist who was now writing about novel ways to date. It was early evening and we were heading for the Boxwood Café at the Berkeley Hotel at Hyde Park Corner, another high flyer in the gastronomic leagues. We were just outside when my phone rang. It was the editor of the section I had just submitted my copy to. She had some questions: 'In the copy, you say the duck was only in the pan for two minutes.'

'Yes.'

'That seems awfully short. Are you sure it was two minutes?'

'Duck cooks quickly, I think,' I said.

Hiqlexic looked over at me questioningly. I am not the sort of girl whose friends would call her for a cooking tip.

'You think or you know?'

'It was flamed for two minutes and then it went in the oven for four minutes.'

'It's just that I looked at a few other duck recipes and they were cooked much more slowly. You said it should it be brown when it comes out of the oven?'

'But this was a breast.'

Hiqlexic was standing virtually on top of me, giving me a
look that said, 'Is it really necessary to be talking about duck

breasts while I'm standing here in the cold?'

'Come on,' he mouthed. The footman was now within earshot, too.

'Breasts brown very easily,' I continued. 'It was definitely four minutes because the men were making lots of "quickie" jokes.'

'Just to check, in the photo are you the blonde in the black dress or the redhead in the black shirt?

'I'm the blonde in the black dress.'

The footman raised an eyebrow and Hiqlexic looked both bemused and impatient.

'And there's a bit of a discrepancy over the parsnips. You say parsnips, but we only have photos of turnips. Should we change the copy to turnips?'

'There were parsnips and turnips, so you can say both.'

'Was that really necessary?' Hiqlexic asked.

'Sorry, it was work,' I replied. He looked at me oddly. 'I'm editing a cookery video. About duck.'

'And turnips, presumably?' said Hiqlexic.

'Parsnips and turnips.'

Another time, I wrote a piece about SeekingArrangement. com for *The Times*. I divulged that I had used the site myself but stopped short of admitting that I had pocketed cash. The next day, I received a text from a guy I had dated more than a year before: 'I knew someone would write about it one day. It could only be you! LOL.'

I am probably not an organised enough person to manage a dual identity, however. I wrote a piece for the *Daily Mail* about men who travel to the Ukraine to pay for relationships. I had used the anonymous Hotmail account that I used for sugar daddy dating to contact a 'bridal agency' in Ukraine for the story. I needed to create a male alias, so I changed my Hotmail settings so that my sender name displayed as 'Simon Johnson', which seemed like a pretty generic fake man's name to use. Obviously, I forgot to change it back, so the next time American Ad Man was due for a visit to London, I left him confused. He got the confirmation for our meeting from a Simon Johnson, greeting him as 'sexy'. That was pretty hard to explain.

Instead of welcoming American Ad Man's visit, as I usually did, I was so enthralled with my new freelance projects that I saw our meeting more as a nuisance than a pleasure. I didn't spot it then, but that was another sign that my motivation for sugar daddy dating was beginning to shift from excitement, novelty and adventure to what I had always insisted would never spur me on – monetary gain.

American Ad Man was staying at the Sanderson, which has to be the most futuristic hotel I have ever been in. His room had been designed in an eclectic mix of French boutique and feng shui, with Japanese shoji screens partitioning different areas. The bed was right in the middle of the room, so you could walk all around it. When I first entered, I thought he just had a room with a bed and nothing else. I looked around for the bathroom or a sign of a wardrobe, but there didn't appear to be any. It reminded me of the hire-by-the-hour love hotels in Japan. Then I found other rooms opening off the main bedroom. A bathroom, a walk-in wardrobe and a small office were hidden behind cream curtains that ran all the way around the walls. You would never know the other rooms were there unless you went feeling your way around. I discovered I could walk from the wardrobe to the bathroom to the office via a little corridor lined with mirrors that ran around the perimeter of the room.

We went to Hakkasan that night, a bustling Asian fusion celebrity favourite in a basement on a tiny street just off Oxford Street. We were joined by one of his American friends and his German wife. Walking there, we brainstormed an explanation for how we knew each other. We came up with a few way-out versions before we remembered that we had both spent time in Japan. Our story was, we clarified one final time before entering the restaurant, that we had met in Japan while I was working as a tax consultant (like my friends, American Ad Man was amused by that part of my personal history). We would say his advertising agency was one of my firm's clients in Tokyo. It was a good job our alibi was based on our real-life backgrounds, because the friend's 40-something wife grilled me suspiciously and clearly viewed me with great disapproval.

I managed to knock a glass of wine over myself, too. I blame the waiter. He stood over our table for ages, going on and on about the dim sum platter being the house speciality and listing all the exciting things inside the dumplings: bamboo and yam beans, ostrich meat and Chinese chives. I was thinking, yes, I know, hurry up, shut up and just let me eat one. I leaned over to take one for my plate, giving him the hint to leave us be. In making my exaggerated gesture, I knocked my wine flying. Thankfully, it fell towards me, which meant the only things it drenched were my dress, my seat and my half plate of dim sum. Had it toppled in the other direction, it would have gone over the wife and that didn't bear thinking about. The waiter rushed for a cloth and stood over me for another five minutes fussing and checking I was OK.

When we got back to the hotel, American Ad Man ordered a bottle of Moët for the room. After the wine at dinner, we hardly touched it. I had become so much more careful about how much I drank since going freelance. I think I used to drink so much because I had no reason not to. It was another rebellious thing I did to escape the boredom and frustration of a job I felt overqualified to do. Now that I was working for myself, I cherished every moment of time and carefully preserved my mental energy. I hated not running at full capacity.

We lay on the bed. I was in my underwear and he started giving me another of his outstanding massages. If I were married to a man who was this good a masseur, I thought dreamily, I would never let him go.

American Ad Man brought up what sounded like his increasingly acrimonious marriage. Each time we met, I noticed he had become more bitter towards his wife. When we'd first met, he'd simply said they led separate lives. Now it seemed she had become the bane of his life.

'Take one piece of advice, sweetie: there is nothing like a woman who nags to drive a man to adultery.'

'You think?'

'All my colleagues would say the same. I would say around 70 per cent of my married colleagues are having affairs.'

'70 per cent?!'

'Easily. And I bet ya they all put it down to nagging.'

'I'll remember that. Not that I think I'll ever get married.'

He laughed heartily, in the way he always did. 'I like your attitude. Go on, what's your latest theory on marriage? I remember you always have a good one.'

'I'm fundamentally against the principle of marriage,' I declared. 'Because a marriage is a lifelong promise and any relationship that's held together by a vow alone can't be based on free will, which is totally the opposite of what love is supposed to be about in the first place. Don't you think?'

'Absolutely. My wife has got me cornered. I can't leave her – it's too expensive. And I can't get a girlfriend because then my wife would leave me and take me for every cent. I should have kept her as a girlfriend and given her all the money she wanted to keep up her lifestyle. It would have been way cheaper than marriage.'

'That's very cynical,' I observed. 'When I say I won't get married, I don't mean it in a bitter way; I just think it's a false basis for love. I think – I hope – relationships can last for ever.

But if it's destined to last and the two people want to be together, it will last. We shouldn't need some ridiculous vow based on a religion that none of us even follow to hold it together.'

'Or social pressure,' he added. 'Divorce still isn't a socially attractive thing to do.'

'It's hardly surprising, though. The idea that we can we make a promise today about how we'll feel in a year, two years or twenty years time is pretty unreasonable. We might have found a higher form of love by then, or we might want to change our lives or . . . I don't know, go and become a monk or something.'

'I like your attitude,' he laughed. 'Don't you want to get married one day, though? Don't you want to call up your girlfriends, all excited, and tell them you're getting married? I know girls back home think like that.'

'Absolutely not,' I replied in disgust. 'I can think of nothing worse than a situation where my most significant triumph is to be defined by someone else, to feel my whole purpose in life depends on being part of them. I want to be with someone because they captivate me or I'm in awe of them and I want to be with them, not because I need them to complete who I am. Getting married so you can show the world that you've "made it", or that you've "bagged a banker" or "bagged a lawyer"? Ugh, I'd despise myself!'

'You're pretty rare,' said American Ad Man. He leaned over the bed and wrapped his arms around me. I knew what he was going to say next. 'I like your attitude!' we chorused and he roared with laughter at my impression of him.

He rolled over playfully on top of me and kissed me. He slipped my bra strap off my shoulder and started kissing my breast and then my neck and my lips. He ran his hands slowly down my back to my pants, hooked his finger around them and gently slid them off. We wriggled around for ages before having sex.

American Ad Man seemed to enjoy the intimacy more than sex. In fact, we didn't actually have sex until our fourth meeting, even though we were always physical. He seemed to love massaging me more than anything else. That and talking about his marriage. He wasn't looking for answers to his problems; he just needed an impartial ear.

I could tell he wanted me to spend the night. I didn't want to stay. I lay on the bed, his knuckles kneading between my shoulder blades, listening to him talk about his wife, wondering how much time I should let pass before making my excuses and leaving. It wasn't that I didn't want to be with him; it was just that I wanted to be with me more, at home, in my own bed, and up early tomorrow going about my new life – my new freelance life, which I loved. I now had more exciting adventures than hotel liaisons with high-flying married men. The only hook attaching me to my sugar daddy dating world now was money.

'Ouuuuuch!' I yelped. He'd found my sciatic nerve again.

Chapter 27
Dropping Arrangements

♥ *May '09*

No sooner had American Ad Man left London than Malaysian Sugar Daddy arrived. He was visiting friends, he said, but he later confessed to me that part of the reason he came was to see me.

My mindset had changed since the last night in Kuala Lumpur at Malaysian Sugar Daddy's apartment, looking fondly over at him with a tear forming in my eye. My interests had moved on from the dreamy, idle philosophising we'd done on the beaches of Penang. I had been caught up in the romance of a foreign country and the emotional upheaval of being made redundant. Back on home ground, consumed by a thousand work-related projects and with a heart set on nothing but my new career, I no longer felt the same pull to him.

He was in the UK for four days and he wanted to stay *with me*! I wasn't used to that. Every time I'd spent the night with a man over the past two years (bar that unfortunate evening of the Rubber Ball with Munich Man), it had been either at the finest of hotels or in their plush apartments. I imagined having to put my laptop away at night and entertain. What would I do for food – cook?! What about friends I'd arranged to see? It's hard to coordinate diaries with married friends. I wasn't ready to have my everyday space occupied by a man whom I didn't consider a long-term part of my life. On an adventure in Malaysia, yes. Back in my own routine, no.

In a self-induced attack of claustrophobia, I said no. Then I felt guilty, so I phoned him back and said yes. He stayed one night. I hardly slept. He hardly slept. He snored. I huffed and puffed. We tossed and turned. I got up in the morning and moaned that I hadn't slept. He suggested going out for breakfast. I said no because I had work to do. At which point, he said, nicely, that he would stay in a hotel for the remainder of his trip. But he told me not to feel bad about it, saying, 'If you have work to do, that's OK. Let me know when you have some time and we can meet then.' I felt so guilty that I couldn't do any of the work I had to do after all.

I did spend one other night with him, but in his hotel, not at my flat again. Then, on his last day, I arranged to spend the afternoon with him before his evening flight. I had done an early-morning news shift at ITN. I was freelancing back at my old job. Yes, back where The Boss was. And, yes, I found that darn inexplicable crush was still as strong as it had been when I'd left the place. I finished at 3 p.m. and met Malaysian Sugar Daddy on the lawn at Lincoln's Inn Fields, behind Holborn. We sat in the blazing July sun and shared a Marks and Spencer's chicken salad.

He proceeded to tell me how he had met a girl from the site the previous night. I think he was trying to spark jealousy in me, but I didn't care.

'How was it?'

'It was a total disaster, actually.'

'Why?' I was only asking to make conversation. My mind was on my morning news shift, preparing my flat for

decorators and whether I had replied to Happily Married
Girlfriend's email inviting me to some scary-sounding Happily
Married barbecue afternoon.

Malaysian Sugar Daddy told me that his date had been
demanding. She'd wanted to know what sort of arrangement
they would have, how often she would see him, whether he
had kids, whether he was looking to settle down and all sorts
of stuff like that. 'She was not like you,' he concluded.

'Was she pretty?'

'Yes. She was 23.'

Nine years younger than me. 'If people want longevity and
a romantically ideal match, they shouldn't use sites like
SeekingArrangement.com. They should go to Match.com,' I
pointed out.

'I didn't want a committed relationship either when I first
joined. But then I met you. You are kind of addictive.'

I wished he wouldn't say things like that.

We walked back to the Tube, where we were to part
company. Suddenly, I felt sad. It was the same feeling I'd had
when I was leaving Malaysia. Malaysian Sugar Daddy had
this habit of suffocating me but then leaving me wanting
more of him when I couldn't have him.

I got a text from him from the plane: 'I have to shut this
thing off in a minute but I think we should seriously think
about a non-serious no-pressure relationship xo.'

Me: 'All good until the r-word.'

Him: 'Well, then, how about an "elationship?"'

Me: 'I will consider! Do "elationships" require you to help
me prepare my flat for decorators?'

Him: 'Yes! Have to shut this off for take-off now! Bye. With
love.'

♥ ♥ ♥

The invitation to return to Kuala Lumpur was always open.

In fact, more than that, it was expected that I would go back. Each time he called, Malaysian Sugar Daddy referred to my next trip. Because he was the one sugar daddy who did know my real profession and my new passion, he knew that I was constantly on the lookout for stories. He was quite entertained that I'd chosen to write about one of his favourite discussion points – prostitution.

'You can work from here,' he used to say. 'You can take all the time you like to write. You'll have someone to cook, to clean. You'll have your own room. Maybe I can help you find some stories here.'

'OK,' I agreed finally. 'I can come in July.'

'July will be unbearably hot. Come now and we can make it an open return date. You can stay for as long as you have time.'

I'd done some research of my own on stories I could follow up out there. If I went back to visit Malaysian Sugar Daddy, I could make a trip to Thailand and pursue a lead for a possible article. I now viewed every personal or professional activity as a potential feature. But I didn't expect or want Malaysian Sugar Daddy to fund that part of my trip. It was taken as a given that he would pay for me to reach Kuala Lumpur. But the Thailand leg of my trip was my personal research and I wanted to both fund and organise that myself.

In fact, by now we had become close enough for me to feel awkward receiving any kind of payment for our arrangement from him. He had given me a 'parting gift' when he'd last come to London, but the time we'd spent together hadn't followed anything like the pay-per-meeting pattern established when we'd first met. Now that I was going to visit him for a second time, neither of us was clear about the other's expectations. Certainly, for me, there wasn't a monetary goal in mind. I just wanted to see him, and see Malaysia again.

Thankfully, he brought it up himself on the phone one day: 'When I was in London I felt very awkward about, you know . . . the arrangement,' he ventured.

'Me too,' I agreed, and we discussed, awkwardly, how we both thought our friendship had progressed to the point where it seemed unnecessary for him to offer me cash to secure my company.

'I would like to see you under more natural circumstances,' I ended. 'It wouldn't feel right for me to accept a gift from you any more. I think we could both relax more, too, if we knew that we were in each other's company only because we wanted to be.'

I meant what I said. If our arrangement ended, he would know that my reasons for spending time with him were genuine, and I would be able to relax in the knowledge that there was no unwritten obligation for me to be on my best behaviour at all times. I think we both hoped the circumstances of how our friendship had formed would hurriedly fade from memory.

'However we met doesn't matter now,' he added. 'You have become a friend and I hope you will continue to be a friend for many years to come, whether we fuck or not. I don't care about money. If I wanted to see a friend and they couldn't afford to come to see me, I would always offer to pay for them. You are no different.'

Even though I was happy to be rid of the arrangement, I was glad because I viewed Malaysian Sugar Daddy as a potential lifelong friend, not because I saw him as a potential lifelong lover. I cared about him deeply and valued his friendship and the quality of his company, but I still kept our relationship at arm's length. I was soon to learn, however, that Malaysian Sugar Daddy read far more into the arrangement to end our arrangement than I did.

As promised, I headed to Kuala Lumpur for a second time

at the beginning of July. Despite there being no arrangement, I found Malaysian Sugar Daddy offered me far more valuable support than a financial agreement could ever have given me. He took an interest in what I wanted to do. He constantly suggested ideas for stories in Malaysia, fixed up another meeting with his reporter friend and offered to find a translator for me for my trip to Thailand in case I needed to interview local people.

As planned, he didn't accompany me to Thailand. When I set off from Kuala Lumpur, full of enthusiasm for the story I was about to research, I thought I would thrive on the time alone. Malaysian Sugar Daddy tried to persuade me to shorten the trip to just three days instead of six, telling me I would find it unbearably hot at this time of year and asking if I was sure I wouldn't get bored? I dismissed him, telling him I wanted to take at least three days out to recharge on a beach, that I love the heat and never get bored.

But when I was there, I missed him. I had never felt so bored in my life and I was so hot I spent most of the days lying flat out under a fan in my beach hut draped in a cold wet towel. I was in a grotty part of the country, unused to tourism, and before long I decided to change my flight and went back to Kuala Lumpur three days early, my tail between my sunburnt legs.

Chapter 28
Brussels

July to August '09

I will always remember American Ad Man as the first sugar daddy who paid me to spend the night with him. And I will always remember how respectful he was and how genuine our relationship seemed in the beginning. We were attracted to each other in the same way we would have been if we had met conventionally. I remember how awkward that first night was, both of us unaccustomed to handling or talking about cash in that context.

Our next meeting, though, just over a year after we'd met, served as my first real awakening to how dangerously addictive it can be to mix sex and money and how ephemeral the high proves to be.

American Ad Man was in Brussels for a week on business. He called me on the Wednesday. He suddenly had some free time on the Friday evening and wanted to know if I'd like to join him, at his expense, of course. I was working a freelance shift at ITN that Friday, from 6 a.m. until 3 p.m. I would need to dash off half an hour early to catch the Eurostar, arriving in Brussels at 7 p.m. and going straight to dinner. Of course, I said yes.

I went to the newsroom that day in one of my Prada dresses from Canadian Greg's New York shopping trip. This was an occasion when a designer dress was worth the price tag. What else would be classy enough for a day in an office yet sexy and glamorous enough to impress my paying date at a top Brussels restaurant later?

It was the black leather sleeveless dress, the one with panels of velvet down the front and back. It really was stunning. I also had on slender, ankle-hugging, over-the-knee, black leather boots and my red leather coat. As I walked out of the building on Gray's Inn Road, heading for the Eurostar terminal, I smelled deliciously of leather.

Typically, American Ad Man again wanted to mix meeting me with whatever other social occasion was on his calendar. He already had a dinner arranged with some colleagues. It was beyond me why he wanted my company enough to put me on a train to Brussels, pay me and then have to share me. We had to come up with another explanation as to why he, a married man, would be bringing a young British girl to a work dinner. We couldn't use the Japan alibi this time, since all tonight's colleagues had worked with him in Japan.

'You could be a family friend who happens to be on a working assignment in Brussels,' he said.

'A family friend with a British accent who happens to be working in Brussels and can't speak French?' I asked, but he dismissed my concerns, insisting it would all be fine and reminding me again that he liked my attitude.

I walked out of the Eurostar terminal in Brussels into a near storm. It was pouring with rain and I was sure that if I hadn't been wearing such weighty clothing I would have been swept off my feet by the wind. The queue for cabs folded round into at least four rows. All I could do was stand in line, my teeth chattering, and wait. I looked good, but I was not warm. I was late before I'd even got into a cab, and then everything that could possibly go wrong did go wrong: a burst water main held up the traffic at the station exit, a bus got stuck on a turn a few streets after that and there were roadworks two streets after that. All the time, the cab driver was speaking to me in full-speed Flemish. He simply refused to believe that I couldn't understand him.

I arrived at the restaurant forty-five minutes late to find a table of ten suited male bankers, two Americans, the rest Belgian. They were a rakishly attractive bunch and my heart fluttered as I sat down. I don't know if it was nerves or bewilderment at my own luck, securing the only female place in a smorgasbord of male power, intellect and testosterone. American Ad Man pulled a chair out for me and they all stood up, like his sailing buddies had when the wife had arrived at breakfast at the Lanesborough. Here, I seemed to be an equally respected figure.

I sat down, taking in the scent of cigar smoke and the gentle, elegant hum of Flemish. My pheromones must have gone into overdrive, because I became the centre of the table's attention. The men were deliciously genteel, asking me plenty of questions, taking an interest. They were so gracious, so different from the raucous bunch at the Lanesborough.

We were in a wonderful but quiet seafood restaurant. I sat against the wall so I could gaze at the other customers. I noticed how many middle-aged couples were in the restaurant and how engrossed they seemed in each other. In a typical upmarket London restaurant, there would be a mix of suited men, young couples and older men with younger women, possibly the occasional group. What struck me so much about the clientele of this Belgian eatery was how enamoured the men seemed to be with the women opposite them. Most couples looked in their mid-50s, yet each of the women had a certain unique beauty about her. They were slim and groomed but not over-the-top glamorous. They were quietly confident and contentedness seemed to spill from them. Most had one hand locked in her man's across the table and in the other a large glass of red wine, relishing it, looking in full control.

Whatever they were doing, they had their men captivated. I felt a pang of envy. Me, the commitment-phobe who thrived on independence and got satisfaction from the feeling that I could capture the short-term attention of many men at one time. Suddenly, I saw a deeper quality in these women than what I had. I couldn't put my finger on it, but it looked like they had the unconditional devotion of their partners. They did not look like new lovers, nor were there any of the flirtatious gestures you might associate with a forbidden encounter. It looked like what they had was genuine affection that had survived years. And these women seemed radiant with it. I couldn't take my eyes off them. It seemed to me that they had the type of relationship I imagined The Boss to have with his partner – fashionable, youthful couples in their 50s, with more wisdom than I could ever achieve at my age, quietly appreciating each other's company.

Suddenly, I wanted to be them – the women in the restaurant. I wanted to be someone's cherished partner, too, to reach for a hand across a dinner table simply because I wanted to and not just because it was the appropriate gesture. But what I had actually done was made myself the fun accessory – the designer girlfriend worthy of admiration but not love. And that was what I'd remain for as long as I kept putting a price on my company.

It was still dark when American Ad Man left for the airport in the morning. There was an envelope beside the bed: 'I still like your attitude! x.' Inside, a fan of euros.

I thumbed through them. The feel of them soothed the pain of the previous night's realisation. But they're euros, I sighed. Foreign currency doesn't quite give the same buzz as sterling, which sings with hair-trigger spending power. When I'd received euros from MissPenelope and The Sugar Daddy, I'd stuffed them in a safe place and waited for the exchange rate to go down. Of course, I never gave foreign currency rates another thought and found my cluster of 500-euro notes months later, screwed up in an elastic band underneath a casserole dish in a very high kitchen cupboard. Knowing me, I thought, I'll find this next batch in an equally surprising place months from now.

Having exchanged some of the contents of the envelope for a pink and grey snakeskin handbag and an Indian head massage at the hotel spa, I boarded a very empty Eurostar back to London. I stared out of the window and momentarily glanced down at my new bag. It looked garish in comparison with the old French farmhouses whizzing by the window, and for a minute I hated it for intruding on the purity of the scenery. The image of those Belgian men pouring out wine for their beautiful yet understated wives in the restaurant last night had stayed with me. Somehow, the designer handbag, the white envelope of cash peeping at me from inside it and the realisation that I was travelling back home alone made what should have been a pleasant memory painful.

I remembered the words of Date One from Sugardaddie. com when he had talked about young women being the 'ultimate trophy'. He had described how younger and older women fulfil different desires – the older woman being wise and powerful and captivating. I realised exactly which of those roles I had played the previous evening. Even though American Ad Man spent an increasing amount of time dwelling on his wife's faults, he was still with her – devoted, supportive, providing.

How did I get into this game of receiving cash for companionship? I wondered. I never actively looked for it. I just went looking for fun, didn't I, after my break-up? I wanted to satiate a thirsty sex drive and do something about my cheeky – though slightly ashamed – preference for older men. How did I get into the money bit? When I discovered that some of the men were willing to pay for what I was doing for enjoyment, I guess.

But, actually, maybe all this superficial sugar daddy dating wasn't really that much fun any more, now that I was in a different stage in my life. The trouble was, though, I was finding it hard to convince my subconscious that this model of pay-as-you-go affairs was anything other than the most logical way to approach relationships. It didn't seem to want me to venture into anything deeper. And so it seemed that every time I experienced a pang of sentimentality or a yearning for romance, it said, 'Cooee! Look at all these powerful men in suits flying around the world. They're not available but aren't they exciting! And look at that pink snakeskin handbag over there. Isn't it niiiiiice! Look at that dress! Imagine it with those shoes! Aren't you lucky you can afford another massage this week?! And look at all those fifty-pound notes!'

Chapter 29
Smothered

♥ **September '09**

Malaysian Sugar Daddy was phoning me more and more. His choice of expressions indicated that his idea of our so-called 'elationship' had gone far beyond my vision, which was of seeing each other a comfortable four times a year. 'You don't realise the impression you left on me from that trip,' he said once when we were reminiscing about our first holiday in Malaysia. Another day, another text: 'Even the pigeons are reminding me of you.' (I'd complained a lot about the pigeons waking me up in the morning with their scratching on the window ledge.) As the weeks went by, I went from feeling contentedly flattered to mildly frustrated and then downright agitated that every other day there was a text infringing on my increasingly precious time: 'Are you free to talk?' 'Text when you're free to talk.' 'Can I call in five minutes?'

Yet, despite all that, there was a consistent pattern whereby I'd pick up the phone in exasperation, with an abrupt warning of 'I can't talk for long!', but then he would instantly defuse me, either by making me laugh within the first minute of the conversation or by saying something meltingly loving or supportive of my new crazy-busy, draining freelance slog. Then it would come flooding back to me how funny, nice, caring, witty and selfless he really was. I would feel his warmth and my sense of being overwhelmed would be soothed. Then, five minutes after putting the phone down, I would go back to being busy and get annoyed by his over-attentiveness again.

One week, he phoned every day for four consecutive days. Somehow, he managed to time each attempt right in the middle of me rushing to a meeting, hammering out sentences to meet a deadline or being in the middle of a newsroom shift or on an evening out. I grew more frustrated. Surely he knew that if I hadn't phoned back, it meant I hadn't had the opportunity to phone back? Why give someone five missed calls when you know perfectly well that all modern mobiles register one, I thought furiously. Each day when I got home, I would have scores of emails to attend to, washing spilling out of my basket, an overgrown lawn to mow and probably a case study to interview for an article. I hadn't even spoken to Only Remaining Single Friend for three weeks. Phoning Malaysia was the last thing on my mind.

But when I did finally phone back – because I was driving down the M4 and had time to kill on the hands-free – I softened as soon as I heard his voice.

'Ah, it is the woman who is impossible to get hold of and even more impossible not to love,' he greeted me. How could I not smile back? It was such a beautiful thing to say. But it scared me, too, because it was further confirmation that he felt more for me than I did for him.

I tried to tell him, look, I just couldn't talk right now and I probably wouldn't be able to in an hour's time either, and tomorrow would be the same and he was making me feel guilty. He told me not to worry about him or feel obliged to call him back. He told me he accepted the way I was, my elusiveness, my brusque telephone manner and the fact that I was impossible to get a commitment out of. 'I don't want to tie you down. If you don't want to talk to me, just don't talk to me. Even when I come to London, if you don't have time to see me, just say you can't see me. You don't have to explain why.'

And so I was put at ease for another week. Until the texts started again. 'Do you have ten minutes to talk?' 'Can I call you now?' Then, a touch of sarcasm: 'Remember me?' Sometimes a niggling 'Any time for me?' or a guilt-inducing simple 'Hello'. They made me feel burdened at first and then downright resentful.

I thought maybe I should tell him that it was over. But how could I say that when there wasn't anything to be over? As far as I was aware, we'd never made a decision to be 'in a relationship'. And by no means did I want to cut him out of my life. He had a remarkable, enlightened mind and he was incredibly trustworthy and reliable. I didn't want to throw him away. I just wanted him to ease off.

I consulted the person I always consult in times of romantic dilemma: 'So, if I tell him I don't want to have a relationship, I'll hurt him, and he'll think that I no longer like him, or I've met someone else, and I don't want to make him feel like that, he's just getting over his divorce, but I've got to make him stop phoning me *every other day*!' I stressed to Only Remaining Single Friend over a Sunday roast in Highgate.

'You do need to say something, babe, because he's clearly stressing you out,' she advised. It was about the tenth time I'd mentioned it. 'Don't get frustrated and tell him he's phoning too much – he will be hurt by that. Be clever about it – massage his ego. He's a man. Tell him that you wish you had more time to speak to him, because you enjoy your chats, and you hope that you can make more time, but your work is really important to you right now.'

I beamed. This, I thought, is why Only Remaining Single Friend works in PR and wins awards for it. She knows just how to tell people to do what you want them to do, while at the same time making them feel good about themselves. I take the much more destructive approach of letting loose with whatever random thoughts come hurtling into my head, without pausing to think how it sounds from the outside.

So off I went and told Malaysian Sugar Daddy just what Only Remaining Single Friend told me to say. It worked. At first. For several days after our conversation, rather than the usual accusing 'You are never free!' tone, I got a lovely, 'That's OK. I know when you don't pick up it's because you're in the middle of something. And I just roll my eyes and think, "That's Helen." I don't want you to feel like you have an obligation to talk to me every day. I'm always happy to hear your voice whenever you have time.' He was so gentle and calm and understanding. There, you see, I soothed myself – a calm, frank approach led to a calm, grudge-free reaction. I shouldn't get frustrated with his telephone demands; I should stay cheerful, friendly and let him know that even though I'd like to speak every day, it's just not practical. I was at ease again.

Until, two weeks later, he told me – in a phone message, because I'd missed the call again – that he'd booked a flight to London. Was I free to meet him for dinner the night he arrived? If not, what about the night after? And then was I also free to accompany him to the south of France the following weekend, to a friend's party? I felt a surge of panic all over again. A whole weekend?! At such short notice?! I wasn't free the night he arrived. I had a family function in the countryside, way, way out of London.

'Well, if you want,' he said when I told him, 'I can arrive a day or two early and we can go together. I would like very much to meet your family, and if you feel more comfortable, you can introduce me as your friend, not your boyfriend.'

I was speechless. Was he joking? Surely! This was a big smack-in-the-face realisation that evidently there was a huuuuuge disparity in how we saw our relationship. How could I not have seen that Malaysian Sugar Daddy had come this far with his feelings? Since when, when . . . when did he start to think that we were ever anywhere near the category of boyfriend? Why . . . why would I ever have contemplated introducing him to anyone in any circle as my boyfriend? Because he was most definitely nothing of the sort. And, and . . . also . . . Introduce. Him. To. My. Family. What was he thinking?!

I had to think quickly. Oh my God, I thought, I don't even mention my dates to my family, let alone bring any of them to a family party. If I did, it would be the main topic of conversation until Christmas. What was I going to do?

♥ ♥ ♥

'You did what?!' gawped Equally Commitment-Phobic Male Friend as I sat white-faced on his patio, clutching a glass of rosé, having just divulged the chain of events leading up to my current crisis (except the bit about ever being involved in an arrangement).

'I told him that I wished I could speak to him more, but, right now, while work is really important, I don't have as much free time as him.'

'Oh, you idiot.'

'Why?'

'Because that's a clear signal for any man that you're really keen on him and to keep going.'

'Is it?'

'Of course it is! If you tell him you wish you could speak to him more, the guy's clearly going to think he's still in there and you feel the same way about him. And if he used the L-word, too . . .'

'He hasn't exactly used the L-word. He said he found me "addictive". He didn't say he loved me.'

'Oh, for fuck's sake. You should be seeing great big red warning lights flashing. "Beware: Man getting too attached." You've just gone and encouraged him more.'

'Oh,' I said, staring into my glass. I was wondering if rosé wine is supposed to have legs in the same way as white does, because this glass didn't have any. 'But I didn't want to hurt him and tell him that I don't have a slot for him in my day-to-day life. [Only Remaining Single Friend's name] told me to say that. It's a nicer way of telling him to back off.'

'You took dating advice off [Only Remaining Single Friend's name]?'

'Yeah.'

And then Equally Commitment-Phobic Male Friend laughed so hard into his pint of Hoegaarden that I thought he might choke. 'You'd better tell him fast that you don't want him to meet your family, because otherwise he'll be checking out wedding venues in Kuala Lumpur before you can say prawn laksa.'

'Oh my God. This is a disaster. I'll tell him it's close family only.'

'No! Tell him you don't want him there. Tell him you don't want to have a relationship. Tell him you don't feel the same as he does.'

I had Female Rejection Syndrome again – softening the blow with words of kindness that only serve to offer hope. Oh, yikes. I had to do it, didn't I? I had to tell Malaysian Sugar Daddy that he couldn't attend a family function with me in the country because . . . well . . . because I didn't feel that my affections warranted that sort of involvement. That's what I would say.

I ignored every single call from Malaysian Sugar Daddy that week.

I don't know exactly how I worded it, but I think it was a mixture of – in no particular order: it's a very small family affair; it will change the dynamics between us; I haven't even told them about you; it will throw up too many questions; I would feel bad if you had to stay in a hotel on your own; I just wouldn't be comfortable.

Malaysian Sugar Daddy got the gist, though, from the flurry of stilted excuses and didn't push the subject. But he still wanted to meet me for dinner the day he arrived. I went on an unplanned drinking session with Equally Commitment-Phobic Male Friend, so I postponed to the next day at the last minute.

Only, the next day, I was in Brighton on a film shoot for another mini-documentary I was working on. I had no idea what time I would finish and had no control over it. We had loose plans to meet at 7 p.m., but I said I would call to confirm during the day. However, I didn't get chance to phone. I was constantly with people and I had other calls and emails to attend to, too. OK, I could have managed a quick text to say 'speak soon running late', but I didn't. I suppose it was my subconscious defiantly letting him know that he was not my number one.

When I looked at my phone for the first time in two hours at 6 p.m., there were four missed calls and two text messages. The most recent: 'Helen, I'm just twiddling my thumbs. Please call me.' Instead of feeling remorseful – as I should have – I was infuriated. Four missed calls is just aggressive, I thought. He knows I'm on a film shoot. Does he expect me to hold my fucking phone when I'm on camera? I warned him that I had no control over what time the shoot would finish.

I gathered up my things – tripod included – and headed to the train station, from where I would go straight to meet him in central London. On principle, I didn't reply immediately.

I heard my phone ringing again as I was running to the

train, camera bags flapping everywhere. I called him back as soon as I'd slumped into a seat. 'You're only an hour and a half late,' he began. I think he was actually teasing, but because I felt hassled I was quick to demonstrate, in whatever way I could, that I did not belong to him and that he had no claim on my time.

'I couldn't get to my phone. You know that. When you called just now, I was running for a train and I had my hands full with three different bags. This is the first time I've had a chance to call you all day. So don't make snide comments like that, please.' I was surprised by how firm I sounded. It was the first time I'd ever raised my voice to Malaysian Sugar Daddy. In fact, it was the first time I'd raised my voice to anyone since entertaining passengers on the Aspen shuttle bus by accusing Hiqlexic very loudly of not being able to connect with other human beings.

Malaysian Sugar Daddy knew what to say to calm me down. He was very good at that. 'I know. It's OK. I was just worried something had come up and you might have had to cancel. Don't get stressed. I'm not angry. I just want to see you.'

No doubt my defensiveness was partly the product of guilt. Deep down, I knew that I could have at least sent a text. I was also aware of how I had unashamedly blown him out the night before – a form of cowardly procrastination on my part. What I was now doing was justifying my bad behaviour in my head. If I could find something to blame him for, it would make me feel less wrong.

Of course, I hadn't had a chance to rationalise all this before meeting him so when I did finally turn up I was still irritable.

Had it been a friend whom I'd kept hanging on all day, I would have been falling over myself with apologies. If it had been one of my dates who was compensating me for my time with an envelope of cash, I would never have let it happen. But, for some reason, I just couldn't bring myself to say sorry to Malaysian Sugar Daddy.

Because there was no longer an arrangement between us, and because I knew his feelings had developed more than mine, I couldn't help feeling like I was there on his terms. Is this what I've become, I thought, someone who only ever considers giving up my time for money? I might not have returned his romantic feelings, but I still valued him as a person. Yet the way I was treating him was far from what he deserved as a friend. I knew I was behaving unfairly, but I couldn't stop myself. It was my way of trying to push him away without having to actually come out and cruelly say, 'I don't feel the same for you.'

He was sitting at a table outside a pub in Holborn with a pint of his beloved real ale. 'Hi,' I said.

'I should have known that your "call you in ten minutes" means "call you in an hour",' he grinned.

His humour reminded me all over again why I enjoyed him so much. He was one of the most generous people I had ever known. I don't mean with money or material goods but with his energy, attention and time.

I smiled back and relaxed and we went on to have a wonderful evening. After dinner, he asked if I wanted to come back to where he was staying, at the Soho Hotel just a few streets away.

This is it, I thought. I have to say it now. Just like Equally Commitment-Phobic Male Friend told me. I still found Malaysian Sugar Daddy as attractive as I always had, but for some reason that wasn't translating into sexual energy as it usually would. It was as if my inner formula for attraction was demanding something else – it wanted something else in the mix . . . something like . . . more passion maybe?

'Well, I'm quite tired,' I heard myself say. Now I was even

angrier with myself. Why couldn't I just *say* it?

'That's OK. You can sleep.'

'Let's get a nightcap in the bar and see how we feel.' I *need* to tell him. I *will* tell him over a drink.

The Soho Hotel has a beautiful bespoke bar, with antique cabinets and mismatched period sofas. Malaysian Sugar Daddy ordered a single malt. I ordered a gin and tonic. He informed me that he had some cocaine in his room if I was feeling tired.

'I don't really want to do a line,' I said. I wished I'd never introduced him to the damn stuff.

'I wish you would let go a little when you're with me,' he said.

'I have important things to do tomorrow.'

'You party with your friends. I wish you would let your barriers down with me.'

'My barriers are up because . . . because I'm putting my barriers up to you! This is all too much. You're too much. I'm sorry . . . You're so loving, you're so affectionate, you're so nice to me, but you want too much from me! I can't give you that level of emotion back. And you're making me hate myself for it!' I blurted out.

Malaysian Sugar Daddy was silent.

'I'm sorry. I should have spoken to you about this earlier,' I added.

'Yes, you should,' he said quietly. And then, 'What are you scared of?'

'Being trapped.'

'But, Helen, you should know that out of all the men you meet I am the one who will allow you to be free. I don't want to possess you. I won't stop you from doing other things, and I don't mind if you have to cancel because you have to do something important with your work or your friends. And I won't stop you dating other people. I love you as a good friend. And I will do even if we stop having sex, or whatever. I just want you to enjoy the time we have together, without feeling obligated. I'm not putting pressure on you. You put this pressure on yourself.'

I put this pressure on myself? Maybe I did.

'I'm sorry,' I said. 'I was awful to you today. I just wanted you to stop crowding me.'

'When I tell you I want to speak to you, it's not to make you feel bad or guilty. It's because I want to hear your voice.'

For a minute, I felt myself relax. I felt my fears being allayed again. But then I stopped myself. I couldn't let myself get into that same frustrating cycle again. No, Equally Commitment-Phobic Male Friend had been right. Malaysian Sugar Daddy said all these things to put me at ease, but I was afraid he did so because he knew that was the only way to keep me. Actions always speak louder than words. I don't think he was ever as casual about our casual relationship as he made out. Maybe that theory of mine on relationships – that we'd all be happier if we kept it casual – only works when you've banned yourself from falling in love.

Malaysian Sugar Daddy may not have intended to trap me, may not have tried to possess me, may not have expected me to cancel things for him, but without even trying he had trapped me. That was because I didn't want to be with him. I didn't love him. I hadn't loved anyone during all my sugar daddy dating experiences.

So I told him. I told him that we could no longer have our 'elationship'.

I left him to go up to his hotel room alone and I walked alone back to Oxford Circus Tube. I was sad. Had I just thrown someone away – someone I nearly loved – just because he was getting too close? 'You put this pressure on yourself,' his voice whispered in my head.

Yes, maybe I did. In Malaysia, I'd loved that he allowed me

to do what I wanted and didn't crowd me. But then he'd been paying me, so I'd somehow felt that I'd have had no right to insist on my space even if I'd had to. Now that he was no longer paying me, I was fighting him. Without an arrangement, he wanted more of me.

As I walked, I remembered how I'd felt when I'd left Set-Up Date: relieved to be alone but somehow guilty that I hadn't given more of myself, guilty for feeling possessive about my time. Being paid for my time assuaged that guilt. Putting a price on my time had only reinforced my belief that personal space was so precious it wasn't to be shared. Terminating our arrangement had obviously given Malaysian Sugar Daddy the idea that I was so enamoured with him that I felt his company was reward enough for all the sacrifices that go with being with someone.

In fact, Hiqlexic put more pressure on me than Malaysian Sugar Daddy did, yet I could endure him. Our relationship was validated in a way that the one with Malaysian Sugar Daddy no longer was: it had a measurable benefit – money. I had yet to see what emotional closeness could bring me.

When I'd got off the Tube and was nearing home, I received a text. I dropped my bag fumbling for the phone, just like I had done when Set-Up Date had texted me in the winter months more than a year ago. 'Feeling melancholic and finishing all the coke.' I remembered the text Malaysian Sugar Daddy had sent me from the airport on his first trip, when I was in the gym. Then he had told me, 'I am drunk and feeling melancholic.' How sad that our 'elationship' had started and ended on such a similar note.

Chapter 30

A Chain and a Pendant

♥ **November '09**

What I was doing, when I look back at myself with wiser eyes, was incredibly dangerous. I was carving out a career as a writer about dating, relationships, the sex industry and prostitution, and at the same time I had a secret life in which I occasionally got paid by men to be their sexual companion/consort/date or whatever I was. It was risky, but in some ways it was a good combination. The money gave me the freedom to do what I really wanted to do, which was to write. And my experiences kept me fascinated with the subject matter. It wasn't all about prostitution. I wrote pieces on sex parties, the merits of older men (*loads* to say about that!), sex and disability, the boom in the online sex industry, the Japanese sex industry. I felt more qualified than any other journalist to write about those things – though I never revealed the depth of my own experiences.

I lived out my two careers in perilous parallel. I would log on to the site every couple of days to check for messages, just as I would routinely scan different news websites for story ideas. By now, I was looking at each message as potential business. How far I had drifted from my original innocent objective of a few exciting dates in fancy cocktail bars with sophisticated older gentlemen.

It was also feeding my cynicism about real relationships. As was apparent from Malaysian Sugar Daddy's last visit, I was starting to view every private encounter with the opposite sex as a duty that deserved payment. I did go on a couple of conventional dates, but . . . take the frustration I'd felt about my meeting with Set-Up Date, multiply that by ten, then square it. It was like going back to school after studying for a doctorate. After I'd experienced the assertiveness of Hiqlexic's holiday booking style, the grand tastes of American Ad Man, the rich mind of Malaysian Sugar Daddy and the full-on pace of Munich Man on a bender, even the logistics of setting up a normal date were a turn-off: 'Where shall we go? What do you fancy? Shall we stay in? Shall we go out?' I had no patience for it. I had grown used to an older, self-assured man taking the lead – and never worrying about the cost.

I hadn't wanted a long-term, conventional relationship before I set out on sugar daddy dating, but now the idea was so remote it wasn't even in the same hemisphere. In my mind, that kind of relationship was an emotional handicap that would suck me dry of inspiration and mould me into someone I wasn't. I had so much freedom now, working for myself and dating multiple men, none of whom asked questions and all of whom paid me. I had all the validation I needed. I didn't need love.

This feeling was compounded by the deflated attitudes to romance I was exposed to. Many of my dates, like American Ad Man, had given up on the idea of passion as a lasting concept. Others, like Malaysian Sugar Daddy, were still smarting after being rejected by a spouse they had believed would love them for ever.

Actually, I was living not a double life but a quadruple one.

I was lying to so many people in the different pockets of my life that I was finding it hard to know who was the real me. I was lying to the men from SeekingArrangement.com about what I did for a living. I was lying (well, not lying – just being economical with the truth) to the editors of newspapers about exactly how close I was to the topics I wrote about.

I lied on 'real' dates when the guys asked about my relationship history. 'No, I haven't been in a relationship for three years,' I'd say. They probably thought I was either desperate, asexual or a closet lesbian. I was lying to friends and colleagues, too, because people thought I was more successful than I was because I always had plenty of money. I was going on holiday every other month and I had a new pair of shoes every time they saw me. But even though I had a degree of financial security, I still felt insecure about my future. I couldn't date sugar daddies for ever – and when I stopped, how would I subsidise my career then? I couldn't talk about any of these concerns with anyone either. You can't sit at a bar in Louboutins and a Gucci dress and moan to a friend that you're worried about your income.

Worst of all, I lied to my family. At the party that Malaysian Sugar Daddy had wanted to come to, I wore Prada but told them it was Zara. If they thought I was buying designer clothes, they'd assume I had massive credit card debts. Everyone knows that most freelance journalists can't pay for Prada, no matter how busy they get.

I couldn't face friends, because there was so much confusion in my head about what I could or couldn't say and who I'd told about what date and where I'd said I'd met him and how much I'd divulged about my choice of Internet dating site.

So I retreated to my own company and concentrated on my work. When that got boring, I would go onto SeekingArrangement.com and fix up a date as entertainment, thriving on the anonymity of an encounter with an intellectually interesting stranger.

And that was how I met Richard.

A chain of events seemed to have been conspiring to get me to give up dating for money. The first was the speck of envy I'd felt towards the wife at breakfast with American Ad Man, the woman who'd tamed the unruly men with her sheer presence; then there were the romantic couples in the Brussels restaurant; the coldness from the men in my life when I'd been made redundant; the jolting realisation, provoked by Malaysian Sugar Daddy, of how scared I had become of any sort of emotional attachment; my lack of interest in having emotionless sex for the sake of it now that I had more fulfilling things in my life to satisfy my sense of adventure; and, recently, my increasing anxiety now that my legitimate and illegitimate worlds were drifting so close they were almost brushing against each other. Richard was the big sparkling pendant at the end of that chain.

He was visiting London from Los Angeles for an antiques auction at Sotheby's. He was staying at the Dorchester on Park Lane – my second favourite hotel after Claridge's. The ground floor is a huge open area. The reception turns into a long, narrow lounge, furnished with comfortable sofas, golden pillars, chandeliers and exotic plants. At the end of that is a decadent piano bar. When I knocked on Richard's door, I was half worried he might not be there. We had arranged the date the night before, through the site. I had no email or phone number and hadn't received a confirmation message that day.

He opened the door. 'Helen, right? Oh, I'm so glad. I was worried you wouldn't come. I tried to confirm earlier, but I couldn't access the website on the hotel's computer because my password's stored in my laptop, which is at home.'

He was 42 and looked like a younger Tom Cruise. My first thought was, what does a guy like you need to do this for? You must be married.

He took my coat – my full-length black sheepskin – and invited me to sit in the lounge area at the back of the room by the window. It was lined with real leather sofas. A side table was loaded with bottles of nearly every type of single malt available. Through some sliding doors was an equally spacious bedroom, dimly lit with green-tinted spotlights. There was a plate of Medjool dates on the table by the bed.

'How long have you been doing this?' he asked as he sat down opposite me.

'This? As in the site?' I asked. Blimey. That was quite an opener. 'Maybe a year.'

'A year?'

'Ish.'

The awkwardness reminded me very much of the first time I'd met American Ad Man, only this time it was me who was being the guarded one (and drastically underestimating the length of time I'd been using the site for).

'Tell me, what made you join? I imagine you have guys coming up to you all the time.'

'Not really,' I answered. 'Well, sometimes, I guess, but I'm not really interested in dating with the goal of a relationship. I just wanted fun when I joined. And I've always preferred older guys. So this seemed a good way to date.'

'I'm interested,' he continued, 'in what you think when you meet me like this. Did you come here thinking there was definitely a payment on the cards for tonight? When I contacted you, did you think you'd definitely sleep with me? I'm curious to know what goes though your mind when you agree to a date on a site like that. Tell me.'

I was squirming, but I liked him for being bold and interested. 'No. I didn't have any expectations. I wanted to have a date for the fun of it. If we like each other and it materialises into an arrangement, then great. If not, then we haven't lost anything. I think some girls do have a set agenda, but they should probably be on a different type of site, if you know what I mean.'

'What's the deal tonight, then? What would make you happy?'

'What would make me happy?'

'Yeah. Should we go for dinner? Should we stay here and get room service? Do you require payment for your company for dinner?'

'That depends where the evening goes, and how we feel we may want to carry it on.' He must have known full well that I wouldn't have the audacity to give a direct answer to that sort of question so early on in the evening. Was he testing me?

'I haven't done this before,' he replied. 'Not like this, anyway. I have a bit of a problem with paying someone for their time. So I'm just curious as to how you feel about this and why you agreed to meet me this evening. I don't mind if you say it's for money. But I just want to be clear, so no one's fooled here. Does that make sense?'

It did make sense. But only after he'd said that. Now it was clear that all his questions were about protecting himself. He was worried he would feel compromised by parting with money for someone's company.

'I'm just looking for an enjoyable evening and enlightening company,' I told him, intending to put him at ease. 'Anything extra is a bonus, not an expectation.'

'So.' He paused. 'If you've done this for a year, how many times has an evening like this turned into a payment?'

'I'm not telling you.' He was asking too many questions. I suddenly thought, in a jolt of paranoia, that maybe *he* was a journalist! Maybe he was covertly gathering psychological profiles on the types who dabble in this lifestyle! 'Very rarely as a one-off date. It usually happens with people I've formed some sort of regular relationship with.'

'Here's the deal, then,' he said. 'I like you. You're an

interesting and beautiful girl. I don't mind giving you something to come to dinner with me tonight. Money to me is . . . whatever . . . I don't have to think about it. But . . .'

'Yes?'

'But the deal is there is no deal. You can leave whenever you like. I can leave whenever I want. You have no obligation to ever see me again. So how much do you want?'

'For what? For the night?!'

'There are no conditions, remember. You're free to leave at any point. We can spend the weekend together or we can spend the next hour together. I am asking what would be a reasonable amount for me to ask you to spend an open amount of time with me?'

He had trapped me. He was staying in full control of the situation while not taking on the burden of naming a figure. He was cleverly protecting himself from the bruise to the ego associated with paying for a girl's company. He was a lot smarter than anyone else I had dated from the site.

'I'm sure you already had a figure in your head that you were willing to part with before you even met me,' I said. 'Let's save both our dignities and leave out the negotiation.' I had nothing to lose. I still wanted to go for dinner with him.

I was right. He already had a pre-stuffed envelope of cash. Being a first-timer, he'd wanted to test to see if the amount he'd settled on was unnecessarily high.

Over dinner – at the Ledbury, a two Michelin star restaurant in Notting Hill – Richard seemed to be making an attempt to map the DNA of my personality. He wanted to know everything about me – not just obvious things like my background, but what made me tick on all levels.

I didn't try to stop him. I wasn't worried about the opinion he would form. My only guardedness stemmed from the fact that I couldn't tell him I was a journalist who wrote about the sex industry. So when he asked questions like, 'Where do you want to be in five years' time?' or, 'What is your real ambition?' I had to make up something bland like, 'To be successful in my career,' rather than saying, 'I want to write, and I want to become the journalist that I set out to be five years ago.'

He would say things like, 'You're so poised all the time. It's very elegant and sexy, but I keep watching for flashes of the real Helen to come through.'

'Nothing that I am doing is forced,' I replied. 'That poise is the natural me. It's a symptom of being reserved.'

He questioned me endlessly on why I didn't want to be in a long-term relationship. I went over the same ground as I had with so many people.

'Everything you say,' he said towards the end of the evening, 'is so rational. There is not one thing you have said all evening with which I disagree or which I can question from a logical point of view. But you know what I think?'

'What?'

'I think you view the world too logically. I think you tuck away your emotions as protection and base all your judgements about the world on reason alone. Imagine yourself on a map of time. If you alter your viewpoint by two degrees, that small movement can have a huge effect on your position twenty years from now.'

'Which way do you suggest I move?'

'Keep your views but soften them. Be open to someone entering your life. I detect that you're someone who is very malleable to your surroundings. You probably adapt very easily to diverse situations.'

You can say that again, I thought. Business meeting with a charity to discuss some research for a story at 4 p.m., date with a view to payment at 7 p.m. Trudging to a press event with a camera kit last week, discussing news agendas in ITN's boardroom the week before, taking MDMA on a beach with a Malaysian lover a few weeks before that . . .

'But I wonder who you are in your natural habitat?' he concluded.

I paused to digest the question. I didn't know. 'I feel like I'm getting a personalised therapy session this evening,' I smiled. 'I take it all on board, by the way.' That last sentence was the understatement of the year.

'I do think I have come into your life for a reason,' he agreed.

'Don't most people usually tell other people they've come into their own life for a reason? But you think that *you've* come into *my* life for a reason,' I quipped. I was hoping to relieve the intensity of the conversation.

'I've had lots of good fortune. Sometimes we need to give things back. There are two things – important things – that you should take away from our evening tonight.'

I tried to focus. I was at that second-bottle-of-wine point where you start to lose concentration on what the other person is saying.

'You need to be kind and gentle on yourself, and you need to open up your heart to the possibility of love.'

'I am open to love,' I protested. 'Just not in the be-all-and-end-all format that most people look for.'

'Just try those two things.'

He got the bill and we climbed into a taxi. We didn't know where we were going. Was I to go back to the Dorchester with him? We stroked hands in the taxi and it felt natural to rest my wine-drowsy head on his shoulder, something I usually consider far too intimate for a first-time meeting. But when we arrived at the hotel, I stayed in the taxi. He had asked such personal things and read me so well that I couldn't go back to his room.

'You find it easier to have sex with someone who doesn't know you than someone who does, don't you?' he said.

'I think maybe I do,' I replied.

The doorman opened the taxi door, but still we didn't

move. I couldn't get out and go upstairs with him.

'We might never see each other again. How weird is that?' he said.

'I know,' I replied. I desperately wanted to see him again but the idea was preposterous. He was a Tom Cruise lookalike billionaire, 42 years old, with no ex-wife and no kids. He was probably the most sought after bachelor in cosmetically enhanced California. And, exactly – he lived in Los Angeles. He was unavailable. Plus, he knew that I had dated men for money and he didn't even know that I had a half-decent career. Why would he pick me?

'Do you want to come to the antiques viewing in the morning?'

'At 10 a.m.?'

'Yes. At Sotheby's. It's a private viewing, so you can't be late.'

It was now 1.30 a.m., and I knew that a 10 a.m. start on a Saturday was usually out of the question for me.

'Give me your number and I can text when I wake up,' I said, thinking that gave me the option to 'oversleep' and reschedule for lunch.

'If you're definitely going to be there, you don't need my number, do you?' he said.

'Oh, whatever,' I said, thinking that that was a clear sign he didn't want to meet again.

He held my face firmly. 'No, I want you to come. But the question is whether you can make a commitment now for the unknown tomorrow. You should open your heart, remember.' He looked me directly in the eye, pecked me affectionately on the cheek and climbed out of the cab, the footman following him with an umbrella to the canopy over the door of the Dorchester.

♥ ♥ ♥

What am I doing?! I thought, clutching a double-shot Starbucks soya latte on the Tube at 9.45 the next morning. What am I doing and who am I?

I had slept awfully. I had deliberately not set my alarm because I wanted to leave it to fate to decide whether I woke early enough to make the 10 a.m. meeting. If not, I had no way of contacting Richard. I had no email, no phone number and he couldn't access the site while he was in the UK. I kept waking myself up through the night, dreaming that I was late.

Eventually, at 8 a.m., I succumbed to the fact that my mind was not going to switch off and allow me to sleep, despite the meagre four hours of wine-induced slumber I'd had. I wanted more of what I'd sampled last night: that fondness I'd felt from him, how intriguing he was. His words. His warmth. Romantic attraction. I know myself well enough to judge that I am more likely to regret what I don't do than what I do. So I got up.

I didn't get there until ten past. He's bound to not be here, I thought. I wasn't even hurrying to the entrance of the auction house. Part of me almost wanted him not to be there – it would have made things simpler. But he was. 'I thought I might have missed you,' I said.

'But you're always late,' he replied without hesitation.

'I forgot I'd told you that.'

'You didn't. I can just tell.'

The private viewing at Sotheby's was an experience I will never forget. The huge galleries were empty. It felt like the echo of our footsteps on the marble floors could be heard around the world. We were guided into a small room and seated underneath a Picasso, which was being prepared for auction with a guide price of £7 million. I stared up at it nervously. Imagine if I knocked that off the wall!

We were offered champagne, which, still delicate from the

night before, we both immediately declined. A suited curator with half-moon spectacles on a chain around his neck guided us through the brochure. He talked directly to Richard, referring to me only as 'your wife'.

After that, we went for lunch at the Wolseley, situated in a Grade II listed building on Piccadilly, and then on to another antiques fair. Richard had arranged to meet his regular antiques dealer at his stall. He was tall and skinny, dressed in tweed and had frizzy hair. He called everyone by name at least twice in every sentence and reiterated every phrase. He talked as quickly and in as incomprehensibly posh a voice as Munich Man. Richard expressed an interest in two rococo tables.

'Richard, this is not unlike the Meissonier you already have, Richard. Not unlike your Meissonier at all, Richard. And this can be repolished, Richard, to the same colour as your Meissonier. It can be repolished quite easily, Richard.'

'Can you negotiate a good deal on that?'

'It's a good price for a table like that, Richard. Tables like that, Richard, are very rare. Very rare. That price is on export. It's a good price, Richard. It's a fantastic table, fantastic.'

Instead of being annoying, his eccentricity was charming. He stood about two centimetres away from us, but somehow it didn't feel intrusive. He was very likeable, even though he didn't shut up.

We stood with him for 40 minutes, talking about the viewing we'd been to that morning and going through the catalogue, and then he fast-paced us around the fair, introducing us to those colleagues he considered fair dealers. I don't know why I was there. Usually, I considered my free time precious, yet I was choosing to spend it at a stuffy antiques fair with a man who wasn't even paying me for my time and whom I might very well never see again. Richard bought two rococo tables – £190,000 for the pair. He paid by debit card. It took ages to get the customs paperwork sorted for their export to the US. By the time we came out, it was 5 p.m.

I felt like I was just hanging out for the day, with no purpose. We were both delicate from our alcoholic indulgences last night. Dinner and wine were out of the question. I wanted to rest, but I didn't want to part company with Richard. What do you do when you're too hung-over for anything energetic and you're with a near stranger?

'We've created an odd sexual dynamic between us, haven't we?' I mused. We had gone back to his hotel and were drinking peppermint tea and eating fresh jumbo olives in the Dorchester's long, open-plan piano bar.

'What do you mean?'

'Because of the depth of connection we've created so quickly, we've gone beyond that initial sexual electricity. Because of how we met and because of the awkward negotiation, I feel I can't have sex with you now. I want to, physically. But it would somehow nullify everything we've built up. To have sex with you now, right at the end of two days in each other's company, knowing it would just be a fleeting encounter, would feel like I was sleeping with you to fulfil that obligation . . .'

'Yeah, I get it,' he affirmed. I didn't need to explain. We were both well aware of the dynamics. 'If we knew each other better, these would be the kind of idle moments when we could get out a book or watch a film.'

'I guess so,' I agreed. 'It's a good gauge of how comfortable you are with someone when you feel it's OK not to have to expend energy in being entertaining or lively or talkative, isn't it?'

'Do you always feel like you have to be engaging in people's company?'

'Mmm. Maybe I do.'

'Isn't there anyone you're comfortable enough with to totally let go and be at your worst?'

I thought about this and there wasn't. Friends? Some, maybe. But, with friends, you get to go home at the end of the day, switch off the social persona. 'You put this pressure on yourself.' I heard Malaysian Sugar Daddy's words in my head again.

And that was when it all clicked into place. Somehow, somewhere in my sugar daddy experiences, I had created a link between spending time with my dates and having to be alert, on guard, entertaining, on my best behaviour. No wonder I was afraid of them intruding into my intimate world. I could only relax alone. These men had validated the quality of my company with Prada, lingerie, first-class airline tickets, expensive restaurants and hard cash. So I felt I had to be at my best at all times. I could no longer remember what it was like to be appreciated unconditionally, or loved that way.

I'd deliberately chosen to forget about love. I had dismissed it as a useless emotion that got in the way of fun and glamour and exciting hotel liaisons – and extra income.

'Are you OK?'

'Excuse me for two minutes.'

I tried to calmly glide to the Ladies. I could feel tears welling up behind my eyes. It was like someone had lifted a veil. I stood in front of the mirror and splashed water on my hot cheeks and neck. 'You find it easier to sleep with someone you're not emotionally attached to, don't you?' That was what Richard had asked me last night. He was right. I had developed a complete and utter phobia of losing my autonomy. I thought a real relationship could only intrude on the sanctuary of my solitude. But, of course, I would do, wouldn't I? Over the last three years I'd spent nights and weekends with men I didn't truly feel passion for. I was attracted to them, yes. But was I really driven to spend time with them, really desperate to get to know them, feeling my heart flutter when they entered the room? No.

I'd only felt real passion about relationships that weren't real: The Boss, whom I knew I couldn't have; and Malaysian Sugar Daddy, who lived in another country. Even then, when I realised that I could have him, I ran a million miles. With fantasy relationships going on in my head with people who were safely out of reach, I could survive very well as a long-term singleton.

It had seemed logical for me to be rewarded for the investment of my time not with love but with gifts and cash. But how pricey those luxuries seemed now that I could see the poisoned attitude they had left in their wake. What happened to that 29-year-old girl who guiltily googled 'younger women, older men, dating', full of wide-eyed fascination about what lay ahead?

She had been starting out on a harmless quest for some temporary rebound fun. She wanted to play the single girl about town for a while. But she'd fed a little seed of commitment-phobia with designer goods and a champagne lifestyle and now it had grown into a great big giant poisonous beanstalk.

I didn't know how long I'd been at the marble sink. I walked back up the stairs to the piano bar.

'Sorry, I'm really feeling the effects of last night's wine,' I lied.

'I don't need an excuse,' he said. 'You're free to go anywhere you like. Remember?'

I smiled. He really did seem to be able to read my mind. God, I hoped he couldn't tell that all that lot had just been going through it.

'What if we have a rule – a no-speaking rule? Would you join me to watch a movie in the room? If we don't speak, we have to relax.'

'I know what will happen, or what we'll be tempted to do,' I said, meaning that if he thought this was his chance to get me into bed, then he could forget it. My emotions were red raw, like fresh blisters.

'There's absolutely no question of that. I won't allow it to happen. I don't want it to happen. Let's try it. You can leave at any time. I won't be offended. And they have a great room-service menu.'

I didn't want to leave him, but I had that urge to run away again, especially given the whirlwind of thoughts thundering through my head. I felt I needed to be alone to deal with them. But then, by being alone, wouldn't I again be feeding my fear of intrusion? I felt overwhelmingly drawn to Richard. He found my vulnerabilities and I wanted him to do more, to bring it all out, like an exorcist. I wanted my muddled emotions out in front of me so I could sort through them. I wanted to examine each piece of rubble created by the popping of this bubble I'd been in for three years.

I agreed to go to his room. We put on an old Audrey Hepburn movie and lay on the bed fully clothed, nestled up against each other. Neither of us watched the film. Richard fell asleep and I lay there pulling apart layers and layers of thoughts. I woke him at the end of the film to say I was leaving.

'I kind of don't want to part company,' he said.

Neither did I. But there was still a strong drive in me telling me to leave, leave and be alone. I need to totally retrain my whole subconscious, I thought. If I ever want to replace envelopes of cash with anything more rewarding, then I need to force myself to stop thinking that a relationship is going to prevent me from being me.

I started to raise myself from the bed. Neither of us knew if we would make the effort to contact each other ever again. His words, 'You need to be kind and gentle on yourself, and you need to open up your heart to the possibility of love,' rang in my ears. I had a flashback to the moment when I'd parted with Greg at the end of my New York shopping trip. We'd had an amazing time, but it had stopped there – no future. Like him, this man was just another sugar daddy diary entry.

'I want to thank you,' I said, as I sat on the edge of the bed with my coat on.

'For what?'

'For being such great company. I feel like I've grown.'

Epilogue

When I left the Dorchester that evening, I took away nothing more than an envelope of cash. But in truth I wanted so much more from Richard than that. I wished I could have given it back and seen what we could have offered each other then, in a different world.

He had triggered powerful emotions in me, far more so than anyone else I'd met over the past three years. I desperately wanted to see him again. I wanted more of the special, intimate attention he paid me. I wanted to know what he'd say next. I wanted to feel him nestle up close as we had when we'd half-watched the film in his hotel room. I wanted to soak up his presence. But I couldn't. I didn't have his contact details, for one thing. What was more, the fact that our relationship had been defined by cold, hard cash right at the beginning meant that we could never really reclaim it and turn it into something less clinical.

The footman closed the cab door and I noticed his white gloves were worn and blackened. Was that just a coincidence? Or was it that I was suddenly seeing flaws in everything that had once seemed so glamorous? I realised then that I had achieved all the exhilaration I had set out to find. I had fulfilled my sugar daddy fantasy a long time ago. By continuing, I was turning a harmless high into something destructive.

Like anything in excess, it was becoming toxic.

During the past three months, I seemed to have been receiving increasingly loud messages telling me that it was time to move on, time to experience a different type of magic and excitement, the kind that can't be bought with Selfridges store cards, that means more than ski trips, hand-made corsets, leather dresses by Prada, Wolford stockings and Veuve Clicquot. I was finally recognising that there were grander pursuits than dates with international businessmen in five-star hotel bars.

When I started out with my guilty 'thing' for older men, I was genuinely interested in my dates, in their minds, and drawn in by their sophisticated lifestyles. But by the end, I'd realised they were just ordinary people with no more knowledge of the world than I had. I continued using the website long after my fascination had faded because they were paying me. I had watched myself go from an innocently lustful, curious 29-year-old to a 32-year-old with a heavily guarded secret, a woman who saw dates as business opportunities.

Cash is startlingly addictive. I will never forget the rush of slipping an envelope layered with fifty-pound notes into one of my scores of handbags, carrying sheafs of notes in my wallet, the joy of breaking into a fifty to pay for a round of drinks. I loved walking through the cosmetics counters in department stores and buying whatever shiny-packaged goodies I wanted. But money and a fast lifestyle are no remedy for a lack of fulfilment. Real satisfaction came only when I started to do things I really felt passionate about: writing and working for myself.

I don't regret accepting money from men or being impressed by flash lifestyles for a while, nor do I disrespect any of the men I met for offering those things. They were attracted by the glamour of a younger woman in the same way I was attracted to the glamour of their out-of-reach lifestyles. Have I had sex for money? Yes. Have I ever manipulated anyone's heart for money? No. Have I ever had sex with someone I wasn't attracted to in some way? No. And for someone from a generation that went on 18–30 holidays and to university freshers' balls and for which rebound fucks were the recommended form of break-up therapy, I think that's pretty rare!

Through my exploits, I discovered that there are many forms of relationship. Most of us like to think ours are based on love and chemistry, but for some it's convenience or financial support or merely companionship. As long as we are honest about the basis of the relationship, then any model is acceptable. I stopped taking money from men not because I changed my view on whether it was right or wrong but because I changed my view about what I wanted. I still maintain that lifelong relationships aren't necessarily the ideal, and I think I would still get annoyed with any man who phoned me as much as Malaysian Sugar Daddy did!

But I did act on Richard's words and adjust my attitude by two degrees. And when I did, I discovered that I had a deep yearning for something immensely more rewarding than what I could get from renting out my own company. Yes, I had a deep romantic yearning. In fact, it had been there all along. It was just that I had barricaded myself in for three whole years. And the reason that I only noticed these great big ugly barriers surrounding Kingdom Helen now was because I was suddenly finding myself imprisoned by them. I'd been so scared of anyone getting through that I'd locked myself in. Richard told me he had come into my life for a reason. And now I could see what the reason was. Someone needed to tell me, 'Get rid of those godawful barricades of steel and let someone come in. You need the company.'

In three years and probably hundreds of dates, I only ever

came close to genuine feelings a handful of times. Malaysian Sugar Daddy, for a while, but it was the escapism he represented that I fell in love with. As soon as he tried to get into my real life, I felt suffocated. Richard, for twenty-four hours – though I don't know if that was because he snapped me out of a three-year obsession or because he looked like a taller, younger Tom Cruise. And, of course, The Boss, who, I now realised, had been a safely unobtainable figure onto whom I could project my repressed romantic yearnings. As long as I nurtured a crush on someone unavailable, I didn't have to risk getting attached to someone I could actually have.

But now that I was 'opening myself up' and 'adjusting my attitude by two degrees' and being 'kind and gentle on myself', I no longer wanted to wrap myself in the protection of an unrequited crush. The only way I had been able to escape my career frustrations was to take the plunge and go freelance. Maybe I needed to take the same approach to my feelings about relationships. Maybe I need to leave the shallow end and plunge into deeper, unknown waters.

Well, that was what my subconscious concluded anyway. And it sent a write-up of the whole giddy whirlwind of a process to my conscience.

It said: 'Miss Helen, *phewwwww*! Don't ever put me through that again. Do you realise you've tried the tasting menus in nearly every Michelin-starred restaurant in London, and a fair few in New York, you've been a VIP Prada customer, you've filled your closet with Louboutins, you've eaten white truffles, you've sipped a £3,000 bottle of Pétrus (from a glass, I was pleased to see), you've stayed in luxury ski chalets, you've taken MDMA on a Malaysian beach, you've been to a fetish nightclub, you've had sex with girls, you've been to three continents with four different men, all of whom paid you. You've met film directors, multimillionaire banking executives, a playwright, a TV presenter. You've upset friends, you've amused friends, you've laughed, you've got angry, you've heard remarkable stories of success, failure, divorce and heartbreak. But, Miss Helen, you have not once been brave enough to try love. All best, your subconscious.'

And my conscious mind said: 'Gosh, that was fun. I'm going to write it all down before I forget. Now, I'm not sure where it's coming from, but suddenly I've got this burning desire to fall in love, since I've not really done much of that before. I don't think I want to date frivolous, wealthy men on a part-time basis any more. And I don't want gifts poured down my throat ever again. I want to choose to be with someone. I want to experience being wooed, not bought. I want to be part of the beautiful, lively, unpredictable game of human sexual attraction. I want to flirt, I want to feel that nervous uncertainty about whether the other person likes me back, I want the not knowing when to make a move, the exhilaration of feeling the object of my lust enter a room. I want heart flutters. I want burning desire.

'In fact, being paid was quite boringly formulaic. You know you're going to see each other on set evenings of each month because there's an arrangement to do so. The attraction doesn't get a chance to simmer. It was ready-made, microwaved romance. Well, now I'm going to learn to cook. Yes, cook! Me! I'm going to aim for Michelin-starred romance with all the trimmings of love and concern and attachment and sharing. And I'll look for the key ingredients that Happily Married Girlfriend once tried to recommend to me. What were they again? "Someone who looks out for you, who you can learn about and who will really love who you are"? Yes, that was it. With love, your consciousness.'